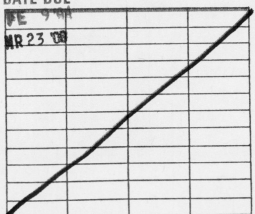

Teaching Disadvantaged Children in the Preschool

CARL BEREITER

SIEGFRIED ENGELMANN

Institute for Research on Exceptional Children
University of Illinois
Urbana, Illinois

Prentice-Hall, Inc., Englewood Cliffs, New Jersey

Current printing (last digit):

10   9

Library of Congress Catalog Card No.: 66-24974

Printed in the United States of America C-89245

PRENTICE-HALL INTERNATIONAL, INC., *London*
PRENTICE-HALL OF AUSTRALIA, PTY. LTD., *Sydney*
PRENTICE-HALL OF CANADA, LTD., *Toronto*
PRENTICE-HALL OF INDIA (PRIVATE) LTD., *New Delhi*
PRENTICE-HALL OF JAPAN, INC., *Tokyo*

preface

A book that prescribes definite teaching procedures and curricula for the preschool education of disadvantaged children is necessarily premature. Nevertheless, we have felt that there is an immediate need for something more than the general precepts and recommendations that now constitute the literature of compensatory preschool education. For the lack of definite guides, preschool teachers across the country have fallen back on what they would like to think are "tried and true" methods of nursery school education. It should be recognized that none of these methods have been tried for very long with disadvantaged children and that none of them have been proved "true" in the sense of accomplishing the objectives of compensatory education.

The methods and curricula set forth in this book have been or are being "tried" in about 14 different classes for disadvantaged children around the country—enough trial, at least, to show that they are feasible. They have been shown "true" to the extent of removing, not merely lessening, the major deficiencies in learning that are characteristic of disadvantaged children.

We wish to acknowledge the valuable contributions of those who worked with us in the establishment and operation of the pilot preschool from which this program emerged—Jean Osborn, Philip Reidford, Margaret Welsh, Louise Herzberg, Ann Bernos, Helen Bereiter, and Therese Engelmann. We are particularly grateful to Mrs. Osborn for her dedication, resourcefulness, understanding, and skill. A number of other individuals and groups helped us in a variety of ways, but we should especially like to acknowledge the generosity of the McKinley Foundation of Champaign, Illinois, in providing space and facilities for conducting the preschool. The research reported herein was supported by the Cooperative Research Program of the Office of Education, U. S. Department of Health, Education, and Welfare.

C. B.
S. E.

contents

*Teaching
Disadvantaged Children
in the Preschool*

the need for a new kind of preschool for disadvantaged children 1

*I*t is summer. A dozen six-year-old children are playing in a first-floor schoolroom. In one corner some girls are busily playing house. Two boys are pursuing each other around the room on tricycles, playing policeman. Three or four children are seated around a teacher who is reading them a story. Others are seated at a table snipping up bits of colored paper and pasting them onto a larger sheet. A couple of boys are wandering around not doing much of anything, but if the head teacher had not stopped to talk to us, she would probably have found something for them to do.

"You wouldn't believe how these children have changed," she tells us.

"In what ways?"

"When they first came in here, they didn't know how to play. They just stood around. And they hardly talked at all. Now you can't shut them up."

We note that there is much vocal noise, but even though our ears have become well tuned to the dialect, there is very little we can understand; nor do the children seem to pay much attention to what others say. The teacher tells us the children were given a school readiness test a few weeks before. Almost all of them were a year or more below average.

"These children will be starting first grade in the fall, won't they?"

"Yes."

"How do you think they'll make out there?"

"It all depends on the first-grade teacher. Some teachers don't seem to understand how different these children are. If a teacher understands. . . ."

"What do they expect of first-grade children in this school?"

The question seems to puzzle her.

One of the girls who has been cutting and pasting brings her production over to show us. She presents it to us with much pride, but says nothing. "That's very pretty. What color is this part?"

"Uh know."

"What color is this other part?"

"Uh know."

"Show me the red part." This she does, correctly and confidently. She can point to every color we name.

"Now show me a part that is *not* red." She points to the red part.

"Lift up your hands." Both hands go up.

"Now, lift up your *hand*." Both hands go up again.

"Is a boy a girl?" She laughs and shakes her head "No."

"No, a boy is not a girl. Say 'A boy is *not* a girl.' "

"A boy a girl."

"What do you think it would take to get these children ready for first grade?" we ask the teacher.

"Time. Time. They have so much to learn. If we could keep them another year, then *maybe* some of them, at least, would be ready to start first grade."

"But then they'd be a year behind."

"That's true. But most of them always will be."

This is a "successful" preschool for disadvantaged children. The teacher is not entirely deluding herself when she says the children have made great gains. And yet this same enthusiastic teacher admits that these children face almost certain failure in school. The children have learned to play. But, in six weeks, they may re-enter the same classroom to find that the housekeeping corner and the tricycles are gone and in their place are desks, pencils, books. The chalkboard, which they had never noticed before, will begin to bear strange characters. Some children will not even know how to look at these characters, let alone interpret them. These preschoolers have learned to "express themselves" through speech. But, in six weeks, a teacher will begin talking to them and asking them questions that call, not for self-expression, but for the communication of knowledge and ideas. She will speak in simple words, but many of those words will be ones that they have never noticed. Like the chalkboard, those words will never have had any function before.

"They have so much to learn," the teacher admits. We refrain from saying "What? Give us a list. And then tell us which of these things you are teaching, and how, and at what rate, and on what basis you decide which of these to teach and which to neglect, and how you expect the neglected things to be learned." We refrain, because such questions are too demoralizing to a teacher who works hard, who tries, and who cares. But these are the questions that need to be asked. They are the questions this book poses and attempts to answer.

Educational Retardation in Disadvantaged Children

With no known exceptions, studies of three- to five-year old children from lower socio-economic backgrounds have shown them to be retarded or below average in every intellectual ability.[1] The degree of retardation is not always large, and sometimes falls short of statistical significance, but differences between lower-class and middle-class children invariably favor the latter group. What is more, the differences are largest in those abilities most relevant to success in school.

On general intelligence tests, disadvantaged children typically score 5 to 15 IQ points below average. An average deficit of 15 points on such scales is grave indeed, and it is found regularly among Southern Negro children and appears to be characteristic of Puerto Rican immigrant children.[2] Such a deficit places the average of the group on what is now coming to be considered the borderline of mental deficiency, so that roughly half of the children in such groups fall into the mentally retarded range. An average deficit of only 5 points, such as is found among more stable lower-class urban populations, is often considered trivial, since it falls well within the normal range. But if the IQ scores of a group are normally distributed around a mean of 95, such a group can be expected to have one-and-a-half times the average number of children falling into the below-80 range, which indicates inability to cope with ordinary schooling, and only half the average number of children with IQs of 130 or more—a common cutting-point for the identification of gifted children.[3]

Although intelligence test scores are most commonly looked at as some kind of "index of brightness," it is more useful for the present discussion to consider them as a very general sort of indicator of how much a child has learned that is relevant to success in school, compared to other children of his own age. Not all items on intelligence tests reflect learning of this kind—items that test short-term memory do not, for instance—but the bulk of them do. Accordingly, a five-year-old child with an IQ score of 85 may be said to be about nine months retarded in over-all school-relevant learning, in that he performs like the average child of four years, three months. An IQ of 90 at the age of five represents six months' retardation; an IQ of 95, three months'.

Compared to this over-all average of three to nine months' retardation, disadvantaged children of preschool age are typically at least a year behind in language development—in vocabulary size, sentence length, and use of grammatical structure. *Indeed, in practically every aspect of language development that has been evaluated quantitatively, young disadvantaged children have been found to function at the level of average children who are a year or more younger.*[4]

The other area in which disadvantaged children seem to be especially retarded is reasoning ability or logical development. Here, too, the amount of retardation is typically a year or more.[5]

Verbal and reasoning abilities—which may be combined under the general rubric of ability to manipulate symbols—have been found to be the major factor in academic achievement throughout the school years.[6] Thus, from the point of view of success in school, disadvantaged children are retarded most in the areas that count the most.

It is also instructive to note the kinds of performance in which disadvantaged children show little or no retardation. These are, principally, immediate memory span and ability to master specific rote-learning tasks.[7] Performance on these items does not rely on previously learned concepts or strategies the way performance on language and reasoning tests does. Therefore, performance of this kind comes closer to demonstrating raw ability to learn. It would appear from this that what disadvantaged children lack is learning, not the fundamental capacity to learn.

The Disadvantaged Child and School Failure

If young disadvantaged children are lacking mainly in learning rather than ability to learn, it might seem that once they enter school, where they have an opportunity to learn, they would catch up. Unfortunately, the opposite seems to be true. All available evidence points to the conclusion that disadvantaged children fall farther behind as they proceed through school. Martin Deutsch and his co-workers have done several studies comparing lower-class and middle-class children at the first-grade and at the fifth-grade level. They find that the differences between lower- and middle-class children are wider at the fifth-grade level and that they show up in a greater variety of areas.[8] Deutsch interprets the results as showing a "cumulative deficit" in which small deficiencies at an early age lead to inferior learning which in turn increases the magnitude of the deficiency—a sort of compound interest effect in reverse.

If anything, the cumulative deficit is probably more severe than the Deutsch data indicate, because by the fifth grade, many more lower- than middle-class children will have dropped out of the comparison, having been placed in special classes for the retarded or having lost a year through grade repetition.

At the higher school levels, the failure of disadvantaged children in academic achievement shows up more dramatically. When special classes for disadvantaged children are instituted in junior high schools or high schools, one of the major difficulties of curriculum planners is finding instructional materials easy enough for pupils who are by that time four years retarded in reading ability.[9] The school drop-out problem is still largely a lower-class problem, and although it has many facets, one of the commonest is again school failure—of adolescents so far behind in basic academic skills that their presence in high school classes is a cruel farce.[10]

Even those disadvantaged children who finish high school are below standard in their achievements. Adequate data are not yet available, but it appears from college entrance examination scores and more indefinite kinds of information that among the more seriously disadvantaged groups, such as southern Negroes, the average high school graduate has something like a seventh- or eighth-grade level of achievement in basic subjects.[11] Although some children from poor backgrounds do excel academically, their number is small. One of the best available indicators of academic excellence is reaching the final selection rounds in the National Merit Scholarship testing program. According to recent statistics, a child from a prosperous home has from 4 to 30 times as good a chance of achieving this distinction as a child from a poor home.[12]

The plight of disadvantaged children, as they slide downward through school, must, of course, be due in part to the failure of schools to provide more effective education for them. Some writers, notably Kenneth Clark, have attempted to explain the poor academic attainment of disadvantaged children entirely on the basis of the inferior quality of schools in low-income areas.[13] This charge may be legitimate, but to claim, as Clark does, that cultural deprivation is a myth is to ignore the overwhelming evidence that disadvantaged children are already well below average in academic abilities at the time they enter school. From the beginning there is a lag in learning that must be overcome if disadvantaged children are to emerge from school with the same skills and knowledge as more privileged children. If the lag is to be made up during the school years, then schools for disadvantaged children have to provide higher-quality and faster-paced education than that provided for advantaged children. Another possible solution is to provide this kind of education before the school years—the motivating idea for preschool education for disadvantaged children.

Given the present persuasion of American education, it hardly seems necessary to argue that the preschool period is a better time to provide superior education. The preschool movement is already underway. The question is simply how to get the most out of it. If the preschool does not succeed in overcoming the educational handicaps of lower-class children, the problem is left in the laps of the public schools, where it is difficult to provide a minimally adequate educational program for disadvantaged children, let alone the superior one that would enable these children to catch up with those who have been more fortunate in their earlier educational experiences.

The Need for an Above-average Rate of Learning

If the point is accepted that disadvantaged children are behind other children in certain developmental aspects, then it follows by simple logical necessity that *they must progress at a faster than normal rate if they are to catch up.* Although this conclusion is not a popular one, there is no conceivable way to contradict it except by denying that disadvantaged children are behind. The only issue open to question is what the nature of this faster-than-normal progress should be.

It is conceivable, for instance, that faster than normal progress could be achieved simply by removing some barrier that has impeded progress— as, for instance, if a deaf child were suddenly cured of his deafness. "Miracle cures" of this kind are sometimes claimed in work with disadvantaged children, as when a child is found to gain 20 points or so in IQ after a few months of preschool experience. Such enormous gains, however, are highly suspect to anyone who is familiar with mental measurements. It is a fair guess that the child could have done as well on the first test except that he misinterpreted the situation, was frightened or agitated, or was not used to responding to instructions unless they were delivered in a certain imperative tone of voice. This suspicion grows if, in looking over what took place during the period of preschool experience, one cannot find adequate sources for the new learning that the gain in intelligence test score supposedly revealed.

This is not to say that what happened to the child was not important or valuable, but only that it represents an exceptional and irrelevant case. The main concern is not with what disadvantaged children can do but do not, but with what they cannot do but should be able to do if they are to succeed in school.

If educators are to deal realistically with the educational problems of disadvantaged children, they must eliminate the magical thinking which has led many otherwise cautious and sensible educators to believe that disadvantaged children can suddenly "blossom forth" intellectually in the same way that they occasionally do "blossom forth" emotionally after brief experience in a favorable environment. Specialists in child development have emphasized for years what a slow and continuous process intellectual development is, what an enormous amount of learning and unlearning, practice, and trial-and-error goes into the smallest step in intellectual growth.

Where genuine learning is concerned, enormous leaps simply do not occur, and leaps of any kind do not occur without sufficient cause. A child does not know how to read at the first-grade level one day and at the third-grade level the next. He may *perform* at the first-grade level the first day and at the third-grade level the next, but the only reasonable inference is that he knew how to read at the third-grade level the day before, yet for some reason failed to demonstrate it. If a child's vocabulary level goes up a whole year in three months, this implies that he has learned on the order of *3000 words during that time.* Such learning may be possible, but it would have to be accounted for. If the child has been exposed only to the ordinary run of verbal experiences during that period, it becomes hard to believe that he has managed to learn four times as many words during that time as the average child.

To avoid falling into magical thinking on this matter, it is best to avoid such ambiguous terms as "development" and "intelligence" and to consider the whole matter in terms of *learning*. Instead of saying that the disadvantaged child is retarded in the development of certain abilities or that he has a low IQ, it is more to the point to say that there are a number of things that disadvantaged children of preschool age have not yet learned but which they will need to know before they enter school if they are not to be seriously handicapped.

The problem of achieving a faster than normal rate of progress then becomes the problem of producing *learning* at a greater than normal rate. This puts the problem on a realistic basis that is more or less familiar to all educators. We all recognize that learning, of some kinds at least, can be speeded up, whereas the term *development* often connotes a process that must go on at its own rate. Furthermore, the conditions that are necessary for learning to take place are in some ways familiar to all educators, whereas the notion of increasing intelligence is often confusing when covered with ideological trappings.

To speak of "accelerating learning" rather than "accelerating development" or "increasing intelligence" is not, the writers trust, to bury issues that need to be faced. To the extent that "development" and "intelligence" involve things that are not learned, they involve things that education can do nothing about. Thus, in viewing preschool education solely in terms of learning, we do not ignore development and intelligence but treat only those aspects of them which can be influenced by education.

The Inadequacy of Enrichment

The most widely endorsed strategy for helping disadvantaged children overcome their learning deficiencies is the one called "enrichment." In broad terms, the strategy of enrichment is to compress into the preschool program the maximum quantity of experiences believed to contribute to the culturally privileged child's superiority in learning. In practice, the strategy is often watered down by the infusion of experiences chosen, not because they are expected to be the most beneficial to the child but because they are ones that, on humanitarian grounds, he is thought to *deserve*—trips to parks, a chance to enjoy certain toys, and so on.

Even in its purest form, however, the enrichment strategy seems doomed to failure—that is, if success is judged not on the basis of the disadvantaged child's progress but on the basis of his demonstration that he is catching up to the more privileged child. The reason is simple: while the disadvantaged child is going through those experiences that privileged children have gone through before him and hopefully is learning from them what the privileged children learned, these same privileged children are not standing still and waiting for him to catch up but are having new experiences and learning new skills from them.

Were it not for the time limitations involved, the enrichment strategy would be perfectly adequate. If privileged children learn what they do from certain experiences, disadvantaged children should be able to learn those things from the same experiences—given enough time. But time is the least available resource in the education of disadvantaged children. A normal preschool program may comprise only 500 hours—a meager time allotment in which to try to overcome disadvantages that accumulate over some 20,000 hours (the approximate number of hours a child is awake between the age of one and the time he enters kindergarten).

There are only two ways to increase the amount that is learned in those 500 hours: by selecting experiences that produce more learning and by compressing more experience into the time available. The normal experiences of childhood—the kind with which the enrichment strategy deals—do not lend themselves well to either of these strategies.

While it is possible to eliminate a number of normal experiences as being of limited educational value, one cannot go very far the other way in identifying "stars" among normal experiences that far outshine others in their power to produce learning. Normal childhood experience, by its very nature, is a day-to-day affair, each new experience adding a little bit to what was learned from others, the whole body of experiences being relatively homogeneous and continuous.

Normal childhood experiences are also not very compressible. When one tries to cram the experiences of baking a cake, building something with blocks, listening to a story, examining a pet rabbit, and a half-dozen others into a half-day preschool session, the experiences are no longer the same as in everyday life. Most early childhood experiences are of a leisurely or low-pressure sort. The high spots are spaced well apart (and many parents know the hysteria and hyperactivity that overtake a child when highly stimulating experiences are not well spaced, as on a holiday). The normal activities of early childhood take up a lot of time. Normally, the young child has a lot of time; but the disadvantaged child who enters a preschool at the age of four-and-a-half has already used most of his up.

The basic fallacy behind the enrichment strategy is the idea that since privileged children learn what they do from certain experiences, disadvantaged children must learn from *the same kinds of experiences*. If this assumption were true, there would be no hope of speeding up the learning of disadvantaged children enough so that they could overcome their relative backwardness. If disadvantaged children are to learn at faster than the normal rate, they are going to have to learn from experiences of some other kind than those that have been responsible for the learning of more privileged children—experiences that are more potent generators of significant learning, experiences of a kind that can be compressed into a small period of time without losing their effectiveness.

The Need for Selection and Exclusion in Preschool Programs

If a child is genuinely a year retarded in some area of developmental learning and if he is to make up the deficit in a year's time, he must learn at twice the normal rate during that year. For this to happen across the whole spectrum of developmental learning is simply out of the question, no matter what kind of educational methods are employed. Not one child in a million progresses at this rate. On the other hand, if a narrow enough area of learning is chosen, it is fairly easy to produce learning at twice the normal rate. For instance, the typical child will learn a half-dozen or so names of states every year until eventually he knows all 50 of them. But, with a little concentrated teaching, a four-year-old child could learn them all and thus have learned at far beyond the normal rate.

Although learning the names of the states is a trivial accomplishment and one that will do practically nothing to offset a child's handicaps in academic abilities, this in no way invalidates the principle that focusing on specific learning goals makes high rates of progress possible. It merely demonstrates that the teacher must be very careful not to waste time on learning that is of small importance.

To take a child who is a year behind in practically every area of learning relevant to school success and bring him within a year to the point where he is on an equal academic footing with the average child is an enormous task. Probably no experienced educator would question this. Nor would he question the necessity of focusing preschool education for such a child on those kinds of learning most crucial for school success. What is harder to accept is the corollary to this proposition: that such focusing requires that other desirable educational goals be abandoned or at least relegated to a definitely secondary position. Yet, this is a necessary corollary. To focus means to narrow, to restrict, to intensify an effect by concentrating effort upon a smaller range. More specifically, it means, in this case, *focusing upon academic objectives and relegating all nonacademic objectives to a secondary position.*

In recent years, this unpleasant necessity has been faced first at the high school level and now increasingly at the elementary school level. Reluctantly, educators at these levels have had to recognize that they cannot do everything for the child that deserves doing and that if they are to provide the quality of academic education that our society demands, they must allow certain other worthwhile activities to be slighted.

Understandably, many conscientious educators are reluctant—and some whom the writers have encountered are downright horrified—to see this academic emphasis and its attendant narrowing of educational objectives extended downward into the preschool. The preschool has become, in some areas, the last bastion of education for the whole child. Here, at least, it would seem that education ought to be based on the total present needs of the child rather than upon the limited objectives of academic preparation.

This concern with the child's over-all development as a human being is thoroughly commendable. The mistake that seems to be inherent in the "whole child" point of view as it exists among educators is contained in the assumption that this concern requires a broad, unfocused educational program that recognizes no priorities and tolerates no omissions. The following are some of the flaws in this assumption:

1. It fails to consider the child's future. A program that is so concerned with the child as he is that it destroys his future cannot claim to meet the child's over-all developmental needs. The threat of school failure that hangs over disadvantaged children is sufficiently grave that if it is not dealt with, practically everything else that a preschool might accomplish stands to be wiped out, including emotional health, social adjustment, interests, and favorable attitudes toward school.

2. The idea that in order to produce a well-rounded child, one must have a well-rounded program reveals an ignorance of the fact that a world exists outside the schoolroom door. Children need physical exercise, social interaction with others their own age, and opportunities for free play. But, if children get ample amounts of these outside of school, it is quite possible that the educational program that contributed most to rounding out the child's total development would be one that included none of these.

3. In the hands of a skillful teacher, favorable attitudes and emotional adjustment can be fostered just as readily through activities that serve specific learning purposes as through activities that otherwise serve only as amusements. This is a point that is well-known to teachers at higher school levels but that many early childhood educators seem not to recognize.

4. According to a view that is gaining increasing favor among developmental psychologists,[14] development is not merely something that happens to a child, much less something that is handed to him by the school; rather, the child is considered to play an active role in his development. From this view, it should follow that a major contribution that education can make to the child's over-all development is to provide him with the tools he needs to pursue his own development more successfully. In other

words, the role of education is not to make the child well rounded by distributing his experiences over a wide range, but to teach the child those specific skills which will enable him to make himself well rounded, which will enable him to get the most out of the experiences and opportunities that are available to him. For instance, it may be less important to provide the child with experiences in playing with different toys than to develop in him those ways of logically organizing experience that will enable him to draw more than temporary amusement out of his play with toys.

5. The teacher who tries to meet all the children's needs is bound to extend herself beyond her range of competence—into realms of social work, psychotherapy, and even medicine. Not only is she likely to do unwitting harm, but she will be shirking the full-time job she has been charged with—that of promoting learning. The teacher may complain that she cannot depend on other people to solve the children's social and emotional problems. But it is perhaps more pertinent to ask whether other people can depend on her to solve the children's learning problems.

6. Finally, it is necessary to recognize that, in the education of disadvantaged children, some sort of compromise between the ideals of all-around development and the severity of the child's deficiencies must be made, as it must with any kind of handicapped child. For many such children, there is more that should be done than can be done through the agency of a preschool, and so any program will have its shortcomings. No matter what is done, many disadvantaged children will leave the preschool with deficiencies for which they will suffer in later years. The only choice is between one kind of lack and another. By devoting a great deal of time to artistic and construction activities, disadvantaged children could probably achieve the level of more privileged children in this regard. Through continuous field trips and other forms of exposure to elements of the physical, biological, and social world, they might acquire in a year's time the breadth of familiarity with the world that other children have. Through continuous verbal interaction with adults, they might overcome some of their deficits in language. Through large doses of stories, records, and dramatizations, they might absorb the substantial literary heritage that many privileged children have. If all the time were devoted to play with toys, blocks, and the like, they might acquire whatever it is that middle-class children get out of their extensive occupation with these things. But any one of these activity areas would use up almost all the time available. Dividing the time between several or all of the areas would mean some gains in several areas but not enough in any one to catch up.

The "whole child" approach amounts to dividing the time, giving the disadvantaged child a smattering of learning in many areas but leaving him with all the deficiencies he had before, only to a lesser degree. This choice has a certain conservative appeal, but the authors are convinced that there is a better choice. The following two chapters will make the reasons clearer. The first of the reasons for this conviction has already been indicated: that for the disadvantaged child's future, academic success in school is of such critical importance that any preschool program that fails to do all it can to ensure this success has failed the "whole child." The second reason (which will be elaborated in Chapter 2) is that the language deficiency of disadvantaged children is not just one among a number of handicaps but is the central handicap from which many of the others derive. By remedying it, it is believed, one can remedy many of the others. On the other hand, there is reason to believe that if the language deficiency is allowed to remain, other handicaps in knowledge and intellectual skills *cannot be remedied.* It is believed, therefore, that the other options mentioned in point 6 above cannot be realized; that a continuous round of field trips, demonstrations, nature, and science projects, for instance, cannot produce in the disadvantaged child the same level of learning that they produce in a child who has the language abilities necessary to organize, interpret, and generalize from such experiences. The final reason for dismissing the "whole child" approach (which will be documented in Chapter 3) is that the language handicaps of even severely deprived children can in fact be overcome in a year's time, with substantial personality and social development taking place simultaneously, whereas there is no evidence that concentration upon some other goal or combination of goals is able to do as much.

Can the Traditional Nursery School Be Adapted to the Needs of Disadvantaged Children?

Almost all preschools for disadvantaged children follow a basic pattern of activities that has grown up over the years in nursery schools serving predominantly upper-middle-class children. Many preschools have taken this pattern over virtually without change. The more experimental preschools have added special features of one kind or another usually designed to provide more language experience, but have retained the basic pattern and a large number of the activities found in the traditional nursery school.

The ingredients of the typical nursery school program should be familiar to most readers. There is usually a period of free play during which the child may avail himself of standard materials and facilities: large blocks, simple toys, a housekeeping corner containing child-size furniture and appliances, a dress-up corner supplied with varied costumes and adult clothing. There is a rest period and a period of outdoor play on playground equipment; a period for juice and snacks and toileting; a session devoted to group singing or rhythm activities; an art and craft period which may be quite free or directed toward some set project; a time during which stories are read to the children; a period in which conversation is carried on, perhaps with the teacher presenting and discussing some object or picture or else the children individually reporting on their experiences or showing off possessions. Some time is usually devoted to group games, finger-plays, and the like. As Sears and Dowley [15] have remarked, differences between one nursery school and another are usually not in the activities carried out but in the way they are handled and in the general atmosphere maintained.

Nursery schools have never been intended to achieve academic objectives in the way elementary schools do, and so it should not be surprising if the traditional nursery school structure is found not to lend itself very readily to such objectives. On the other hand, this traditional structure has become so familiar and accepted that it seems as if it represents what is normal for young children to do, and gross deviations from what is normal and natural must always be approached with caution. However, if a maximally effective educational program is to be designed for disadvantaged children, we must be free to explore new possibilities and criticize traditional methods.

With this in mind, two questions must be raised concerning the traditional nursery school pattern as a model to be followed in planning education programs for disadvantaged children: (1) How well does this type of school lend itself to the focused and rapid learning of academic skills that disadvantaged children need? and (2) How valid is the premise that the traditional nursery school represents what is normal and natural in childhood experience?

As to the first question, several reasons have already been advanced which suggest that the traditional nursery school program is not well suited to providing focused and rapid learning. Its emphasis on experience rather than achievement of specific goals best serves a diversified rather than an intensely focused educational program. It does not provide an ordered sequence of activities that keeps the child working at the upper limit of his abilities. The same basic activities and content are retained for long periods of time, many throughout the preschool period. Finally, the activities that make up the traditional program were not chosen because of their effectiveness in achieving academic goals; they represent an accumulation of activities that seem to work and that are compatible with certain principles of child development.

Research done to evaluate the effects of the conventional nursery schools generally supports these expectations. As summarized by Sears and Dowley,

> The evidence suggests, but not strongly, that certain social participation skills are enhanced by a good nursery school experience and that

in certain cases these effects can be observed several years later. Language and intellectual development may be influenced, apparently, particularly if the home or out-of-school environment of the child is meager in stimulating qualities.[16]

These results are what one might expect from a type of school that provides a wide range of generally beneficial experiences—small gains spread over a wide area. A number of recent results from preschools for disadvantaged children that have followed the traditional nursery school line, in whole or in part, support the same conclusion—small improvements are found in virtually every area of development that is evaluated.

This is not the impression that some of the more enthusiastic reports of such studies have conveyed. A good deal is made of average gains in IQ of six to eight points and of comparable gains on language tests. Such enthusiasm is dampened by those studies in which preschool and nonpreschool control groups are followed into kindergarten. The typical finding then is that the nonpreschool groups make gains of approximately equal magnitude when they enter kindergarten, whereas the preschool group makes no further gains, so that the advantage of the preschool group is largely erased.

This finding has puzzled many investigators, but when it is put together with some other fairly consistent findings from preschool studies, a reasonable explanation emerges. The significant average gains shown during the preschool period are not, typically, shared by all the children in the preschool program, but are mainly accounted for by children who had very low initial scores. These children often show such enormous gains that even though children with higher initial scores show little or no gain, the scores when averaged together suggest a substantial gain for all the children. As noted in a previous section, these "magical" gains of 15 or 20 points in IQ are highly suspect. It would appear that there are a fair number of disadvantaged children who do not perform at all near their capacity on mental tests until they have had enough experience in some kind of school situation to respond appropriately to testing. It is not just a matter of doing badly the first time; if they are tested again a year later without any school experience in between, they will do just as poorly as before. But as soon as they have undergone a period of adjustment to schooling, whether at the preschool, kindergarten, or first-grade level, their scores go up to the level of other children with the same background.

From the point of view of overcoming basic lacks in academic preparation, this kind of gain in test performance is of no consequence. What is important is the final level of performance and how it compares with the performance of children who wait until kindergarten for their first school experience. On this basis, the advantages of a traditional preschool experience are shown to be very slight and, what is more significant, the children end up well below average on tests that are predictive of academic success. The writers have analyzed results from eight different experimental classes for preschool children that have followed traditional patterns. They find that a very simple rule fits all the results quite closely. The rule is that, on the average, disadvantaged children who have gone through a preschool will progress *half* the way from their initial IQ level to the normal level of 100. Thus, if they start with an average IQ of 86, they may be expected to end up with an average IQ of 93. If they start with an average IQ of 92, they may be expected to end up with an average IQ of 96. So far, this rule has never been more than 2 IQ points in error.

Notice that according to this rule, no group will ever reach an average IQ of 100 if it starts out below that point. No traditionally taught group on which the writers have seen data ever has done so. Those few cases where disadvantaged groups have risen to an IQ level of 100 or above through preschool training have all involved radical departures from the traditional preschool model.

Of course, the fact that traditionally taught groups progress only half the way from their initial level to the normal level in a year of preschool experience would not be discouraging if, during a second year, they could progress the rest of the distance. But the typical finding is that they do not show any relative progress at all during the second year. The writers interpret this as evidence that the gains obtained during the first year were mainly due to improved responsiveness to testing and that gains of this kind occur only once.

The justification for adhering to the traditional model of preschool education, therefore, cannot rest on its tested effectiveness in producing the kinds of gains in ability that disadvantaged children need, nor on its ready adaptability to the pursuit of such gains. It would appear, rather, that the traditional approach owes its wide acceptance to its seeming consonance with "the true nature of the child." It is easy to get the impression that any gross departure from the traditional approach would run contrary to the natural order of child development. The value of blocks or the sandbox for a three-year-old is no more seriously questioned than the value of the rattle for an infant. The design of Child Development Centers for Project Head Start clearly reflects this attitude. Certain materials and activities and a certain general kind of schedule are taken to play the same sufficient and healthful role in the development of poor children as they do in the development of more privileged children. To suggest that disadvantaged children may need something entirely different seems almost to suggest that they are not children, that the same laws of child development do not hold for them as for other children.

What is overlooked in this view is the extent to which the traditional nursery school is a uniquely upper-middle-class institution designed to provide not what *all* children need, but what *upper-middle-class* children need to round out their rich diets of experience. That is, instead of providing, as many people seem to assume, those experiences which are most characteristic of a privileged childhood in our society, the traditional nursery school in many respects provides those experiences which are *not* characteristic of child life in privileged home environments.

The following are some of the more obvious contrasts between the traditional nursery school environment and what is generally conceived of as the typical upper-middle-class home environment:

1. Whereas the upper-middle-class child often spends most of his time at home with adults and has fewer than the average number of playmates of his own age, the nursery school stresses peer-group relationships and a reduced amount of adult-child interaction.

2. Whereas the home environment is especially rich in verbal experience, the nursery school stresses seeing and doing.

3. Whereas the child at home is subject to many prohibitions, the nursery school encourages, within limits, greater freedom and independence.

4. Whereas the child at home is sometimes prevented from developing physical skills and courage by overly protective parents, the nursery school attempts, through greater permissiveness and more carefully designed play equipment, to engage the child in more active and venturesome physical activities.

5. Whereas the child's parents may discourage messy activities, the nursery school gives the child the opportunity to play with clay, sand, water, finger paints, etc.

6. Whereas the child's parents may demand high levels of achievement, the nursery school allows the child to set his own standards.

7. Whereas the home environment is future-oriented, the nursery school stresses enjoyment of the present.

8. Whereas the home environment fosters competitiveness, the nursery school fosters cooperation and discourages comparisons of one child's performance with that of another.

9. Whereas at home the flow of information tends to be from the parents to the children, in the nursery school the flow is from the children to one another and to the teacher.

10. Whereas the home environment is highly reality-oriented, the nursery school encourages fantasy and dramatic play.

What is especially interesting is that, in complementing or offsetting the upper-middle-class home environment, the nursery school has taken on many of the characteristics of the lower-class home environment. In fact, in reading down the list of contrasts between the home and the nursery school environment, one finds that, in almost every case, the same contrast could be drawn between the upper-middle-class and the lower-class child's environment: adult versus peer contacts, verbal versus non-verbal experience, regulation versus freedom, physical restraint versus physical freedom, neatness versus messiness, future versus present orientation, competition versus noncompetitiveness, teaching versus nonteaching, reality versus myth and pretense.

This is not to say that the typical nursery school resembles a slum, but only that it provides, in a highly refined form, a great many of the outstanding cultural influences of the lower-class environment. The nursery school may, in fact, capture most of what is best in lower-class culture —for, indeed, it has many commendable aspects. But it is ridiculous to call the experiences provided by such a school compensatory when they are administered to children from lower-class backgrounds. If one wanted to provide a truly compensatory program, in the sense that it would make up for the lacks and offset the excesses of a lower-class environment, a good beginning could be made by taking the ten characteristics listed above and adopting the opposite of each.

This confusion between characteristics of the middle-class home and characteristics of the middle-class nursery school is especially unfortunate when it comes to finding ways of dealing with the central problem of improving the academic aptitudes of disadvantaged children. In looking for the secret of the middle-class child's academic talent, the nursery school is about the last place one should consider. Although a good nursery school may help the upper-middle-class child develop his intellectual abilities, it is well known that he already has these abilities before he gets to nursery school and that he is not hampered intellectually if he does not attend a nursery school. To the extent that environment has anything to do with the superior academic abilities of the child from a privileged background, the crucial factors must exist somewhere in that complex of verbalism, parental stimulation and control, competition, achievement motivation, perfectionism, and orientation to the future which constitutes the stereotyped environment of the upper-middle-class home—not in the nursery school, which, if anything, acts as a countervailing influence on these factors.

All this should elicit a very strong skepticism, not only about the specific features and activities of the typical nursery school but also about its whole structure and orientation as they apply to preschool education of disadvantaged children. It should encourage the serious and open-minded educator to consider entirely new approaches which are truly compensatory and which focus directly upon the crucial problems of disadvantaged children.

Summary

The gist of this chapter is contained in five major points:

1. By the age of three or four, disadvantaged children are already seriously behind other children in the development of aptitudes necessary for success in school.

2. Disadvantaged children must somehow "catch up" in the development of these abilities, or they will enter elementary school with handicaps that will spell failure for a large percentage of them and a limited future for all of them.

3. If they are to catch up, they must progress at a faster than normal rate.

4. A preschool program that provides the usual opportunities for learning cannot be expected to produce learning at above normal rates.

5. A short-term preschool program cannot be expected to produce above normal gains in all areas of development at once; a "well-rounded" program is therefore incompatible with the goal of catching up: selectivity is necessary.

Taken together, these points indicate that radical departures from established practices of early childhood education are needed. It was shown that preschools for disadvantaged children that are patterned after the familiar upper-middle-class nursery school have not succeeded in meeting the challenge of providing a faster than normal rate of learning in areas significant for school success. An examination of the structure of the upper-middle-class nursery school suggested an important reason for its inadequacy as a model of preschool education for disadvantaged children: the nursery school complements the influences of the privileged home instead of duplicating them, and thus exerts many of the influences of a lower-class social environment while minimizing many of the influences that have been responsible for the superior intellectual development of upper-middle-class children. It is therefore incompatible with the requirements for a compensatory educational program for disadvantaged children.

Notes

1. An extensive annotated bibliography of relevant studies is provided in B. S. Bloom, A. Davis, and R. Hess, *Compensatory Education for Cultural Deprivation* (New York: Holt, Rinehart & Winston, Inc., 1965). Perhaps the most convincing evidence comes from the consistent failure of efforts to develop "culture-fair" tests on which children from lower-class backgrounds would *not*

obtain lower scores than middle-class children. See W. Coleman and A. W. Ward, "A Comparison of Davis-Eells and Kuhlmann-Finch Scores of Children from High and Low Socioeconomic Status," *Journal of Educational Psychology,* 46 (1955), 465–469; R. D. Hess, "Controlling Cultural Influence in Mental Testing: An Experimental Test," *Journal of Educational Research,* 49 (1955), 53–58; D. I. Marquart and L. L. Bailey, "An Evaluation of the Culture Free Test of Intelligence," *Journal of Genetic Psychology,* 86 (1955), 353–358.

2. Susan W. Gray and R. A. Klaus, "Interim Report: Early Training Project," George Peabody College (mimeo), 1963; A. Kennedy, V. Van de Riet, and J. C. White, Jr., "A Normative Sample of Intelligence and Achievement of Negro Elementary School Children in the Southeastern United States," *Monographs of the Society for Research on Child Development,* 28 (1963), No. 6; G. S. Lesser, G. Fifer, and D. H. Clark, "Mental Abilities of Children in Different Social and Cultural Groups," Final Report, Cooperative Research Project No. 1635 (Harvard University), 1964.

3. The issue of "cultural bias" in intelligence tests is not very pertinent to this discussion. We are not concerned with the disadvantaged child's "real" intelligence, whatever that may be, but with his chances for success in school. In this regard, the cultural bias of intelligence tests merely reflects the cultural biases of the schools—the tests, in other words, measure the kinds of abilities that are important in schools as they exist, without regard to whether or not these abilities have any universal relevance. See K. Eells, "Some Implications for School Practice of the Chicago Studies of Cultural Bias in Intelligence Tests," *Harvard Educational Review,* 23 (1953), 284–297; J. B. Stroud, "Predictive Value of Obtained Intelligence Quotients of Groups Favored and Unfavored in Socioeconomic Status," *Elementary School Journal,* 43 (1942), 97–104.

4. See references in note 2 above and, in addition, S. J. Weaver, "Interim Report: Psycholinguistic Abilities of Culturally Deprived Children," George Peabody College (mimeo), 1963; Mildred C. Templin, *Certain Language Skills in Children* (Minneapolis: Institute of Child Welfare, 1957); Mildred C. Templin, "Relation of Speech and Language Development to Intelligence and Socioeconomic Status," *Volta Review,* 60 (1958), 331–334; Dorothea McCarthy, *Language Development of the Preschool Child* (Minneapolis: Institute of Child Welfare, 1930). A number of as yet unpublished studies using the Illinois Test of Psycholinguistic Abilities have consistently found disadvantaged children to be a year or more retarded on the auditory language subtests.

5. Few comparative studies on reasoning abilities have been carried out on preschool children. Kennedy, Van de Riet, and White (*op. cit.*) found that southern Negro children had relatively more difficulty with reasoning items than with practical or rote memory items on the Stanford-Binet intelligence test. See also C. Higgins and Cathryne M. Silvers, "A Comparison of the Stanford-Binet and the Colored Raven Progressive Matrices IQ for Children with Low Socioeconomic Status," *Journal of Consulting Psychology,* 22 (1958), 465–468; J. Siller, "Socioeconomic Status and Conceptual Thinking," *Journal of Abnormal and Social Psychology,* 55 (1957), 365–371.

6. D. E. Lavin, *The Prediction of Academic Performance: A Theoretical Analysis and Review of Research* (New York: Russell Sage Foundation, 1965).

7. I. J. Semler and I. Iscoe, "Comparative and Developmental Study of the Learning Abilities of Negro and White Children Under Four Conditions," *Journal of Educational Psychology,* 54 (1963), 38–44; A. R. Jensen, "Learning Ability in Retarded, Average, and Gifted Children," *Merrill-Palmer Quarterly,* 9 (1963), 123–140. Unpublished studies using the Illinois Test of Psycholinguistic

Abilities have characteristically found disadvantaged children to be normal or even above average in ability to repeat digits (a test of immediate auditory memory)—a feature of their ability profiles that markedly distinguishes them from mentally retarded children.

8. M. Deutsch, "The Role of Social Class in Language Development and Cognition," *American Journal of Orthopsychiatry,* **25** (1965), 78–88; M. Deutsch and B. Brown, "Social Influences in Negro-White Intelligence Differences," *Journal of Social Issues,* **20** (1964), 24–25; B. R. Brown and M. Deutsch, "Some Effects of Social Class and Race on Children's Language and Intellectual Abilities: A New Look at an Old Problem," New York Medical College, Institute for Developmental Studies (mimeo), 1965. See also R. T. Osborne, "Racial Differences in Mental Growth and School Achievement: A Longitudinal Study," *Psychological Reports,* **7** (1960), 233–239.

9. NCTE Task Force on Teaching English to the Disadvantaged, *Language Programs for the Disadvantaged* (Champaign, Ill.: National Council of Teachers of English, 1965).

10. J. C. Bledsoe, "An Investigation of Six Correlates of Student Withdrawal from High School," *Journal of Educational Research,* **53** (1959), 3–6; D. Schreiber, *The School Drop-out* (Washington, D. C.: National Education Association, 1964).

11. R. T. Osborne (*op. cit.*) found Negro children in a southeastern state to be on the average three to four years retarded in basic subjects by grade 10, the amount of retardation having increased steadily from grade 6. This suggests a leveling-off at the seventh- or eighth-grade achievement level. The same estimate is indicated by unpublished data from predominantly Negro colleges in the South. The average achievement level of entering freshmen is said to be tenth grade or below. Considering that college entrants represent a select group, it seems reasonable to estimate the terminal achievement of the average student in the high schools from which these students graduate at several grades below this.

12. R. C. Nichols, "The Financial Status of National Merit Finalists," *Science,* **149** (1965), 1071–1074.

13. K. B. Clark, "Education Stimulation of Racially Disadvantaged Children," in *Education in Depressed Areas,* ed. H. Passow (New York: Teachers College Bureau of Publications, 1963), pp. 142–162.

14. J. McV. Hunt, "Motivation Inherent in Information Processing and Action," in *Motivation and Social Organization: Cognitive Determinants,* ed. O. J. Harvey (New York: The Ronald Press Company, 1963); R. W. White, "Motivation Reconsidered: The Concept of Competence," *Psychological Review,* **66** (1959), 297–333.

15. Pauline S. Sears and Edith M. Dowley, "Research on Teaching in the Nursery School," in *Handbook of Research on Teaching,* ed. N. L. Gage (Chicago: Rand-McNally & Co., 1963), pp. 814–864.

16. *Ibid.,* p. 850.

cultural deprivation
as language deprivation

2

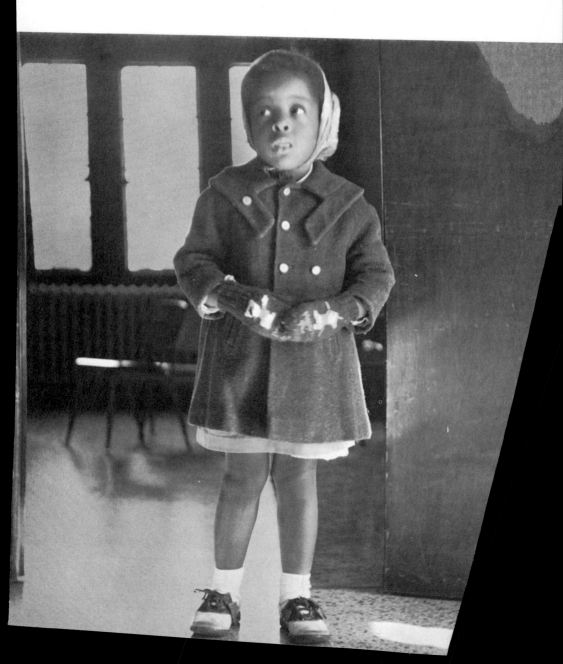

*I*n spite of its wide use, *cultural deprivation* is not a well-accepted term. Mentioning the term in any group of six or more educated adults will usually call forth at least one protest that it is not true that lower-class people do not have a culture—they merely have a different culture.[1] The term has a legitimate meaning, however, which is too important to be brushed aside.

In order to use the term *cultural deprivation,* it is necessary to assume some point of reference. In most dealings with people of different cultures, it is inappropriate to assume a fixed point of reference. To say that the Trobriand Islanders are culturally deprived by our standards is to misuse the term, for it makes no sense to apply our standards to a culture so remote from our own. In dealing with lower-class people in ordinary American communities, however, the various subcultures share many common values and standards, and, with respect to these shared points of reference, it is both legitimate and useful to speak of *cultural deprivation.*

The standards of the American public schools represent one such point of reference. There are standards of knowledge and ability which are consistently held to be valuable in the schools, and any child in the schools who falls short of these standards by reason of his particular cultural background may be said to be culturally deprived. It does not matter that he may have other knowledge and other skills which in other contexts might be valued more highly. There are no schools in our society in which the knowledge and skills peculiar to lower-class groups valued and fostered. In fact, one of the recurrent themes in American tion has been the resistance of underprivileged minority groups ir leaders to efforts to provide them with a special kind of educa- gned to perpetuate their working-class values and status and to ldren to it.[2] Religious and ethnic identity, yes, but lower-class . Any educational program so conceived would quite prop- rded as a means of *depriving* poor people of a chance to ac- cultural benefits necessary for the improvement of their hoosing the standards of the schools as a common refer- t an arbitrary choice. The choice was made when the schools were established as the uniform means of educating all children.

Studies of young disadvantaged children force us to recognize that merely providing lower-class children with access to standard American formal schooling is not sufficient. They are still deprived of many important opportunities for cultural learning which are ordinarily provided through the home rather than through the school. Because of this, the children are not able to profit maximally from the opportunities that the schools provide. Even though technically they are receiving the same education as middle-class children, in fact they are not. Gross evidences of this fact are seen in the numbers of lower-class children who are held back in school, placed in low-level, slow progress classes, channeled into nonacademic terminal secondary school programs, and so on. The low level of academic achievement of lower-class children provides less conspicuous but even more persuasive evidence of deprivation.

If schools for lower-class children did not teach reading and writing on the grounds that lower-class people do not value these skills very highly anyway and that such skills are not of much importance for the unskilled tasks that the children will eventually be expected to perform, probably even the most anthropologically minded among us would grant that children educated in these schools would be culturally deprived in a genuine sense—deprived of opportunities for cultural learning to which everyone in our society is entitled. If this is a case of cultural deprivation, it should not take extreme subtlety of mind to recognize that the situation is basically the same if children receive instruction in reading and writing in school but fail to learn it or fail to learn it to the usual standards because they have been denied prerequisite learning experiences afforded other children in our society.

Cultural deprivation is thus a useful term in discussions of preschool education for disadvantaged children. It is not just a synonym for *disadvantage*. It allows us to focus on those disadvantages that are relevant to education, while recognizing that the child may be disadvantaged in other ways or may be merely "different."

Even by this restricted definition, cultural deprivation in young children may have many facets. But it is possible to rank different elements of cultural deprivation according to how seriously they handicap the child in school learning and according to the amount of effort that may be necessary to alleviate them. For instance, the child who does not know what a sheep is might encounter an occasional difficulty in understanding something that came up in the course of school learning, but it is hard to imagine any very formidable or basic difficulties that might arise as a result of this particular bit of cultural deprivation. Moreover, the lack is one that could be easily remedied, and very likely would be, the first time it came up in the course of school work. On the other hand, if the child did not understand the meaning of the word *or*, he would experience innumerable and serious difficulties with instructions, concepts, and problems; and this lack is not one that can be remedied on the spur of the moment with a picture, example, or brief explanation.

Assigning priorities to different aspects of cultural deprivation is of great importance when it comes to planning a compensatory preschool program. Should a half-day be devoted to a field trip in which the child will have the opportunity to find out what a sheep looks, smells, feels, and acts like? Should time be so used if this same child also does not understand the use of *or* and other basic words of this kind which may take many hours of instruction to teach? Without some basis for assigning priorities, ignorance of *sheep* and ignorance of *or* are on an equal footing. Indeed, anyone familiar with the more unstructured approaches to pre-school education for disadvantaged children is probably aware that more time is devoted to learning about sheep, fire engines, supermarkets, guinea pigs, hair ribbons, freight trains, and similar impedimenta than is de-voted to such elementary necessities as learning the meaning of *or*.

Sensory Deprivation versus Cultural Deprivation

In an area where facts are few and speculation runs high, it is perhaps inevitable and to the good that people should look far afield for bodies of fact and theory that might be relevant. The price paid for this intel-lectual speed-trawling, however, is that some farfetched ideas occasionally capture the imaginations of people who do not understand them well enough to appreciate their fundamental irrelevance. Such has been the case with sensory deprivation, which threatens to fasten itself firmly onto the concept of cultural deprivation in the minds of many educators.

Sensory deprivation is a well-established phenomenon, although its operation is not yet well understood. When chimpanzees and some other mammals are raised from birth either in no light at all or in plain white light (passed through lenses that destroy all patterning), nerves in the visual system are found to deteriorate irreversibly.[3] Animals reared under these conditions are also found to have difficulties in learning certain kinds of visual discriminations which they should be capable of making despite their losses in visual acuity. There is also evidence from extensive experiments with rats that the amount of visual stimulation they receive during the early weeks of life influences the size of the visual cortex (the part of the brain involved in processing visual information) and its chemical composition, although it is not established to what extent be-havior is affected or to what extent the effects are reversible.[4]

Some evidence of the same effects has been found in human children. Infants raised in an almost totally blank visual environment and given a minimum of handling were found by Dennis [5] to be grossly retarded in such basic aspects of development as learning to sit, stand, walk, and speak. They were also less healthy than physical conditions should have warranted, suggesting a general systemic depression resulting from the sensory deprivation.

From these dramatic findings, inferences have been made that the intellectual backwardness of disadvantaged children may have its roots in sensory deprivation and that the major hope of salvaging these children lies in providing them with an abundance of varied sensory experiences. This inference, however, has very little to recommend it beyond its simplicity. In the first place, sensory deprivation does not appear to have major neurological effects except in very early infancy when nerve cells are not fully developed. Animals that have better developed visual systems at birth, such as the cat, do not show these effects. In order for sensory deprivation to be shown as relevant to disadvantaged children, therefore, it would have to be shown that this deprivation occurs very early. On the contrary, Pasamanick and others have found no evidence of social class differences in rate of development during the first two years of life.[6]

Secondly, sensory deprivation studies have dealt only with very drastic amounts of deprivation far beyond any that occur in ordinary life, lower-class or otherwise. There is no evidence that moderate reductions produce any damage. In fact, evidence accumulated by Berlyne [7] suggests that there are optimum levels of stimulation and that extreme deviations, whether above or below such levels, may be harmful. Determining the optimum level is not easy. For all we know, lower-class children may be closer to it than middle-class children.

Thirdly, there is ample evidence, again summarized by Berlyne,[8] that free organisms will tend to seek out an optimum level of stimulation, withdrawing from excess and seeking stimulation when they are not getting enough. One thing that all studies of sensory deprivation have had in common is that the subjects involved have not been free to seek additional stimulation. It is therefore very risky to draw a parallel between these subjects and the slum child who is free to roam the streets.

It would seem that those who have attributed sensory deprivation to lower-class children have not seriously considered what the term implies. It has nothing to do with the educational quality of the stimuli available, but only with their variety, intensity, and patterning. On these purely quantitative bases, automobiles passing in the street are as good as story books, old shoes are as good as dolls, and trash cans are as good as toy drums.

What may be called the "sensory deprivation fad" appears to have originated in a misinterpretation of J. McV. Hunt's influential book, *Intelligence and Experience.*[9] Hunt made extensive reference to the sensory deprivation studies as one kind of evidence that experience influences intellectual development, and although he has continued to cite this evidence in discussions of cultural deprivation, he has never maintained that cultural deprivation as we know it is caused by sensory deprivation. In fact, he has hypothesized that during the critical first year of life, when sensory deprivation might have an effect, lower-class children are likely to be exposed to more stimulation than middle-class children.[10]

There is little reason to suppose that disadvantaged children have suffered on the sensory account. The source of their backwardness in learning, therefore, must be sought in the *content* of the experiences they have had. It might be possible to construct a machine that would present a child with carefully chosen, though meaningless, changing patterns of shapes, colors, intensities, sounds, smells, tactile experiences, and so on, thus ensuring that the child would have no sensory deprivation whatever. But if this machine provided the only experiences the child received, one would expect him to function like an idiot, for he would not have had a chance to learn anything of value. He would have acquired an organically well-developed brain with nothing in it.

Verbal versus Nonverbal Factors in Cultural Deprivation

Although a lack of verbal learning is the outstanding characteristic of culturally deprived children (as was indicated in Chapter 1), there is a widespread opinion that the roots of cultural deprivation lie deeper than this, that the verbal deficiencies reflect a more basic lack of concrete, nonverbal learning experiences. According to Hunt,

> Our traditional emphasis in education upon arithmetic and language skills can well lead us astray in the attempt to develop a program of pre-school enrichment. If Piaget's observations are correct, spoken language—that is to say the motor side of the language skill—comes only after images, or the central processes representing objects and events, have been developed out of repeated encounters with those objects and events. . . .[11]

> Counteracting cultural deprivation at this stage of development (three to six) might best be accomplished by giving the child the opportunity to encounter a wide variety of objects, pictures, and appropriate behavior. The setting should encourage him to indulge his inclinations to scrutinize and manipulate the new objects as long as he is interested and should provide him with appropriate answers to his questions. Such varied experiences would foster the development of representative imagery which could then be the referents for spoken words and later for written language.[12]

In keeping with this view, Hunt has strongly endorsed Montessori methods, which consist very largely of nonverbal types of sensory and manipulative experience, for the preschool education of culturally deprived children.

Hunt's view is nicely in accord with a long-standing inclination of early childhood educators toward concrete, nonverbal experience, and it is not surprising that it has received wide endorsement. On the other hand, there is no convincing evidence that lower-class children are, in fact, lacking in concrete experience. No one could deny, of course, that lower-class children have fewer than the normal number of toys and games and that they are not surrounded with the large number of gadgets, appliances, and furnishings found in middle-class homes. But it has not been shown that these are necessary or even the best sources of concrete learning experience. The kinds of perceptual and logical organization that Piaget considers essential for the development of intelligence are general enough that they can be provided by almost any sort of concrete experience.

On rational grounds, it can be claimed that specially designed play materials provide opportunities for concrete learning that are superior to those provided by a haphazard collection of household junk; but, by the same token, it can be argued that the highly gadgeted and automated environment of the modern prosperous home is a very poor one for concrete learning. The laws according to which the physical world operates— and it is these, according to Piaget, which influence the intellectual development of the child—are extremely hard to discern in such an environment. One pushes buttons, and the television set and automatic washer come alive, but the average adult in the home, not to mention the preschool child, is usually ignorant of how they work and utterly confounded when they break down. As a laboratory in which to study the basic workings of the physical world, the typical lower-class environment seems superior to the typical middle-class environment, because the physical events that occur in it are more intelligible.

A more fundamental question is not whether disadvantaged children lack adequate concrete experience but whether concrete experience is the crucial factor in the development of academic aptitude that Hunt, following Piaget, makes it out to be. The surest way of answering this question would be to run controlled experiments in which some children are deliberately deprived of concrete experience and others are not and to vary opportunities for verbal experience in the same way. Clearly, such an experiment cannot be carried out on human children, and there is no point in carrying it out on animals, because verbal experience has no great influence on animal behavior.

However, some kinds of physically handicapped children provide "natural" experiments in enforced deprivation. Children who have been blind from birth are cut off from the major source of concrete sensory experience, and, moreover, they are often so restricted in getting about that they are further prevented from making the full use of the senses that remain. On the other hand, they are not deprived of verbal experience. With children who have been deaf from birth or an early age, the opposite is true. They are cut off from relatively little concrete experience, but develop virtually no language during the early years and thus have no access to verbal learning. If concrete experience is as vital as Hunt and others have claimed, then blind children should be markedly inferior to deaf children in intellectual competence.

A large number of studies on the intellectual and academic performance of blind and deaf children have provided convincing evidence that the opposite is true: *blind children, on the average, show little or no intellectual and academic deficiency, whereas deaf children are typically about 10 points below normal in IQ and show gross inadequacies in academic achievement.* Deaf children are from two to five years retarded in achievement throughout the school years, and, even with a longer period of schooling than is given to normal children, they do not, on the average, progress beyond the seventh-grade level.[13] These results correspond quite closely with those found for more severely culturally deprived children. The parallels do not end at this point. When one looks at their profiles of aptitude and achievement scores—at the kinds of performance on which they are strongest and weakest—remarkably similar patterns emerge for the deaf and for the culturally deprived.

A comparison of blind with deaf children thus reveals that children can be quite markedly deprived of concrete sensory experience and yet develop normal intellects and function well academically, whereas if they are deprived of language experience, they are seriously handicapped in these areas even though they have full access to concrete experience.

Even more striking evidence of the importance of verbal factors is provided when one looks at social-class differences among deaf children. If social-class differences in opportunities for concrete experience are as important as they have been made out to be, then one should expect to find that deaf children from poorer homes would be very markedly inferior in intelligence to deaf children from more privileged homes, since learning for deaf children would depend almost entirely on opportunities for concrete experience. No direct investigations were found, but indirect evidence could be obtained from comparisons of deaf children in day schools and deaf children in public residential schools—the latter children more often coming from low-income and rural backgrounds. Such comparisons did not reveal any differences related to social background.[14] This finding was reinforced by a study by Bereiter correlating the intelligence of 300 deaf children in a public residential school with the educational level of their nondeaf parents. The correlation so obtained was much lower than that obtained in other studies using hearing children and their parents and was, in fact, lower than that obtained in a study using children who were reared apart from their parents.[15] Thus, although deaf children usually live at home until the age of five, their level of intelligence does not seem to bear the relation to the socio-economic level of the home that it does in the case of hearing children.

In light of the substantial intellectual and academic retardation found in deaf children, this finding may be interpreted as meaning that deaf children are culturally deprived in much the way that lower-class children are deprived, regardless of their home backgrounds. It would appear from this that social-class differences in opportunities for concrete experience either do not exist or are not important, whereas lack of opportunity for language experience has serious effects that closely correspond to those found in cultural deprivation.

It may seem farfetched to compare the deaf child, who often has no language at all, with the disadvantaged child, who usually does have a language, even though an immature and nonstandard one. To understand how the two can turn out to be academically handicapped in about the same degree, it is necessary to consider in more detail the role of language in intellectual development.

For purposes of getting along socially and of self-expression, language is a convenience but not a necessity for the young child. It is quite possible to make one's wants known, to enter actively into play and other social relationships, and to give vent to one's feelings without language. Young deaf children do this, and it appears that lower-class children also rely to a considerable extent on nonverbal means for these purposes. People who work with disadvantaged preschool children report a considerable number of children who at four years of age hardly speak at all. Language is apparently dispensable enough in the life of the lower-class child for an occasional child to get along without it altogether. Yet, such children are often indistinguishable from their peers in other areas of behavior.

Language becomes a virtual necessity, however, when one moves from the social uses of language to the transmission of knowledge from one person to another and to the performance of certain operations with concepts. From what is known about verbal communication in lower-class homes, it would appear that the cognitive uses of language are severely restricted, especially in communication between adults and children. Language is primarily used to control behavior, to express sentiments and emotions, to permit the vicarious sharing of experiences, and to keep the social machinery of the home running smoothly. These are important uses of language. Many lower-class people are more skillful in them than better-educated middle-class people. But what is lacking by comparison is the use of language to explain, to describe, to instruct, to inquire, to hypothesize, to analyze, to compare, to deduce, and to test. And these are the uses that are necessary for academic success.

If this characterization of verbal communication within the lower-class home is accurate, the parallels between deaf and culturally deprived children become much clearer. The culturally deprived child may be exposed to social uses of language from which the deaf child is barred, but in this area the deaf child is able to compensate for his lack by non-verbal means of communication. With regard to the important cognitive uses of language, however, both kinds of children are seriously deprived—the deaf child because he cannot understand what is said, the lower-class child because he is not sufficiently exposed to language in its cognitive uses.

Thorough research on verbal communication within families remains to be done. There is evidence that verbal communication of any sort between parents and children is limited in lower-class homes, and, of course, the larger size of families, the frequent lack of fathers in the home, the fact that mothers often work, and the crowded conditions that force children out of doors and away from adult contacts would all contribute to such a lack. Studies by Strodtbeck [16] indicate that lower-class mothers make more use of simple imperatives ("Leave it alone"; "Shut up") and less use of explanations and statements in dealing with their children. In some very interesting research by Hess,[17] middle- and lower-class Negro mothers were asked to teach their children certain things in an experimental situation. The lower-class mothers seemed generally at a loss as to how to do it, could not give clear explanations or directions, and did not know how to motivate the child, again falling back on simple imperatives devoid of instructive content. From the protocols cited by Hess, it would appear that the lower-class mothers had never attempted this kind of teaching before. The "errors" they made were very much like those one observes in novice teachers who are unaccustomed to talking to children.

Bernstein [18] has theorized that the speech of lower-class people follows a linguistic code that is ideally suited to maintaining social relationships, that is adequate for sharing familiar experiences and opinions, but that is inadequate for expressing personal or original opinions, for analysis and careful reasoning, for dealing with anything hypothetical or beyond the present, and for explaining anything very complex. He sees this linguistic code as growing naturally out of the conditions of lower-class life and serving a useful purpose in it, but he also sees the child who is brought up in such an environment as being trapped by the restrictions of this linguistic code and unable to operate at the high conceptual and logical level that is required in formal education. Bernstein's theory has especially alarming implications for the lower-class child because it suggests that the child does not merely lack certain of the language skills that middle-class children have; he has learned a self-perpetuating language code that effectively bars him from acquiring these skills.

Bernstein's theory and Hess's observations on the inability of lower-class mothers to teach combine to suggest a more fundamental reason for the deficiencies of lower-class children in school-relevant learning. When a cultural group possesses a distinctive body of knowledge and beliefs which the older generation feels obliged to pass on in some organized fashion to the younger generation, it is reasonable to suppose that the group will develop the language and teaching skills that are needed for such a purpose. Among disorganized and dispossessed minority groups, however, the culture appears to center around attitudes, interests, a style of life, and a scattering of unorganized beliefs and superstitions so unformalized that they may be transmitted without explanation, argument, or detailed exposition. Deliberate teaching is not a normal or necessary part of the adult role in such cultural groups, and neither the skills nor the language peculiar to teaching are developed and maintained. By contrast, in middle-class American society, as in most self-maintaining societies, nearly every adult can and does teach. It is a normal part of the adult role performed almost without awareness, particularly in the adult's relations with children.

Cultural deprivation, then, has a double edge. The lower-class child is not without culture, but he is deprived of that part of culture that can only be acquired through teaching—the knowledge, the meanings, the explanations, the structured beliefs that make up the conceptual furniture of culture. Beyond that, the child spends his early childhood in an environment where teaching does not take place and where the language with which teaching is carried out is not used; therefore, he may not even learn *how to be taught,* and when he is exposed to teaching, he may behave much as if he were mentally retarded or devoid of language altogether.

Some Language Problems of Culturally Deprived Children

All that can be concluded about disadvantaged children from their test performance is that their use of language is similar to that of the average child a year or so younger. The several studies that have attempted to render a more descriptive account of the language of disadvantaged children show much the same thing. In such characteristics as sentence length, word variety, and the use of various grammatical categories and constructions, the language of disadvantaged children resembles that of other children at a lower age level.[19] From this the natural conclusion would be that lower-class and middle-class children speak essentially the same language, but lower-class children are about a year behind in their mastery of it.

As the linguist Chomsky has pointed out, however, descriptive studies of the kind referred to above do not really tell us what a child *can do* with language. A certain grammatical construction may not appear in a sample of the child's speech, and yet he may be fully capable of understanding and using it when the need arises. Conversely, a certain term or construction might appear, but the child's use of it might be so restricted to a few special cases that it would be misleading to credit him with mastery of it.[20] Chomsky goes on to say that

> if anything far-reaching and real is to be discovered about the actual grammar of the child, then rather devious kinds of observations of his performance, his abilities, and his comprehension in many different kinds of circumstance will have to be obtained, so that a variety of evidence may be brought to bear on the attempt to determine what is in fact his underlying linguistic competence at each stage of development.[21]

No systematic research of the kinds Chomsky deems essential has yet been carried out on disadvantaged children, but the writers have made use of two "devious kinds of observations" that may help to throw light on questions of basic linguistic competence. One of these is the Cognitive Maturity Test developed by Engelmann, which tests the child's ability to repeat sentences of various kinds and to answer questions using information contained in the sentences. The other kind of observation is more informal, based on efforts to teach children various language skills. These attempts provide particularly revealing evidence of what children *can* do, as contrasted with what they *do* do, with language.

These observations are quite limited, being based on intensive work with only 30 disadvantaged Negro preschool children and on less intensive work with perhaps 50 more. However, there are no other data currently available that go much below the surface in describing the nature of language deprivation.

The speech of the severely deprived children seems to consist not of distinct words, as does the speech of middle-class children of the same age, but rather of whole phrases or sentences that function like giant words. That is to say, these "giant word" units cannot be taken apart by the child and re-combined; they cannot be transformed from statements to questions, from imperatives to declaratives, and so on. Instead of saying "He's a big dog," the deprived child says "He bih daw." Instead of saying "I ain't got no juice," he says "Uai-ga-na-ju." Instead of saying "That is a red truck," he says "Da-re-truh." Once the listener has become accustomed to this style of speech, he may begin to hear it as if all the sounds were there, and may get the impression that he is hearing articles when in fact there is only a pause where the article should be. He may believe that the child is using words like *it, is, if,* and *in,* when in fact he is using the same sound for all of them—something on the order of "ih." (This becomes apparent if the child is asked to repeat the statement "It is in the box." After a few attempts in which he becomes confused as to the number of "ih's" to insert, the child is likely to be reduced to a stammer.)

If the problem were merely one of faulty pronunciation, it would not be so serious. But it appears that the child's faulty pronunciation arises from his inability to deal with sentences *as sequences of meaningful parts.* Even a sophisticated adult will have difficulty pronouncing a very long word if he is unable to deal with it in parts (the reader might take a try at EMPIANASROFLALILIMINLIAL, reading it aloud once and then trying to repeat it from memory). In the Cognitive Maturity Test, children are called upon to repeat sentences of varying degrees of complexity. The severely disadvantaged child will tend to give merely an approximate rendition of the over-all sound profile of the sentence, often leaving out the sounds in the middle, as is common when people are trying to reproduce a meaningless series—this in spite of the fact that the words themselves are often very simple, like "A big truck is not a little truck."

It may be objected that the child cannot say the sentence because he cannot understand it, and questioning of the child often discloses that he does not understand those sentences he cannot produce. But his inability to produce certain sentences also prevents him from learning to understand them. For instance, after dozen of repetitions of "His father said he could have candy or a cookie," the child may come no closer to rendering the last three words of the sentence than "a-uh cookie." It will then become evident from questioning that the child does not understand that a choice is involved. But if the child is unable to produce *or* differently from *and,* he is in a poor position to learn the difference.

The culturally deprived child is often able to follow fairly lengthy commands. Among the 15 children in the initial Bereiter-Engelmann study were more than the average number for their age who could correctly execute the following instructions taken from the Stanford-Binet intelligence test: "First you put the pencil on the chair, then shut the door, then bring me the box." Where they had difficulty was in distinguishing between commands that differ *only with respect to structure words or inflections:* "Show me the one that is yellow" versus "Show me the one that is not yellow"; "Lift up your hand" versus "Lift up your hands"; "Pick up the red one and the green one" versus "Pick up the red one or the green one."

Braine [22] and Fraser and Brown,[23] in their studies of the grammar of younger but more privileged children, have noted that, among these children also, it is the smaller connectives and other structure words that are lacking. To this extent, the culturally deprived child resembles a culturally privileged child of a younger age. But there is a very important difference. The culturally privileged two-year-old uses a "reduced grammar." He leaves out words that he does not know and forms condensed sentences out of the words he does know how to handle. Thus, even though his sentences may consist of only two or three words, they are distinct words, and he is able to recombine them flexibly because they exist for him as independent entities. Disadvantaged children, on the other hand, often blend the words together with noises that take the place of words and inflections they do not know, so that all the words tend to become fused into a whole. This leaves no distinctive units that can be recombined to generate new sentences.

The culturally deprived child does with sentences what the culturally privileged child does when he is trying to say a big word—he approximates the whole sequence of noises. But the culturally privileged child seems to acquire very early the notion that sentences are made up of words, so that he imitates the noises that occur *within* words but not the noises that occur *between* familiar words. Thus, the culturally privileged child builds up his sentences by adding words to them as he masters them: from "Mommy read" to "Mommy read book" to "Mommy read me book" and eventually to "Mommy, I want you to read me this book." The culturally deprived child grappling with such a sentence would probably start off with some amalgam like "re-ih-bu," with which he would then be stuck. The words "me" and "this" would be lost in noise, as they would be in any other sentences where they occurred, and thus it would be difficult for them ever to emerge as distinct, usable words.

The inflexibility that results from this way of treating words within statements is nowhere so clearly illustrated as in the culturally deprived child's inability to reverse the elements in a statement. For the child who treats sentences as patterns of words, it is a fairly simple matter to learn that the phrase "Harold and Tyrone" can be transformed into "Tyrone and Harold" without changing its sense. Given a few examples, such a child can then go on to handle any problem of the kind "What's another way of saying '_____' and '_____'?" But this task has proved to be one of the most difficult to teach culturally deprived children. When asked "What's another way of saying 'Green and red'?" they will persist in saying "Green and red." Correcting the response does not seem to help. They treat "Green and red" as if it were a three-syllable word, so that to transform it to "Red and green" makes no more sense than to transform "Wonderful" into "Fulderwon," and the generalization of the pattern to other instances is just as hard for them to grasp.

Perhaps the strongest indication that this "giant word" syndrome is not merely a manifestation of immature language comprehension is that the children have a strong tendency to revert to it even after they have been taught to handle certain patterns of discrete words. This shows up most clearly in arithmetic, where the entire vocabulary is new and the children cannot be accused of lapsing back into imitation of the way they hear the same thing said at home. Children in the Bereiter-Engelmann preschool had learned to handle equations of the form "Two plus one equals three," making substitutions to create other equations, e.g.,

"Two plus zero equals two." Even here, some children would continually lapse into amalgamations: "Two pluh wunic'k three." Having done this, they were no longer able to substitute other numbers for the "one," it having become fused with the beginning sounds of "equals."

Combating this tendency to fuse separate words into indivisible wholes has been one of the continuing struggles in teaching effective language to culturally deprived children. One hears a considerable amount of talk about the value of encouraging culturally deprived children to speak in sentences. But this does not really seem to be the problem, if by speaking sentences is meant uttering extended strings of sounds which can be interpreted as sentences. The problem is to get the children to speak in words and to make statements that consist of words rather than amalgamated noises.

The difficulty that culturally deprived children have in treating words as separate entities within statements can go a long way toward explaining many of their other language problems. For instance, vocabulary growth should be slower even when there are ample opportunities for learning. As the new word is used in different sentences, it becomes fused with different noises and therefore becomes unrecognizable as the same word. The "giant word" syndrome would also help to explain the difficulties deprived children have in learning to read, for in reading also the word is the basic unit, and the child who cannot deal with words as unitary things in his spoken language should be expected to have difficulty in mastering a code which is, in essence, a code for translating clusters of printed characters into spoken *words*.[24]

The "giant word" hypothesis is consistent with Bernstein's description of the restricted linguistic codes employed by lower-class speakers and is supported by his research. In comparing pauses and hesitations in the speech of lower- and middle-class adolescent boys, Bernstein concluded that lower-class boys used longer phrase units in their speech, which might imply that their speech consists of larger "chunks" that are treated in speech as if they were single words.[25] This leads to a more fluent but much less flexible use of language.

In keeping with Bernstein's theory that lower-class language is mainly an instrument for the maintenance of social relationships, the writers have found culturally deprived children to be strangely indifferent to the content of verbal utterances while being acutely concerned with the effect that their utterances have on other people. A question that begins with "Can you tell" or "Do you know" is invariably answered "Yes," often before it is completed. These beginnings are evidently recognized as signals that "Yes" is the desired answer. *Yes-no* questions have to be used with great circumspection in the teaching of these children because the children are so adept at and intent upon "reading" the teacher's expressions and inflections for clues to the desired response. The children may even succeed in giving correct answers without fully understanding what *yes* and *no* mean. Several children have been encountered who responded alternatively with "Yes" and "No" or the corresponding head motions, but who did not know which kind of motion went with "Yes" and which went with "No."

Lack of experience in the expository uses of language was sometimes revealed in the children's limited control over voice volume. These children typically showed two levels of volume: one a barely audible mumble used for replying to questions (a self-effacing, "keep out of trouble" tone of voice), the other a loud shout used for commanding attention or voicing complaints and taunts. They lacked the middle range of volume ordinarily used for conveying information.

In terms of the child's intellectual competence, however, the most damaging aspect of this social-centered language is the child's inability to talk to himself. As previously noted, he can often follow complicated instructions. Providing he is able to make use of nonverbal helps, such as pointing, manipulating, and gesturing, he can also give directions to someone else. But, within his own behavior, he often cannot relate what he says with what he does. At a teeter-totter, he can follow the direction to "Push it down" or "Lift it up," but if asked to tell what he is doing, he may say that he is pushing it down when he is lifting it up. As Luria has shown through extensive investigations, the ability to control one's own behavior through language does not come about automatically as one learns to say and do various things. The ability to integrate the two must itself be learned.[26] With culturally deprived children, it appears that speech develops as a form of social behavior that is more or less independent of motor behavior. This does not prevent the child from becoming proficient in motor skills, but it becomes a serious handicap when motor acts must be coupled with judgments, as in drawing, writing, and solving problems involving manipulation of objects. The culturally deprived child then shows much the same dissociation between language and action that has been observed in mentally retarded children.[27]

As Luria and Vygotsky have explained, controlling one's actions through one's own words is a necessary step toward the mastery of dialectical reasoning, which in essence is controlling verbal behavior through an "internal dialog" by means of which one may solve a problem, working a step at a time.[28] This is a use of language quite different from its social uses, and the deficiencies of culturally deprived children in this use are most striking. At the most elementary level, these deficiencies show up in the child's inability to use an *if-then* rule.

In the initial Bereiter-Engelmann experiment, disadvantaged children easily learned the rule "If it has a beginning and an end, it's a word" (beginnings and ends being appropriately designated so that the rule was valid). But even after the children had learned to identify beginnings and ends correctly, they could not with any consistency apply the rule. Simple as the rule appears, its application requires an internal dialog, a chain of verbal steps on the following order: "Does it have a beginning? Does it have an end? Did I answer both questions 'Yes?' If I did, it is a word. If I didn't, it is not a word." The children could not ask themselves these questions. If the teacher asked them, they could answer the first two questions, but they could not use their own answers to these first two questions in order to answer the third question. Because of this inability to use the information gained from verbal operations in subsequent operations, they were effectively limited to "one-shot" intellectual acts. There is a striking similarity in this phenomenon to that noted by Bloom and Broder [29] in the problem-solving processes of select college students who were encountering academic difficulties. Faced with problems that could be dealt with by a "one-shot" approach, these students were able to perform adequately, but when faced with complex problems that could not be solved except by a sequence of steps, such students would brood a while and then say "I don't know the answer to that one." Answers either had to be grasped at once, or they were inaccessible.

This ability to carry on a dialog through which information is accumulated and used—a dialog either with others or with oneself—would seem to constitute the very core of verbal intelligence. All other aspects of language—vocabulary, fluency of expression, standard usage, and the like—are subordinate to it and of little account in academic performance except as "fuel" for such dialog. Thus, culturally deprived children, lacking the most rudimentary forms of constructive dialog, are cut down at the very trunk of academic aptitude. Whatever they possess in the way of expressive language, even though it is also inadequate, serves only to cover a deficiency that is much more profound.

Studies by Loban and others have been cited as evidence that culturally deprived children do possess all the necessary elements of English grammar and syntax, even though they make scanty use of some of them.[30] What is crucial, however, is not the extent to which their language is technically capable of conveying thoughts and information but the extent to which the children themselves are able to use language in this way. A clever philosopher might be able to rewrite Aristotle using only the vocabulary and grammar of a culturally deprived child. But this same child might not be able to express any ideas whatever in an ordered, cumulative sequence.

As the preceding observations suggest, many disadvantaged children of preschool age come very close to the total lack of ability to use language as a device for acquiring and processing information. Language for them is unwieldy and not very useful. For some of them, speaking is clearly no fun, and they manage as far as possible to get along without it. Others enjoy social speech and use it a good deal in play and social intercourse, but seldom for purposes of learning or reasoning; their language, *as they use it,* is not adequate for these purposes.

Social and Emotional Deprivation

Many preschool programs for disadvantaged children are based on the assumption that the central problems of disadvantaged children are not intellectual or cognitive at all, but are problems of social and emotional adjustment. The writers do not know of any evidence to support the assumption. All of the emotional and behavioral disorders that are found in other children can be found in disadvantaged children, of course, and some of them are found in greater numbers. *But there are no emotional or behavioral disorders that have been shown to be uniquely associated with poverty, lower-class status, or minority-group status in preschool children.* A teacher of disadvantaged children, therefore, may expect to have the same kinds of personality problems to deal with as she would with any other preschool children, and should be able to deal with them in the same ways.

Since the view that disadvantaged children are "emotionally deprived" or "socially deprived" is very widespread, however, it may be worthwhile to point out some of the misunderstandings on which this view is based.

1. Cases of very severe personality disturbance are probably more common among poor children. Because these cases are so dramatic, they tend to color one's whole perception of disadvantaged preschool groups. It would be a mistake to build a whole program around children of this kind, however, to the neglect of the vast majority of disadvantaged children whose major problems are not in the area of emotion.

2. Older disadvantaged children often do show personality problems directly associated with their lower-class or minority-group status (feelings of inferiority or resentment). Older children frequently show the damaging effects of school failure on personality development. The symptoms have seldom begun to develop among preschool children, however,[31] and it is difficult to see what preventive measures could be taken within the domain of the school other than providing a solid skill foundation and fostering self-confidence.

3. It is fairly easy to *produce* emotional disturbances in young children. Many of the symptoms of maladjustment that are sometimes conspicuous in preschool classes for disadvantaged children (such as tantrums, uncontrollability, withdrawal, and clinging) arise directly from inept or misguided management practices. Strodtbeck has reported the results of an experimental preschool class in which the major em-

phasis was on "mothering"—holding the children and nurturing any interest they manifested in training materials. Strodbeck notes,

> The absence of the principal teacher from the classroom in order to per-
> form this mothering, coupled with the permissive atmosphere, seemed to
> release sibling rivalry and regressive behavior. It wasn't until the eleventh
> week that tantrums were brought under control. The quasi-therapeutic
> milieu proved to be helpful neither as therapy nor as education.[32]

Similar children in other classes that were run in a more controlled fashion showed no such emotional disturbances.

4. Perhaps the most widespread misunderstanding comes from a failure to distinguish between behavior that reveals inappropriate social learning and behavior that indicates more deep-seated personality disturbances. Physical aggression, for instance, may be a danger sign in middle-class children, but, for many lower-class children, it may be merely a routine way of settling disputes. Preschool disadvantaged children are likely to show distressing tendencies to hit, bite, kick, scream, run wildly about, cling, climb into laps, steal, lie, hide, ignore directions, and defy authority. These are quite inappropriate behaviors for the classroom, and they will have to be replaced by more appropriate ones. This is not always an easy task for the teacher, but she should see the task for what it is: *teaching naïve children how to act in a new situation,* not of administering psychotherapy to malformed personalities.

When viewed in this way, the inappropriate social behavior of disadvantaged children may be regarded as but another facet of cultural deprivation, as another way in which disadvantaged children lack the kinds of learning necessary for success in school. It is an important aspect, for until disadvantaged children have learned the appropriate ways to behave in school, it may be impossible for them to progress in academic areas. But, in practical terms, it is a minor problem compared to the lack of prerequisite language learning, because it may be remedied so much more quickly and simply. A large number of eight-week summer preschool classes for disadvantaged children have made great progress in teaching appropriate social behaviors in school, while making virtually no inroads against the children's lacks in verbal learning.

Summary

This chapter has explored a number of different aspects of deprivation in young lower-class children. Cultural deprivation was defined as a lack of those particular kinds of learning that are important for success in school. In this respect, it is legitimate to speak of lower-class children as being "deprived" of culture, even though they may have a culture which is complete and adequate from other points of view.

Cultural deprivation was distinguished from sensory deprivation, which pertains only to the quantity of sensory stimulation an organism receives during the crucial early stages of neural maturation. It was shown that there is no reason to believe that sensory deprivation is a factor in the deficiencies of lower-class children and that it is largely irrelevant to cultural deprivation, which has to do with *what* the child has learned rather than with the amount of stimulation he has received.

The relative importance of concrete, exploratory learning and verbal learning was investigated. Evidence was cited which suggests that lack of concrete learning has relatively little to do with the intellectual and academic deficiencies of disadvantaged children and that it is the lack of verbal learning, in particular the lack of those kinds of learning that can only be transmitted from adults to children through language, that is mainly responsible for these deficiencies. Thus, there is justification for treating cultural deprivation as synonymous with language deprivation.

The language deficiencies of disadvantaged children were seen to consist not of deficiencies in vocabulary and grammar as such but of failure to master certain uses of language. Language for the disadvantaged child seems to be an aspect of social behavior which is not of vital importance. The disadvantaged child masters a language that is adequate for maintaining social relationships and for meeting his social and material needs, but he does not learn how to use language for obtaining and transmitting information, for monitoring his own behavior, and for carrying on verbal reasoning. In short, he fails to master the cognitive uses of language, which are the uses that are of primary importance in school.

Two special weaknesses of the language development of lower-class children were noted. One is the tendency to treat sentences as "giant words" that cannot be taken apart and recombined. This leads to an inflexible kind of language that does not make use of the full potentialities of the grammar and syntax, and it makes the learning of new vocabulary and structures more difficult. The second weakness, which may well be an outgrowth of the first, is a failure to master the use of structural words and inflections which are necessary for the expression and manipulation of logical relationships. The problem for culturally deprived children is not so much learning to speak in sentences as learning to speak in sentences that are composed of discrete words.

Many educators assume that the disadvantaged child's basic problems are social and emotional rather than intellectual or cognitive. It was pointed out, however, that there is no evidence that underprivileged status has any unique effects on personality development in young children. Its effects, if any, are probably only to increase the incidence of the same kinds of personality disturbances found in children of all social groups. The widespread use of the terms *social deprivation* and *emotional deprivation* seems to be based on misunderstandings arisings from (1) generalizing from a few extreme cases, (2) projecting the problems of older disadvantaged children on to younger ones who do not, in fact, show them, (3) blaming the home environment for behavior disturbances that are actually the result of inept or misguided management in the preschool itself, and (4) interpreting normal lower-class behavior as symptomatic of severe maladjustment. The inappropriate social behavior that many disadvantaged children reveal in school is best interpreted as but another aspect of cultural deprivation, as a lack of particular kinds of learning that are important for success in school.

Notes

1. See B. Mackler and M. G. Giddings, "Cultural Deprivation: A Study in Mythology," *Teachers College Record,* **66** (1965), 608–613.

2. L. A. Cremin, *The Transformation of the School* (New York: Alfred A. Knopf, Inc., 1961).

3. A. H. Riesen, "Effects of Stimulus Deprivation on the Development and Atrophy of the Visual Sensory System," *American Journal of Orthopsychiatry,* **30** (1960), 23–36.

4. E. L. Bennett, Marian C. Diamond, D. Krech, and M. R. Rosenzweig, "Chemical and Anatomical Plasticity of Brain," *Science,* **146** (1964), 610–619.

5. W. Dennis, "Causes of Retardation Among Institutional Children: Iran," *Journal of Genetic Psychology,* **96** (1960), 47–59.

6. Hilda Knobloch and B. Pasamanick, "Environmental Factors Affecting Human Development, Before and After Birth," *Pediatrics,* **26** (1960), 210–218. See also Nancy Bayley and H. E. Jones, "Environmental Correlates of Mental and Motor Development: A Cumulative Study from Infancy to Six Years," *Child Development,* **4** (1937), 329–341.

7. D. E. Berlyne, *Conflict, Arousal, and Curiosity* (New York: McGraw-Hill Book Company, Inc., 1960).

8. *Ibid.,* pp. 200–209.

9. J. McV. Hunt, *Intelligence and Experience* (New York: The Ronald Press Company, 1961).

10. J. McV. Hunt, "The Psychological Basis for Using Preschool Enrichment as an Antidote for Cultural Deprivation," *Merrill-Palmer Quarterly,* **10** (1964), 209–248.

11. *Ibid.,* p. 239.

12. J. McV. Hunt, "How Children Develop Intellectually," *Children,* **11** (1964), 89.

13. S. A. Kirk, *Educating Exceptional Children* (Boston: Houghton Mifflin Company, 1962); I. S. Fusfeld, "A Cross-section Evaluation of the Academic Program of Schools for the Deaf," *Gallaudet College Bulletin,* **3** (1954); C. P. Goetzinger and C. L. Rousey, "Educational Achievement of Deaf Children," *American Annals of the Deaf,* **104** (1959), 221–231; H. R. Myklebust, *The Psychology of Deafness* (New York: Grune & Stratton, Inc., 1960); Mildred C. Templin, *The Development of Reasoning in Children with Normal and Defective Hearing* (Minneapolis: University of Minnesota Press, 1950); Mildred C. Templin, "A Qualitative Analysis of Explanations and Physical Causality,"

American Annals of the Deaf, **99** (1954), 252–269; H. Z. Wooden, "Deaf and Hard of Hearing Children," in *Exceptional Children in the Schools,* ed. L. M. Dunn (New York: Holt, Rinehart & Winston, Inc., 1963), pp. 339–411; S. C. Ashcroft, "The Blind and Partially Seeing," *Review of Educational Research,* **29** (1959), 519–528.

14. Myklebust, *op. cit.;* Templin, *The Development of Reasoning . . . ;* S. P. Quigley and D. R. Frisina, "Institutionalization and Psycho-educational Development of Deaf Children," *Council for Exceptional Children Monographs,* Series A, No. 3 (1963).

15. C. Bereiter, "The Relative Importance of Verbal and Nonverbal Factors in Cultural Deprivation: Evidence from Children with Sensory Handicaps," (Urbana, Ill.: Institute for Research on Exceptional Children [mimeo], 1965).

16. F. L. Strodtbeck, "Progress Report: The Reading Readiness Nursery: Short-term Intervention Technique" (Chicago: University of Chicago, Social Psychology Laboratory [mimeo], 1964).

17. R. D. Hess and Virginia Shipman, "Early Blocks to Children's Learning," *Children,* **12** (1965), 189–194.

18. B. Bernstein, "Social Class and Linguistic Development" in *Education, Economy, and Society,* ed. A. H. Halsey, J. Floud, and C. A. Anderson (New York: Free Press of Glencoe, Inc., 1961); B. Bernstein, "Elaborated and Restricted Codes: Their Social Origins and Some Consequences," *American Anthropologist,* **66** (1964), No. 6, Part 2.

19. Mildred C. Templin, *Certain Language Skills in Children* (Minneapolis: University of Minnesota Press, 1957); Mildred C. Templin, "Relation of Speech and Language Development to Intelligence and Sociometric Status," *Volta Review,* **60** (1958), 331–334; W. Loban, *The Language of Elementary School Children* (Champaign, Ill.: National Council of Teachers of English, 1963); W. Loban, *Problems in Oral English* (Champaign, Ill.: National Council of Teachers of English, 1965).

20. N. Chomsky, Formal Discussion of "The Development of Grammar in Child Language" by W. Miller and Susan Ervin, *Society for Research in Child Development Monographs,* **29** (1964), 35–39.

21. *Ibid.,* p. 36.

22. M. D. S. Braine, "The Ontogeny of English Phrase Structure," *Language,* **39** (1963), 1–13.

23. R. Brown and C. Fraser, "The Acquisition of Syntax," *Society for Research in Child Development Monographs,* **29** (1964), 43–79.

24. J. B. Carroll, "The Analysis of Reading Instruction: Perspectives from Psychology and Linguistics," in *Theories of Learning and Instruction,* 63rd Yearbook of the National Society for the Study of Education, Part I (Chicago: University of Chicago Press, 1964).

25. B. Bernstein, "Linguistic Codes, Hesitation Phenomena, and Intelligence," *Language and Speech,* **5** (1962), 31–46.

26. A. R. Luria, *The Role of Speech in the Regulation of Normal and Abnormal Behavior* (New York: Liveright Publishing Corp., 1961).

27. N. O'Connor and Beate Hermelin, *Speech and Thought in Severe Subnormality* (New York: The Macmillan Company, 1963).

28. Luria, *op. cit.;* L. S. Vygotsky, *Thought and Language* (Cambridge, Mass.: M. I. T. Press, 1962).

29. B. S. Bloom and Lois J. Broder, *Problem-solving Processes of College Students* (Chicago: University of Chicago Press, 1950).

30. Loban, *The Language of Elementary School Children* and *Problems in*

Oral English. More recent linguistic findings, however, suggest that this is indeed an oversimplification of the disadvantaged child's language problems, particularly in the case of lower-class Negro children. In studying urban Negro dialects, Stewart has identified a number of dialect levels, the lowest of which is spoken by most children but usually not by their parents. This dialect is evidently maintained by children and passed on from one generation of children to another with little adult influence. It should therefore not be surprising that this dialect, besides being structurally simpler than adult dialects, should also be exceedingly limited in its cognitive usefulness. See W. A. Stewart, "Urban Negro Speech: Sociolinguistic Factors Affecting English Teaching," in *Proceedings of Conference on Urban School Dialects and Language Learning* (Champaign, Ill.: National Council of Teachers of English, 1965).

In a report given at the 1965 meeting of the National Council of Teachers of English, Beryl Bailey of Hunter College noted two important characteristics of lower-class southern Negro dialects: (1) the presence of an enormous number of homonyms (words that sound the same but have different meanings) arising from the tendency to omit final consonants; and (2) the strong influence of Creole grammatical structure, which is essentially uninflected, depending on words at the beginning of the sentence to indicate person, tense, number, etc. A dialect that has numerous homonyms should itself be difficult to learn as a first language, presenting manifold possibilities of confusion comparable to those encountered by a deaf child in trying to learn English through lip-reading, where a great many different words look the same (are produced by the same observable mouth movements). Faced with such difficulties, it is entirely possible that lower-class Negro children would be retarded in the learning *of their own dialect,* even if they were provided with the same amount of language experience as children from standard English-speaking homes. If Bailey is correct in her hypothesis that Negro dialects have a Creole grammatical structure, this would indicate that standard English is a foreign language to the lower-class Negro child as regards grammatical structure, even though it uses much the same vocabulary. This would tend to support the position set forth in this chapter that the crucial problem for such children is learning the grammar of English rather than increasing their vocabularies.

31. D. P. Ausubel and Pearl Ausubel, "Ego Development Among Segregated Negro Children," in *Education in Depressed Areas,* ed. H. Passow (New York: Teachers College Bureau of Publications, 1963).

32. Strodtbeck, *op. cit.*

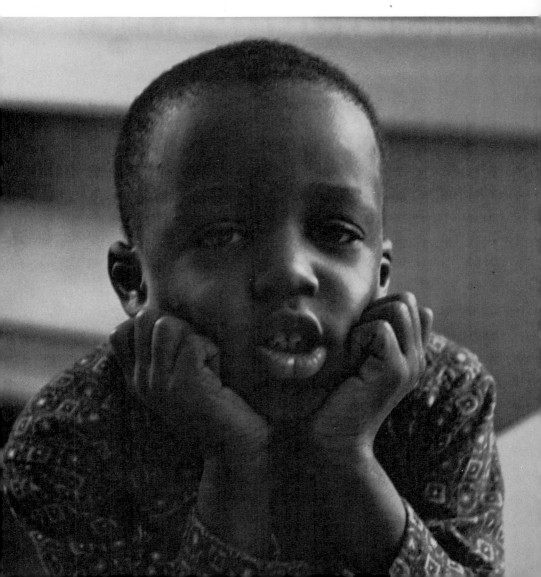

academic objectives 3
for the preschool
and an approach
to achieving them

At the preschool level, there are usually no definite goals that children are expected to reach, no norms of accomplishment on the basis of which a child may be said to have fallen short or exceeded the mark. Whereas a third-grade teacher might be able to say, for instance, that her class had completed the year's work in arithmetic by April 15 (or, alternatively, that they had failed to complete it by the end of the term), there are no such statements which a nursery-school teacher can make, and, indeed, to many nursery-school teachers such statements would be unthinkable.

Yet, it is just such definite goals that are needed if a preschool is to accomplish the task of bringing the disadvantaged children up to a level necessary for later school success. This section will be devoted to setting forth certain minimum standards of academic attainment according to which the success of a preschool program may be judged. In an effective program, most children should be able to exceed these goals. An occasional child will be unable to reach them in a year's time no matter how he is taught; but it should be recognized that every child who falls short of any one of these goals represents a failure of the program. What the goals represent, then, is the writers' best judgment as to what a child who is about to enter first grade should be able to do if he is to have an adequate chance of succeeding in later schooling. No divine wisdom is claimed for these standards; they are offered here because it seems essential for teachers, if they are to be maximally productive, to have tangible goals.

Minimum Goals

1. Ability to use both affirmative and *not* statements in reply to the question "What is this?" "This is a ball. This is not a book."
2. Ability to use both affirmative and *not* statements in response to the command "Tell me about this _____ [ball, pencil, etc.]." "This pencil is red. This pencil is not blue."
3. Ability to handle polar opposites ("If it is not _____, it

must be _____") for at least four concept pairs, e.g., big-little, up-down, long-short, fat-skinny.

4. Ability to use the following prepositions correctly in statements describing arrangements of objects: on, in, under, over, between. "Where is the pencil?" "The pencil is under the book."

5. Ability to name positive and negative instances for at least four classes, such as tools, weapons, pieces of furniture, wild animals, farm animals, and vehicles. "Tell me something that is a weapon." "A gun is a weapon." "Tell me something that is not a weapon." "A cow is not a weapon." The child should also be able to apply these class concepts correctly to nouns with which he is familiar, e.g., "Is a crayon a piece of furniture?" "No, a crayon is not a piece of furniture. A crayon is something to write with."

6. Ability to perform simple *if-then* deductions. The child is presented a diagram containing big squares and little squares. All the big squares are red, but the little squares are of various other colors. "If the square is big, what do you know about it?" "It's red."

7. Ability to use *not* in deductions. "If the square is little, what else do you know about it?" "It is not red."

8. Ability to use *or* in simple deductions. "If the square is little, then it is not red. What else do you know about it?" "It's blue *or* yellow."

9. Ability to name the basic colors, plus white, black, and brown.

10. Ability to count aloud to 20 without help and to 100 with help at decade points (30, 40, etc.).

11. Ability to count objects correctly up to ten.

12. Ability to recognize and name the vowels and at least 15 consonants.

13. Ability to distinguish printed words from pictures.

14. Ability to rhyme in some fashion to produce a word that rhymes with a given word, to tell whether two words do or do not rhyme, or to complete unfamiliar rhyming jingles like "I had a dog, and his name was Abel; I found him hiding under the _____."

15. A sight-reading vocabulary of at least four words in addition to proper names, with evidence that the printed word has the same meaning for them as the corresponding spoken word. "What word is this?" "Cat." "Is this a thing that goes 'Woof-woof'?" "No, it goes 'Meow.'"

These objectives specify kinds of learning that are likely to be missed by any educational program that is not deliberately planned to produce them. They are kinds of learning that do not arise easily and naturally from casual conversations and experience.

The first nine goals pertain to words and constructions that occur in ordinary speech, and so they could be learned in the course of informal conversation, as indeed they are learned by the culturally privileged child in his home. But, in casual conversation, it is easy for the child to escape learning them. Sentences that contain "not" are usually spoken with inflections or accompanying nonverbal cues that convey the idea of negation. Prepositions and conjunctions usually occur in situations where the context makes precise understanding of them unnecessary. If the teacher asks the child whether he would like her to read this book *or* that book, the child does not need to be able to distinguish *and* from *or* to realize that the teacher is not proposing to read both books at once. Thus, though these elements may occur frequently in ordinary conversational speech, they occur only occasionally in a way that induces learning. The child has to extract linguistic gold out of very low-grade ore unless the language is refined for him. A preschool program could therefore put a great deal of stress on oral language and produce a good deal of learning in some aspects of language, yet fail to achieve objectives one through nine.

Objectives 10–15, which have to do with numerical and reading skills, are more obviously ones that cannot be achieved without some special effort. Children may learn *one, two,* and *three* as discrete concepts through ordinary conversation—"Would you like one cookie or two?" etc. But the counting operation itself, which is absolutely essential to arithmetic, cannot be learned except through counting, which is not a normal part of casual conversation. Similarly, for the reading or prereading skills that comprise objectives 12–15, some special experience is required. Certainly direct teaching is needed to learn the alphabet. The other objectives might be achieved merely through reading books to the child, but an enormous amount of reading would be required, and it is still doubtful whether the effort would succeed for the child who is generally retarded in language development.

Possible Strategies for Attaining the Objectives

There seem to be only two strategies available by which the academic goals that have been set forth can be achieved within a limited span of time. One strategy is to compress an enormous amount of miscellaneous verbal experience into the limited time available in the hope that this will make it possible for the disadvantaged child to grasp those more elusive elements of language that are too widely scattered in his ordinary language experience for him to learn them. The other strategy is to plan activities which focus as directly as possible on the objectives, bringing the concepts to be learned to the forefront and ensuring that the child receives an amount of exposure, practice, and correction sufficient to teach what is intended.

The first approach has been called "verbal bombardment." The second approach is simply direct teaching or instruction. Either approach involves profound departures from what is usually found in preschool education. The first requires a "supercharged" verbal environment, with the teacher playing a forceful role, placing herself as the pivotal figure in verbal interactions. The children cannot be relied upon to learn through conversation with one another, because the concepts to be learned can only be learned from a person who already knows them. Activities that disrupt the learning process have to be severely curtailed. The second approach entails even more drastic departures, for it means running the preschool more in the fashion of a regular school, with lessons of some kind, lesson plans, provisions for practice and feedback, performance criteria for the children to meet—in short, the armamentarium of instruction that is employed at later times when one sets about to teach a child to read or do arithmetic.

The "verbal bombardment" approach has the advantage that one does not have to figure out specific ways to teach the various concepts and operations. Correspondingly, it has the disadvantage of being more wasteful, and it entails the possibility of missing certain specific objectives in spite of intensive efforts. The direct-instruction approach ensures that every objective can at least be attended to, and it gives the teacher better day-to-day control over pupil progress so that she will know what objectives need additional attention.

The major questions that early childhood educators have raised about the use of direct instruction with young children are whether it is feasible at all and whether it is good for such young children to be subjected to procedures that are ordinarily reserved for older children. The image of four-year-old children attending classes, following prescribed instructional routines, actually working, is strange and even frightening to many educators. There are precedents for such an approach, however. In the education of deaf children, it is commonplace to begin direct and fairly formal instruction in reading, writing, lip-reading, and speech at the age of four or five. Formal instruction of younger children seems to work well in schools for the deaf, not because of the characteristics of the children but because of the small size of classes and the fact that the instructional content is appropriate for young children. Since these two conditions can also usually be met in preschools for disadvantaged children, direct instruction should receive serious consideration as an approach to the attainment of educational objectives. The next section summarizes the results of an experiment by the writers, using the direct-instruction approach.

Results of an Academically Oriented Preschool Program

The fifteen children who composed the first class to be taught according to the curriculum presented in this book were selected with the assistance of teachers in a predominantly Negro school district in a community where the Negro population has, by northern standards, an exceptionally low per-capita income. These children were chosen on the basis of having older brothers or sisters who were encountering school problems and on the basis of coming from homes which, in the judgment of teachers visiting them, were especially unfavorable educationally. At the time the school began, the children had a median age of 4 years, 6 months. On two language tests administered at this time (the Auditory-Vocal Automatic and the Auditory-Vocal Association subtests of the Illinois Test of Psycholinguistic Abilities), the children scored at about the three-year level.

From the first day, the children were given an intensive, fast-paced, highly structured program of instruction in basic language skills, reading, and arithmetic. Each of these three subjects was taught as a separate class, each with its own teacher, the children circulating in groups of five from class to class. Classes were 15 minutes in length, expanding to 20 minutes as the children became better adjusted to the routine. The only other major educational activity was singing, where specially written songs were employed to give additional practice in skills being taught in the classes.

By the end of six weeks, most of the children had developed into well-motivated learners. They had made rapid progress in the mastery of basic language and numerical operations, and were quite conscious and proud of this, though relatively little effect showed up in their out-of-class behavior. These tendencies were reflected in their performance on the full Illinois Test of Psycholinguistic Abilities (ITPA), which was administered at this time. On the two tests that had been administered previously, which were tests of verbal reasoning and mastery of grammatical inflections, they showed gains of about eight months. But on the Vocal Encoding subtest, a measure of ability to use descriptive language in a relatively free situation, they were extremely low—about a year retarded.

Slowly, their school learning began to influence out-of-class behavior. Ten weeks later, selected subtests of the ITPA were readministered. On the reasoning and grammar tests, the children showed additional gains of three to four months, but on the Vocal Encoding test, they had gained approximately a year. They had begun to use well-articulated sentences and to talk *about* things, rather than merely using language to express wants and feelings. By that time, too, the children had progressed from not knowing how to count past five to being able to solve simple equations involving addition and subtraction, and from not being able to tell whether two printed characters were alike or different to being able to sound out a few three-letter words.[1]

At the end of seven months of schooling, the children had come up to approximately normal on the verbal subtests of the ITPA, with the exception of the subtest measuring vocabulary, and were about six months above average in Vocal Encoding—the measure of free, descriptive use of language.

At the end of nine months, the duration of a normal school term, the children were for the first time administered a standardized achievement test, the Wide-Range Achievement Test,[2] chosen because it had norms extending down below the first-grade level. In reading, 11 of the children scored at or above the beginning first-grade level. In arithmetic, 11 scored at or above the beginning second-grade level, and only one scored below the first-grade level.[3] In spelling, which had never been taught, four of the children scored at the beginning first-grade level, although the average level was about .5, corresponding to the middle of the kindergarten level. Thus, though the children had not yet entered kindergarten, they were, according to the two most basic tests (reading and arithmetic), ready at that time to enter first grade.

As is usually the case with novel curricula, standardized tests oriented toward traditional achievements do not get at all of the significant areas of accomplishment. The arithmetic test, for instance, does not reveal the extent to which the children were capable of handling equations with unknowns in the middle ($7a = 42$, $7 + b = 8$) or to formulate mathematical expressions for solving word problems. The reading test was based on the traditional sight-word vocabulary, whereas many of the children were able to read and interpret whole stories using phonically regular vocabularies. No language tests were available which tested the children's ability to solve complex deduction problems.

One of the most sensitive indicators of the effects of the program was the response of visitors, of whom there were a number throughout the course of the year. Early in the program, visitors saw the children as typical of culturally deprived preschool children, and were impressed at their ability to use sentences and at their progress in such rudimentary skills as counting and recognizing letters of the alphabet. Later, when the children were struggling with reading and arithmetic, visitors seemed to be less and less impressed, not because of what the children were doing but because the visitors seemed now to perceive the children as average children who were having a tough time. Finally, as the children became proficient in basic skills and went on to master tasks well beyond their years, visitors began reacting to them as if they were culturally privileged, academically talented children and began raising questions as to where this would all lead, how we would help the children develop their creative abilities, and so on.

The impression that the children had become transformed into culturally privileged children was deceptive, of course. They had made remarkable progress in certain areas that were the focus of the program and that the project staff believed to be of central importance for the academic future of the children, but, in many other areas, they were still well below children of more fortunate backgrounds. Vocabulary was one of these, and the most detectable. More generally, their mastery of language and verbal reasoning lacked the solidity and wholeness that characterizes the child reared in a linguistically rich environment. This was expected, for there was no magic whatsoever in the gains made by the children. What they learned was what they were taught, and it was impossible in the two available hours a day to teach all the skills that separated these children from more privileged children. Thus, the program did essentially what we urged in Chapter 1 that a preschool program for disadvantaged children should do, and no more: it achieved an above normal rate of learning in certain specific areas which had been chosen as most critical for academic success.

The IQ scores of the children are a crude indicator of the over-all, as opposed to the specific, effects of the program—or, more precisely, of what the specific effects amount to when averaged in with all the other factors measured by intelligence tests. The children were first tested on the Stanford-Binet two months after school began. The reason for this delay was to eliminate from the data the irrelevant six-to-eight-point gain that is expected merely from the children's becoming adjusted to schooling. At that time, the average IQ was about 93. When the children were retested after seven months of school, their mean IQ had risen to slightly above 100. As we have noted previously, this sort of gain is a rarity in preschool experiments, the usual gain being halfway to 100. On the other hand, an average IQ of 100 is remarkably low for children who were performing at the academic level of these children. We take this as a further indication of the focused character of the learning. Academically, the children may have been performing at a level commensurate with an IQ 10 or 20 points higher, but to have taught the children in a two-hour period per day enough over a broad area to bring the average IQ up to 110 or 120 would have been an impossibility. It was gratifying, therefore, that what they did learn was sufficient to bring them up to the average IQ level when weighed in with the deficiencies they still carried with them.

Comparison with Other Approaches

The most useful short-range comparison between different preschool programs would be based on their success in achieving the fifteen objectives listed at the beginning of this chapter. No such comparisons are available, however. In fact, the only empirical basis for comparison of preschool programs that is currently usable is their success in raising the IQ. This is an inadequate basis of comparison, not because the IQ is too narrow but because it is too broad in what it covers. Gains in IQ could come about from increases in vocabulary, from improvements in visual and spatial perception, from increased general knowledge, as well as from improved motivation or attitudes. Still, IQ scores that are based on individual tests like the Stanford-Binet and the Wechsler Intelligence Scale for Children provide information of some significance because they are broad enough in their coverage to make it impossible for any trivially narrow learning to raise the total IQ very much, and the tasks are sufficiently complex that basic intellectual skills pervade all of them.

As was noted previously, most preschool programs have failed to produce gains in IQ scores beyond what is to be expected from improved responsiveness to test-taking situations. The writers are aware of only three exceptions, and all three of these cases represent radical departures from traditional nursery school methods in the direction of providing more intensive and more direct educational experience. One of the exceptions is the Bereiter and Engelmann preschool described in the preceding section.

A second exception is an experimental class under the direction of Weikart. The term "verbal bombardment," used previously, is taken from Weikart's description of this class.[4] It represents the alternative to direct instruction as a means of speeding up learning—the concentration of large amounts of verbal experience into each class period and the subordination of all other activities to verbalization. The teachers talked with or to the children continuously, whether the children talked back or not. Because of the unstructured nature of the approach, it is not possible to specify what the children learned, but, in the first trial of this approach, the average IQ rose from below 90 to over 100. The lowness of the initial scores is somewhat suspect, and perhaps half of the gain might be attributed to improved test-taking responsiveness, but the level eventually achieved is nonetheless remarkable. *It is worthy of note that this successful experiment followed two years of experimentation with a more traditional, activity-oriented preschool program which produced disappointing results quite typical of those achieved in other such experiments.*

The most extreme gains reported in any research are those of Smilansky in Israel.[5] In Israel, the culturally deprived population consists of children of peasant immigrants from surrounding Arab nations. Their problems, however, seem to be comparable in kind and degree to those found in culturally deprived groups in America—severe language handicaps, IQs of around 85, and a general lack of the kinds of knowledge and skills expected in the European-type schools of Israel. Although the specific methods and curriculum of the experimental schools have not been reported, the approach seems to be closer to the one used by Bereiter and Engelmann than to any other approach used in this country. The program was based on an analysis of the skills needed for success in school. These were then taught through what Smilansky calls "direct promotion." As nearly as the writers can make out, "direct promotion" means teaching in the most direct and forceful manner possible toward the achievement of specific goals, as distinguished from indirect, experience- or activity-oriented approaches. Thus, it appears to coincide rather closely with the term "direct instruction," as we have employed it. The program was clearly academically oriented, and appears to have contained a good deal of straight academic content—reading, arithmetic, and language training. Gains in IQ of over 20 points were achieved in a year's time, bringing the IQs of the children up to about 105.

The program in Israel was actually a kindergarten rather than a pre-kindergarten program, kindergarten not being a standard feature of the educational system. It is interesting to note that this experiment again followed upon a history of failure with traditional procedures. Special kindergartens had previously been introduced for culturally deprived children, and they were patterned after child-centered American models. As in America, these programs had achieved modest gains in IQ, but had left the children still seriously handicapped when they entered school. It appears that Israel is about 15 years ahead of this country in providing preschool education for disadvantaged children, and so it is disheartening to find American education setting out to repeat Israel's failures while ignoring the successes that followed the introduction of more intensive educational methods.

The available research is certainly not adequate for making a strong case for any particular kind of approach. The research results, however, do support the points made in the first chapter: that some new kind of preschool education is necessary to remedy the educational handicaps of disadvantaged children; that it must be an intensified and highly purposeful kind of education focused upon academic needs rather than upon global developmental objectives; and that the traditional nursery school model is not an adequate one for this purpose.

As between a "verbal bombardment" approach and a more articulated curricular approach, the choice seems to depend on how specifically objectives can be identified and on the availability of workable curriculum plans and methods. Lacking these, a general "bombardment" approach is the best alternative. But the main stream of progress in education at all levels today seems to be in the direction of more careful analysis and constructive planning of curricula rather than toward mere intensification of effort. This is the spirit in which the writers have undertaken to search for ways in which the fundamental intellectual skills that young children need for academic success could be taught.

Meeting the Broader Needs of the Developing Child

The most serious doubt that can be raised about a direct teaching approach is that although it may succeed in achieving the specific academic objectives toward which it is aimed, it may do violence to other needs of the child. We have already stressed the importance of realizing that school is not the only source of learning and that the child's other needs may be adequately met outside of school; but the issue is too important to be brushed aside quite so lightly.

To avoid a long excursion into the byways of child development, we shall attempt to deal directly with those questions that have most often been raised concerning the use of intensive direct instruction of preschool children in academic subjects.

Does intensive instruction produce excessive stress or anxiety in the children?

The view that anxiety and stress are evils to be avoided is grossly out of accord with current psychological thinking and evidence.[6] Their causes and degree are of great importance. When we say that a problem or learning task is "challenging," we imply that it induces a certain amount of stress in a person, thereby motivating him to strive to solve the problem or execute the task. The child who experiences no such stress is in trouble educationally, as is the child who experiences too much stress. Furthermore, the child whose stress is based on fear of failure, concern over pleasing the teacher, or sheer competitiveness is more likely to get into difficulties than the child whose stress is related to curiosity or a desire to achieve competence.

The disadvantaged children in the Bereiter-Engelmann experiment were characterized initially by an unhealthy lack of stress concerning all things intellectual or academic. There were for them no challenging problems, no intellectual skills they felt eager to attain. In this, they were quite different from culturally privileged children of the same age who are often extremely eager to test and improve their intellectual competence and who are disturbed by contradictions and gaps in their knowledge. Thus, a major task of the preschool was to promote productive kinds of stress and anxiety while keeping them within bounds where the children could handle them.

Initially, the stress had to be applied externally. The children were continually exhorted to try hard, to pay attention, and to think. Tangible rewards were given for such efforts. In time, however, as the children discovered what it meant to learn something or figure something out, success in these efforts became its own end, so that the focus of anxiety and stress shifted to the tasks themselves. By the end of seven months, the simplest way to motivate most of the children was to tell them that a problem was difficult and that they probably would not be able to solve it. Stress, therefore, had not been minimized, but it had been shifted to productive channels, and the children had developed the competency to deal with it.

Evidences of excessive stress did occasionally show up in some children —manifested by thumb sucking, tearfulness, or withdrawal tendencies. These were invariably signals that something had gone wrong in the teaching, that the child had failed to master something he needed in order to handle the tasks confronting him. The signs of excessive stress usually disappeared as soon as the educational lack was made up (through extra instruction, a return to an earlier stage in the curriculum, or a shift to some other kind of task). Thus, it was not teaching itself that produced excessive stress, but only ineffective teaching, which presented the child with tasks beyond his capabilities.

The only sure way to avoid the harmful effects of faulty teaching, of course, is to avoid teaching altogether, but this argument holds for teaching at any level, and if taken seriously, would require complete abandonment of the teaching enterprise. As it is, the disadvantaged child will have to encounter teaching at some time, and if he is without the necessary competencies, he is sure to experience crippling stress and anxiety at that time.

Related to this concern over anxiety and stress is a sort of moral principle that seems to be held by many preschool educators to the effect that the young child should not be burdened with the concerns for achievement and competence that are borne by older children and adults: do not deprive the child of his youth, in other words. We shall not argue the general merits of this principle, but only point out that this is not a principle that is embodied in middle-class child-rearing practices. For good or ill, middle-class children are typically imbued early with a sense that they must achieve intellectual competence, that they must keep up with other children in learning and hopefully excel them. This not only gives them a head start in learning over lower-class children, but also motivates them to work harder and take learning more seriously when they enter school. Thus, the well-meaning teacher who is concerned about protecting the right of the disadvantaged child to "be a child" must realize that she may be putting the disadvantaged child in a poor competitive position with respect to middle-class children who have been reared by parents who do not share these laissez-faire attitudes.

Does an academically oriented preschool violate the child's need for a close affectional relation with a teacher?

In the preschool conducted by Bereiter and Engelmann, classes were generally run in a business-like, task-oriented manner. Each period the children shifted to a different teacher for a different subject. The school thus resembled more nearly a high school than an elementary school, and was certainly in striking contrast to the "mother and her brood" atmosphere of many nursery schools. This business-like atmosphere has struck some one-time observers as coldly impersonal and quite out of tune with the affectional needs of young children. People who have observed the school more frequently, however, have reported just the opposite impression—that if there is a danger, it is that emotional ties between children and teachers in such a school may become too intense. Social psychologists have long noted that highly motivated long-term involvement in a common task tends to produce very strong bonds between the people involved—as witness combat teams in wartime compared to the more idle military groups in peacetime. The reason that emotional ties in task-oriented groups are less obvious to the casual observer is that they are mostly implicit and are not talked about, demonstrated, or dealt with explicitly.

The three-teacher arrangement seems to have important advantages for the children. They come to know each teacher well; if a certain teacher does not relate well to the children, they can tolerate her and learn from her, but invest their emotional capital elsewhere. Thus, potentially neurotic relationships can be avoided, and much less depends on the personal adequacy of each individual teacher. An important benefit for the child's later adjustment to school is that he learns how to learn from a variety of people. The children in the writers' experimental preschool eventually got so that they could learn from practically anyone who could teach.

It is ironic that many educators should feel that disadvantaged children have special need of a close "mothering" type of affectional relationship in the preschool, when the home life of many disadvantaged children is such that motherly affection is the only kind of adult affection they regularly receive. A preschool might better essay to provide other kinds of affectional relationships which disadvantaged children lack. These would be characterized by mutual respect, shared intellectual interests, invested hopes, and fatherly pride. These are aspects of parent-child relationships which are important in middle-class homes but which lower-class homes often cannot provide. A task-oriented preschool is ideally structured to provide adult-child relationships that have these characteristics.

May not a premature introduction to school-type
learning cause the children to dislike school?

A child's first encounters with school-type learning are likely to have far-reaching effects on his attitudes toward school. This is true, however, whether the first encounters come in the preschool, in the first grade, or even later. What is important is that the first encounters be successful, rewarding, and reasonably free of pain. A well-planned and well-staffed preschool ought to have a better chance of assuring favorable first encounters with academic learning than the typical elementary school class. There are fewer children per teacher, shorter periods of instruction, and greater opportunities for flexibility in programming. For the promotion of positive attitudes toward schooling, therefore, it would seem important *not* to wait until the child enters first grade to introduce him to school-type learning.

An unstructured, play-type nursery school may lead the child to like nursery school, but since it does not include school-type learning activities, it cannot foster any attitudes, positive or negative, toward them. It may, in fact, give the child an unrealistic conception of school that will make him more likely to respond negatively to his first encounters with academic learning in elementary school.

How does what the child learns in school transfer to his out-of-school life?

Since the major objective of an academically oriented preschool is to develop skills needed in school, it is not really essential for the child to apply them outside of school. It would be desirable for several reasons if he did, but the program is not a failure if he does not. Some educators, however, are not so much concerned that learning will not transfer as that it will—that the child will become alienated from his parents and peers by a display of "bookish" habits and cultivated diction.

The idea that lower-class people are actively antagonistic to intellectual pursuits and "good" English seems to be greatly exaggerated. It ignores the enormous range of variation that already exists and is tolerated within lower-class groups. A lower-class Negro community, for instance, will often include some who are illiterate and unskilled and who speak a very primitive variety of regional Negro dialect. But it will also include others who have high-school educations, who read books, who work at jobs which (though they may be low-paying and of a service nature) bring the person into contact with the world of affairs and ideas, and who speak a variety of English which (though it may be recognizably Negro in certain of its characteristics) is no more remote from the "King's English" than that of the vast majority of middle-class people. The range of acceptability, in other words, is wide enough so that there is little danger that a preschool program will take a child outside that range. What is more likely is that the child will develop skills and a way of talking that will place him at the higher-status end of that range.

The kinds of learning most likely to alienate a child from his peers and to generate resentment at home are those which produce conflicts in values and social behavior, those which carry the implication that the parents' ways are inferior and that the child is "too good" for them. At the preschool level, hostile reactions are most likely to be touched off by genteel mannerisms and half-baked moral precepts that the child brings home with him. The lower-class parents whom the writers have worked with, like most parents, are pleased when their children come home showing evidence of precocious skills or knowledge. This is what school is expected to produce, and so it is merely taken as evidence that their children are succeeding.

Does highly structured teaching prevent the child from generalizing his learning beyond the tasks he has been taught?

Three of the largest gains made by children in the Bereiter-Engelmann preschool were on tests that require generalization far beyond the tasks that were taught: Vocal Encoding, a test of ability to describe objects under rather free conditions; Visual-Motor Association, a nonverbal reasoning test; and Visual Decoding, a test of ability to recognize in pictures objects of the same class. More generally, the children showed a marked tendency to incorporate school learning into their unguided activities, even though little time was allowed in the school program for unguided activity. Whenever a teacher paused for a few minutes in the course of a lesson, the children almost invariably launched into active discussion that was related in some way to the lesson. If the pause came during an arithmetic lesson, they might begin talking about how many boys, girls, men, women, grown-ups, and children were in the room, how many would be there if so-and-so were not absent, and so on. If the pause came after reading a story about a cat and a rat, they would burst into discourse about their experiences with one, the other, or both. There was thus every indication that the classroom work interacted with their own experience, even when no effort was made to establish such relations.

However, transfer of concepts and skills to other situations should not be expected to happen automatically. Everyday language and mathematical language represent formal systems that are related to the real world by transformational rules. These rules are not intuitively obvious. A large part of formal education is devoted to the mastery and use of them. The preschool, therefore, can do no more than make a small start on this task.

What about creativity and self-expression?

This question is stated vaguely, because it seems that the concepts of creativity and self-expression have only a very vague status in the context of early-childhood education. On one level, the terms are synonymous with freedom of the child to do as he wishes. If this is what is meant, then clearly a highly structured teaching program suppresses creativity, as indeed it should. The disadvantaged child has ten other hours a day for this kind of "creativity," and the preschool hours are better devoted to remedying his educational lacks.

At another level, creativity refers to divergent thinking—the production of new structures or ideas as contrasted with the production of predetermined "right answers" of the kind usually called for in reading, arithmetic, and logic. The available evidence suggests that divergent thinking is best developed through tasks that specifically call for it.[7] There is no evidence (or even convincing argument) for the belief that divergent thinking is fostered by simply allowing children to talk, paint, stack blocks, mould clay, etc. The curriculum set forth in this book does not place strong emphasis on divergent thinking tasks (since they take lower priority than the mastery of skills fundamental to convergent thinking), but the reader will discover relevant tasks scattered throughout the program: inventing new verses for songs, generating explanations for events in stories, thinking up new words that rhyme with other words. Needless to say, the alert teacher will also reinforce any novel insights or ideas that arise spontaneously from the children.

What about the development of social skills and peer-group relations?

Although fostering social development is the major goal of many nursery schools and is only a minor goal of an academically oriented preschool, there does not seem to be much difference between the two in what is actually done. In the traditional nursery school, the children learn to play together under the monitoring influence of a socially adept teacher. In the academically oriented preschool, the children learn to work (but also to play) together under the monitoring influence of a teacher who counts social skills among her other qualifications as a teacher. If there is a difference between the two kinds of schools in what they can accomplish in fostering social development, the difference should be in favor of the academically oriented school. Disadvantaged children are usually not seriously lacking in ability to play together, but they are totally unaccustomed to working together in a school-type setting, and this is something that will be expected of them when they enter the elementary grades. Not only did the children in the Bereiter-Engelmann preschool learn the social behaviors appropriate to school, but they showed striking gains in ability to get along with each other at play and while traveling to and from school. They learned to cooperate, to respect each other's property and feelings, and generally to enjoy one another's company. No special credit is claimed for these gains, however. They are to be expected whenever children interact over a period of months under intelligent supervision.

Summary

This chapter began by proposing 15 specific tasks that a disadvantaged child should be able to perform by the end of a preschool program if that program is to be considered successful in preparing him for the academic demands of the first grade. These tasks range from being able to distinguish words from pictures to being able to perform certain kinds of *if-then* deductions. All tasks involve kinds of learning that are not readily acquired through casual language experience or typical nursery school activities.

Two possible strategies were suggested for producing the necessary learning in the limited time available: (1) "verbal bombardment," which consists of cramming an extraordinary amount of teacher-directed verbal experience into each class period; and (2) direct instruction, consisting of deliberately planned lessons involving demonstrations, drill, exercises, problems, and the like.

An experiment in the application of direct instruction to a group of 15 severely deprived four-year-olds was reported. From being over a year retarded in language abilities at the beginning, these children progressed within nine months to the normal level in language test scores and IQ, and scored at the second-grade level in arithmetic and at the first-grade level in reading. An examination of the results of other preschool experiments disclosed only two that had achieved results of this order, and both of these experiments also involved radical departures from conventional nursery-school procedures—one using the "verbal bombardment" approach and the other using direct instruction.

A number of possible objections to the use of direct instruction at the preschool level were considered. The discussion may be summarized by the following major points:

1. A direct-instruction approach does not minimize stress on children, but tries to direct it into productive channels and to develop in the children the ability to handle it.

2. A direct-instruction approach does not provide the children with "mothering," but does permit the development of close affectional ties of a kind that are more productive of growth and that compensate more directly for the deficiencies in parent-child relationships often found in lower-class homes.

3. Because a preschool is generally in a better position than the typical first-grade class to assure that a child's first encounters with school-type learning are successful and enjoyable, it is probably undesirable to defer the introduction of school-type learning until the first grade.

4. The emphasis of an academically oriented instructional program is on knowledge and skills that the child will need to apply in school. Therefore transfer to out-of-school behavior (in both its positive and negative aspects) is not a major issue. Transfer of learning to other kinds of school tasks cannot be taken for granted, but must itself be taught.

5. If creativity is equated with freedom, the disadvantaged child usually has too much of it already. Divergent thinking is best developed through tasks that directly call for it. Tasks of this kind are included in the direct-instruction program, though they occupy a minor place.

6. Social learning is promoted in much the same way in academically oriented preschools as in traditional preschools, with the important difference that an academically oriented preschool teaches children not only to play together but also to work together, as they will be expected to do in the elementary school.

Notes

1. C. Bereiter, S. Engelmann, Jean Osborn, and P. A. Reidford, "An Academically-oriented Preschool for Culturally Deprived Children," in *Preschool Education Today,* ed. F. M. Hechinger (New York: Doubleday & Company, Inc., 1966), pp. 105–135.

2. J. Jastak, *The Wide-range Achievement Test* (Wilmington, Del.: C. L. Story, 1946).

3. Because the children had been taught an equation form of notation for arithmetic problems rather than the conventional vertical form and used a multiplication table rather than memorizing multiplication facts, the test was modified accordingly. Consequently, the scores are not precisely comparable to the norms. Assuming that the children could not have performed any multiplication problems without the table, scores would have been lowered about two-tenths of a grade level had the table not been used. This would have put the mean at about 1.9.

4. D. P. Weikart, "Perry Preschool Project Progress Report," Ypsilanti (Michigan) Public Schools (mimeo), June, 1964.

5. S. Smilansky, "Progress Report on a Program to Demonstrate Ways of Using a Year of Kindergarten to Promote Cognitive Abilities, Impart Basic Information, and Modify Attitudes Which Are Essential for Scholastic Success of Culturally Deprived Children in Their First Two Years of School," University of Chicago, School of Education (mimeo), undated.

6. L. J. Cronbach, *Educational Psychology* (New York: Harcourt, Brace & World, Inc., 1963), pp. 590–595.

7. J. J. Gallagher, *Teaching the Gifted Child* (Boston: Allyn and Bacon, Inc., 1964); E. P. Torrance, *Guiding Creative Talent* (Englewood Cliffs, N.J.: Prentice-Hall, Inc., 1962).

management
of the preschool

The problems of managing a preschool vary considerably depending on the time, personnel, and physical facilities available. The present chapter deals primarily with problems of management under one of the more common types of administrative arrangements—a preschool for approximately 15 four-year-old children with three teachers, operating two hours a day, five days a week, for an academic year. At the end of the chapter, suggestions are made for adapting the program to a longer school day, a shorter school term, a smaller staff, and to children of different age levels. Most of the management procedures, however, are unaffected by these variations.

In a preschool that is concerned with enabling every child to extract the maximum amount of learning from every minute of the school day, efficient and intelligent management becomes of the utmost importance. Time lost in getting the educational program underway at the beginning of the school term, in carrying out the normal maintenance functions of feeding and toileting, and in coping with individual and group behavior problems is time irrevocably lost from the central business of teaching. Even the best-planned instructional program can fail to achieve its objectives because of a shortage of time resulting from poor management. At best, under the management procedures outlined in this chapter, there are some 20 minutes a day in which the children are not actively engaged in relevant learning activities. With inept management, however, it is quite possible to have a school in which there are only 20 minutes a day during which any given child *is* actively and attentively engaged in relevant learning activities.

Scheduling

What activities are included in the daily schedule?

In the standard program, one hour each day is devoted to intensive direct instruction, divided between three subject-matter areas—language, arithmetic, and reading. For these "major activities," the children are divided into three small groups called *study groups*. During the other hour of the day, the study groups are merged to participate in the "minor activities," which include snack time, music, and a semistructured "expressive" period.

How are the subjects scheduled?

Each study group consists of about five children (the number varying according to the needs of the children), and each study group engages in six periods of activity each day. A schedule of activities is presented below:

	Group 1 5 Children	Group 2 5 Children	Group 3 5 Children
Period 1 (10 minutes)	Unstructured Activity		
Period 2 (20 minutes)	Language	Arithmetic	Reading
Period 3 (30 minutes)	Toilet, Juice, and Music		
Period 4 (20 minutes)	Arithmetic	Reading	Language
Period 5 (20 minutes)	Semistructured Activity		
Period 6 (20 minutes)	Reading	Language	Arithmetic

According to the schedule, Group 1 merges with the other groups during Period 1, the get-ready period. During Period 2, Group 1 is in language, Group 2 is in arithmetic study, and Group 3 is reading. For Period 3 (toilet, juice, and music), Group 1 again merges with the other groups, after which the large group again splits into the three study groups. This time, Group 1 studies arithmetic, Group 2 studies reading, and Group 3 studies language. Through the merging and dispersal of the smaller groups in this way, each child receives small-group training in the three major subjects and enjoys the three large-group periods.

Teachers are assigned subjects, not groups. Each of the three teachers —A, B, and C—teaches a particular subject. She does not teach all major subjects to one group. A teaches language to all groups, B teaches arithmetic, and C teaches reading. Referring to the schedule above, teacher A meets with the study groups in the order of 1, 3, 2; teacher B meets in the order of 2, 1, 3; and teacher C meets in the order of 3, 2, 1. Children sometimes spend themselves during a particular study period, and are relatively lethargic during the next. If such a trend is allowed to continue for a long period of time, the progress in the second study subject will suffer. For this reason, the schedule is routinely shuffled every six weeks or so, thereby changing the order of classes for each group and equalizing the "lethargy" effect for each subject.

At what time should the school day begin and end?

Assuming that volunteer car-pool drivers will transport the children to and from school, the two-hour preschool day should be scheduled so that it does not conflict with the schedule of the drivers. These drivers are often parents of school-age children, which means that they must send their children to school in the morning, prepare lunch, and be home when the children return from school. The preschool should be scheduled so that its two-hour day fits comfortably within the schedule of the car-pool drivers, which schedule varies from community to community.

The preschool can convene either in the morning or the afternoon, but the morning is preferable. In the morning, the children are generally more alert. In the afternoon, they may need a nap, and the two-hour program provides no time for naps. Another advantage of the morning preschool is that it does not follow activities which the children may find more enjoyable. The morning preschool can be more easily appreciated by the children as a job, because in the morning they start their day in the same way as their older siblings who go to school. They have the same morning ritual. The purpose of the school is more obvious, there-fore, than if the school were scheduled in the afternoon when the ritual associated is not shared so fully by school-age siblings.

How much time should be devoted to intensive study?

The schedule calls for three 20-minute study periods; however, during the first month of the program, when the children are becoming ac-quainted with the learning situation and the rewards that issue from it, the length of class periods should probably not exceed 15 minutes. The length should then be increased to 20 minutes. If at any time during the school term children find it difficult to maintain the pace of the 20-minute schedule, periods may be temporarily shortened to 15 minutes. The practice of retaining the 20-minute periods and slowing the pace within the periods should not be adopted. Both teachers and children may develop bad work habits. Everyone should enter the study periods with the attitude that they are going all out, whether the period lasts 15 minutes or 20 minutes.

Staffing

Who should teach?

The plan calls for three teachers for every 15 children. In addition to the teachers, the preschool may have an aide to tutor children who are having trouble in a particular area or who have been absent for a long period of time and are behind their group. The teachers and the aides should be talented. The *ideal* preschool teacher, unfortunately, is not an abundant commodity. Teachers who are less than ideal must often be considered. The candidates usually divide into three groups: the nursery-school teacher, the elementary-school teacher, and people who have not received formal training in education.

In general (with many exceptions), nursery-school teachers are not desirable for work in the intensive preschool. They must usually unlearn a great deal before they can become effective, and the unlearning process may take some time. Their training has provided them with a deeply ingrained bias against "forcing" the child in any way; the intensive preschool is premised on "forcing" the child. Their conception of child development and the emergence of skills is usually diametrically opposed to the viewpoint on which the intensive preschool rests. Equally dangerous, nursery-school teachers often have a strong devotion to nonverbal activities—games and crafts. In other words, they are inclined to reinforce those very tendencies that deter the culturally deprived child from mastering language. Thus, they tend to perpetuate the core deficit of cultural deprivation.

The elementary-school teacher more or less "speaks the language" of the intensive preschool. She is more inclined than the nursery-school teacher to work toward specific learning goals, to maintain discipline, and generally to *teach*. Obviously, not all elementary-school teachers are good candidates for the intensive preschool, but, as a group, elementary-school teachers have far less to unlearn. Since they have taught, they more readily appreciate the value of techniques that make the teaching go more smoothly. Elementary-school teachers are reasonably good candidates.

The nonprofessionals who may be considered for work in the preschool can be classified roughly in three groups: people who seem to be motivated by compassion; people who, as parents, have demonstrated that they know how to teach and handle young children; and parents of the children in preschool. People who are strongly committed to social welfare are understandably attracted to a problem of such social dimensions as cultural deprivation; however, they are poor candidates for the preschool because they may find it extremely difficult to behave in a professionally sound manner. They may hug a child and try to give him needed love, although their behavior will merely set up jealousies and competition for her love among the children in the class. They may find it impossible to think about teaching logical reasoning to children who need help—who smell, who live with violence and vice, who need medical help, and who have been deprived of so many of the bright horizons of childhood. These people find it difficult to accept the educational fact of life that children can learn to read even when they must play at home on a dirt floor.

People who have no professional status but who have demonstrated that they understand young children are generally good candidates for the intensive preschool. The demonstration that these people have raised (in the not-too-distant past) or are raising intelligent, unspoiled children provides very good evidence that they understand how to teach and how to discipline children. These people have not learned a great deal about education that must be unlearned. They are generally less defensive and more willing to learn.

Parents of the children in the preschool may come under consideration for work as teachers' aides. As a rule, they should not be accepted. While it is obvious that the parents should be educated in how to teach their children, it is equally obvious that the intensive preschool is by design a poor place in which to instruct them. Parents, especially those who lean toward the middle class and are therefore more likely to be candidates for teachers' aides, usually rely on shame and other motivating practices which are poor in stimulating self-confidence and learning. Correcting the parents is difficult because they are understandably sensitive about their competence. Also, children have a tendency to regress when their parents are around (the common, cooperative-nursery-school phenomenon).

Which characteristics should be sought in teachers and teachers' aides?

Candidates for work in the preschool should show promise. They should express an interest in teaching and making children more intellectually competent. They should be self-confident—yet not harsh or inflexible. Their confidence should take the form of a frank belief that they can, within limits, make children do what they want them to do. They should not be particularly concerned with discipline problems or the individuality of the children. Perhaps most important, they should not be defensive or afraid to learn. If a teacher has worked with disadvantaged preschoolers before, she should not suppose that she is an expert or that she can learn nothing from the other teachers and the administration. She should indicate willingness to have her sessions audited and willingness to consider more effective techniques for presenting different tasks. She should recognize that even the best teachers have blind spots that can be removed only through the help of others.

Physical Facilities

What kind of space is needed?

A preschool may have to satisfy certain space requirements that are imposed by the state or sponsoring agency. Aside from these requirements, the operation of the standard, work-oriented preschool calls for at least three rooms, the largest of which can serve both as a "homeroom" (for unstructured activities and other large-group activities—juice and music) and as a classroom for small-group study. Or the largest room can serve exclusively as the "homeroom," in which case there would be four rooms in the school—a homeroom and three study rooms. The homeroom should have at least 400 square feet of floor space, and should be equipped with a piano and (like the other rooms) a chalkboard. The most important characteristic of the rooms is their acoustical properties. It should be possible for loud vocal activity to go on simultaneously in every room without interfering with speech comprehension. If acoustical tiled ceilings are impossible, cheap pile rugs on the floors or even on the walls, if necessary, will achieve the desired effect.

Ideally, the study rooms should be as small and plain as possible, perhaps no larger than 100 square feet of floor space. Uncluttered surroundings help ensure that the child will not get caught up in the glitter offered by an object-rich environment. Small rooms reduce the child's temptation to explore and run about.

In addition to the homeroom and study rooms, the school should have bathroom facilities and perhaps modest kitchen facilities (primarily a refrigerator). A floor plan of a four-room preschool is shown in Figure 1.

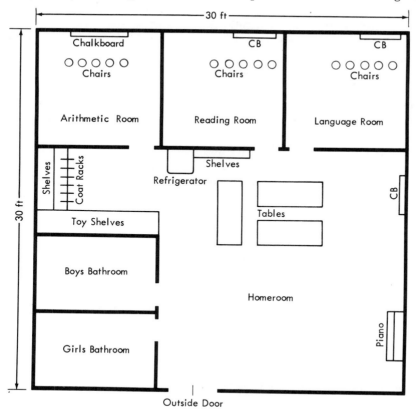

Figure 1

What kind of toys and equipment is needed?

The tendency to overstock a preschool with "interesting" toys is based on a misunderstanding of the child's deficit and a desire to "make up" for the lack of holiday experiences the children have had. The practice of providing an object-rich environment is ineffective in compensating for the child's toy deficit and in stimulating learning. Concrete objects are merely vehicles of concepts. Sometimes toys are good concept vehicles; sometimes they are not. However, presenting the child with many toys and thereby blindly bombarding him with a wide range of sensory experience is not an effective way to present any concept. What the child must learn is not formless; he does not assimilate a little of this concept and a little of that one. He learns very specific rules. The value of any toy should be judged accordingly. A good toy does not teach a little bit of everything. If it is good, it is a good vehicle for *one* concept. It should be presented in such a way that the child learns this concept.

An object-rich environment stimulates the culturally deprived child to attend to the glitter of superabundant stimuli. He darts from one object to another, treating each only in terms of sensory gratification—in terms of movement, sound, or feel. The concepts contained in this clutter are often lost because the child may never be motivated to consider the toy according to any criterion other than sensory gratification. When the toy no longer "feels good," another one is selected. By minimizing the inducement of noise in the environment, the preschool can be far more effective in directing the child not to the vehicle of the concept but to the concept itself. Sterilizing the environment is a firm requirement of the work-oriented preschool. Toys should be limited to form boards, jig-saw puzzles (which are usually favorites with the children), books, drawing and tracing materials, Cuisenaire rods (to be handled during free time under the direction of the teacher), and a miniature house, barn, and set of farm animals. Paper, crayons, and chalk (but no paint) should be available for expressive play. Motor toys, such as tricycles and wagons, and climbing equipment are not necessary for the program, but may be required by the sponsoring or licensing agency.

In addition to play equipment, the preschool should have first-aid equipment and extra clothes (for children who wet or have similar accidents and for children who are not adequately dressed, especially in cold weather).

Getting Started

How should the program be presented to the parents?

The parents should be required to accept certain definite responsibilities as a condition of their child's acceptance into the preschool. These should include agreement to:

1. Attend all parents meetings (of which there will be at least four)

2. See to it that their children attend school regularly

3. Get their children ready on time for the car-pool driver or bus

4. See to it that their children receive adequate rest and get to bed at a reasonable hour

5. Encourage their children, and not shame them, call them dumb, or compare them unfavorably with other siblings

6. Not allow their children to communicate with a nod or a single word, but require them to speak in full sentences

These responsibilities, important in their own right, encourage parents to take the preschool seriously and not as a baby-tending service designed to *relieve* them of responsibility.

Parents will be less suspicious if the preschool is presented to them matter-of-factly as a "proposition" rather than as an outright gift.

How should car pools be organized and handled?

Local groups (especially those concerned with community affairs) are good sources for drivers. Drivers should not drive more than once a week and should pick up no more than five children. Reserve drivers should be on hand for every day of the week, and regular drivers should clearly understand the procedure for calling in when they are not able to drive. Arrangements should be made so that they can call up at the last minute (sometimes necessary when cars will not start in winter).

Drivers should be provided with a list of the children they are to pick up and, if possible, a map showing the quickest route. They should know what type of car behavior is expected of the children (see page 78) and the procedure for picking up children and taking them home. The drivers should be instructed to honk when picking the children up, thus placing the burden on the parents to get the children ready and allowing the driver to stay in the car with the other children. When dropping the children off, the drivers should always let them out on the side of the car away from the street and wait until they are inside the house before driving away (unless another arrangement has been made with the parents).

At least three meetings for car-pool drivers should be held: (1) a get-acquainted session held before the school term begins (during which the basic procedures are explained in detail); (2) a second one after the school has been operating for about two weeks (the primary purpose of which is to iron out any difficulties and discuss the various children); and (3) a session at the end of the school year (in which the progress of the children is summed up and the drivers are thanked for their cooperation). In addition to attending business meetings, the drivers may be invited to a Christmas party. They may want to buy presents for the children they drive. However, they should be encouraged, instead, to put the money into a pool from which identical presents for all the children in the preschool can be purchased.

How should the children be grouped?

Because of the vast range of individual differences in initial abilities, some children will be able to progress further in three months than others will in nine. Therefore, if every child is to progress at near his maximum rate, grouping according to rate of progress is an absolute necessity.

Work with small homogeneous groups minimizes boredom and delay for the faster children and minimizes discouragement and incomplete learning among the slower children. In addition, it enables the teacher to study each child more carefully and detect possible problems. It drastically reduces discipline problems. It makes it easier for the teacher to attract and hold attention. It allows more rapid feedback and corrections of responses, and a greater number of responses from each child.

Initially, three groups of five children each are recommended. Later, it may be advisable to reduce the size of the slowest group to three or four to permit more personal attention to each child and to increase the size of the fastest group accordingly.

Initial groupings are best made on the basis of language abilities. Two scales of the Illinois Test of Psycholinguistic Abilities are good initial indicators when taken together—the Auditory-Vocal Association scale and the Auditory-Vocal Automatic scale. If it is not expedient to use the ITPA, the following test can be presented. It is an abridged version of Engelmann's Cognitive Maturity Test, which has been found to discriminate rather well between those children who are relatively facile with language and those who are not.

A. Have the child repeat the following statements after you. If he does not repeat a statement properly, present it again, as many as four times. After the production of the statement (or after it has been tried four times) ask the question indicated.

1. Puppies are baby dogs.
   What are puppies?
2. A big truck is not a little truck.
   Is a big truck a little truck?
3. Babies eat and cry.
   Do babies eat? Do they cry?
4. She ate the pie because she was hungry.
   Why did she eat the pie?
5. He got the wood so he could build a fire.
   What did he get?
6. There were many cars going to the city.
   Where were many cars going?

7. It is in the box.
   Is it on the box?

B. Present the following questions and instructions.
   1. (Examiner shakes head "No.")
      This means "No."
      (Examiner nods head "Yes.")
      What does this mean?
   2. (Examiner claps.)
      What am I doing?
      (Examiner walks.)
      What am I doing?
   3. Do what I say:
      Hold up your hands.
      Touch your ear.
      Hold up your hand.
      Touch your ears.

After the children have been in school for a month, regroupings should be considered on the basis of performance in class. While the initial screening test is capable of doing a reasonably good job of classifying the children, the children change. Babblers may suddenly develop into rather articulate speakers. Lethargic children may become surprisingly well motivated. On the other side of the scale, those who were ahead initially may, for motivational or other reasons, begin to lag. A troublesome problem is raised by the child who progresses rapidly in one subject and slowly in another. A compromise of some kind is the only solution, perhaps with the child receiving some individual work in a free period on those tasks that are giving him trouble.

Regrouping should be approached with an experimental attitude. If the child is not completely satisfactory in his present group, a change may be just what he needs. Such a change does not necessarily mean dropping the child down to a slower group. If the child is lacking only in motivation and not ability, a move to a faster group may encourage him to perform better. A different child may view a fast group as a threat. He would rather identify himself with a group in which he is more confident and is not "running scared" to keep up with the others. It is not uncommon to move the best-performing child in the 2-group to the 1-group only to discover that the move has sapped him of his self-confidence and changed what had been a self-assured child into a worried, wee-voiced shadow. Moving him back to the "little pond" will probably revitalize him.

The greatest danger in ability grouping is that it will encourage teachers to set lower standards for the slower groups. The same seriousness of purpose, the same concern for maximizing the rate of learning should prevail in every group. The administrative arrangement by which every teacher teaches one subject to every group rather than teaching all subjects to one group should help to avert this danger.

What kind of snacks should be planned?

The sponsoring agency may specify the kind of food to be served during the preschool's snack time. If not, the selection of snacks should be guided by the fact that culturally deprived children are not typically in good health. Most are anemic, and some may have kidney and other disorders that are related (at least indirectly) to malnutrition. The ideal juice-time snack would consist of something like pork liver (which is very high in iron), raisins, and milk; however, compromises are usually made— if for no other reason than to make snack time an enjoyable activity. Good snack items include raisins (seedless), peanut butter, oatmeal cookies, crackers with cheese, molasses cookies, and graham crackers. Vitamin-enriched canned juices or milk (perhaps sweetened) make good drinks. Canned juices are the easiest and quickest; milk may be more beneficial. A handy reference book in planning snacks is the U.S. Department of Agriculture's handbook, *Composition of Foods,* which details the nutritional value of all common raw, processed, and prepared foods.

How should medical examinations be planned?

The type of examination may be specified by the sponsoring agency; if not, the children should receive a full examination, including blood tests and chest X-rays. Examinations should be arranged early. If the sponsoring agency is not paying for the examination, state, township, or county help should be sought. Unless this is done, there is a good possibility that the examination may create resentment among the parents. The reason is that those parents who are on welfare rolls may receive the examination free, while parents not on welfare will have to pay for the examination.

The children will be far less apprehensive about going to the doctor if they have a good idea about what will happen and if they are given a job to do during the examination. They should rehearse the examination, and, during rehearsal, the emphasis should be on the job which the children are to do. "Remember to say 'Thank you, Dr. Teller' before you leave. And 'Thank you, nurse.' " The critical part of the examination can be acted out, with one teacher playing the role of the doctor and another playing the nurse. The "doctor" pinches each child on the arm, simulating a hypodermic shot.

As noted above, the culturally deprived child is typically not in good health. Measures should be taken to do something about the more serious illnesses disclosed by the medical examination. Highly contagious conditions such as ringworm, pink eye, and impetigo should be watched carefully. Children with these diseases should not be allowed to attend school unless they are receiving proper treatment. A public-health nurse is a very helpful person to consult on problems of contagion and sanitation. Eye and ear problems that may not be medically serious should nevertheless be attended to because of their significance for school performance. Watch especially for ears clogged with wax. A doctor may not even remark on this condition, thinking it trivial, but it may interfere seriously with language learning.

A word of warning: concern over the health of the children can be carried too far. Sometimes children will come to school with coughs and signs of a bad cold. It should be remembered that when the symptoms of flu or cold are manifest, the condition is usually past the stage of highest communicability. If the child has a fever or shows signs of being seriously ill, he should be taken home or to a doctor's office. If every child who has any symptoms of illness is sent home, however, the attendance record of the preschool will be ridiculously poor, and the learning performance of the children will suffer accordingly.

What kind of orientation should teachers receive?

The teacher orientation should concentrate on what to do on day one. The point should be made repeatedly that on the first day of school— not on the second or the fifth—the program begins in full force. The rules of behavior outlined in the following section are to be enforced. The beginning tasks in language, reading, and arithmetic are to be presented.

It is generally accepted in early-education circles that children must be worked into a program slowly if emotional stability is to be retained, but there is no experimental evidence to support this supposition. Furthermore, it often seems that the slow working-in process is designed to help teachers who do not know how to begin teaching on day one. They rely on the working-in process to provide encounters from which they can slowly develop a routine. Since this routine is born of contingency, it usually lacks clear focus and direction. The children, meanwhile, derive no great security from the process. Regardless of what school is like on the first day, it will be different from what the children have known before, which means that they must learn a new set of behavioral rules to deal with it. It makes sense that these rules should be ones that will serve them through the rest of the year. Otherwise they will learn rules that have to be unlearned later, and this *can* produce maladjustment and insecurity. Although the children do not "need" to be worked into a program, many teachers do.

Orientation meetings, held just before classes start, are not suited for discussions of basic issues and long-range goals. Teachers are usually too anxious about the beginning of school to pay attention. These matters should have been discussed long before. The aim of the orientation program should be to provide an understanding of how to begin and what to do.

At least three teacher meetings should be held. Rules of behavior (which are outlined in the following section) should be reviewed in detail during the first meeting. It should be emphasized that these rules are easier to enforce on the first day than on the second or third (the children are usually more tractable at first, so that the first day should represent an opportunity rather than a threat). During the second meeting, each teacher should demonstrate the tasks she plans to present on day one. The final meeting should concentrate on a walk-through rehearsal of the first day's activities. It should be held in the preschool. Special attention should be paid to ways of moving the children quickly and quietly from activity to activity.

After this kind of orientation, the teachers usually have little difficulty initiating the program on day one.

Establishing Appropriate Schoolroom Behavior

What kind of behavior should be expected of the children in school?

Except when the children are instructed to yell or sing loudly during the instruction periods or the music period, they should be quiet and restrained—no running, hitting, yelling, or tussling. Even during the unstructured activity periods, the activity should be kept in a low key. Letting off steam during free periods does not pacify children, but merely stimulates them to blow off more steam and makes it more difficult for them to get back to work during the next study period.

CAR BEHAVIOR

Children should sit quietly on the seat. "No feet on the seat" is the rule. Unfortunately, car-pool drivers sometimes allow children to break the rule. Drivers should not be expected to discipline children; however, they should report any misconduct in the car. These reports should be investigated and the problems corrected.

BEHAVIOR BEFORE AND AFTER CLASSES

On their way to the homeroom, children should be required to walk single file, without pushing or crowding, behind the teacher. If they go up or down stairs, they should hold the rail. In the morning, the children should be helped with boots and heavy clothing; however, as the school year progresses, they should assume greater responsibility for dressing.

The school should have several spare winter coats for children who may come to school in below-zero weather without them. After the children are assembled in the homeroom, the morning ritual should be presented. The ritual should change as the children become more sophisticated. In the beginning, it may involve repeating a simple statement, such as "These are hands." Later, it may involve a more difficult statement, such as "One plus zero equals one." As the children learn the days of the week, the ritual may consist of completing the statements "Today is _____. Tomorrow will be _____." and answering the questions "What is today? What will tomorrow be?" About ten minutes should be allowed for dressing in cold weather, five in warm weather. The going-home ritual should be designed so that the day ends on a pleasant note. An orderly follow-the-leader game from the homeroom to the cars satisfies the requirements nicely.

TOILET BEHAVIOR

Complete conversion of the children to habits of middle-class cleanliness is impossible in some cases and impractical in many others. However, children should be required to wash hands before leaving the bathroom and before eating. Children who are inclined to interrupt study classes because they have to go to the bathroom should be taken to the bathroom before the class convenes and should not be allowed to go during the class period.

SNACK-TIME BEHAVIOR

Since the preschool operates on a rather tight schedule, children must not dawdle over their food. They should be allowed to eat at their own rate—within limits. Dawdling beyond these limits should be discouraged by taking the remainder of the snack from the offender (only after he has been warned on several occasions). Children should be required to finish their entire snack before leaving the table. Crushed raisins on the floor are not very pleasant. One child (selected on some type of rotation basis) should play the part of the garbage man and carry the container around to where the others are seated. The children should deposit their empty paper cups, napkins, and any other garbage in the container, holding the cup upright during the process so that no juice is spilled on the floor. Children should never be allowed to take snack items from the table, because these items (contrary to the rules) will usually be eaten during the next study period. Also, children should not be allowed to eat snacks which they bring from home. If a child brings an all-day sucker, the teacher should explain "I'll wrap it for you, Tyrone, and you can have it when you go home." Gum chewing should not be permitted because it interferes with the children's articulation.

BEHAVIOR DURING MUSIC AND UNSTRUCTURED ACTIVITIES

The atmosphere during music and unstructured activity should be more relaxed than during the study periods. The activity should be enjoyable. However, certain restrictions should be imposed. The children should be required to *sing*. They should be required to remain seated in a small circle or to carry out the actions associated with the various songs.

During unstructured periods, children should have their choice of listening to a story read by one of the teachers, looking at a book, drawing, or playing with a toy (see page 72). Children should be held responsible for returning play materials. Crayons and pencils are most conveniently kept in a large open box. Books, paper, toys—all should have a special place on an accessible shelf.

Clean-up time should never become a production, and the study schedule should never be delayed for clean-up. If clean-up requires more than two minutes, the teacher should finish the clean-up later. Unstructured periods should end promptly and should not be prolonged while some children finish their drawings. Children should not learn that their pleas for more time *may* work, because this encourages procrastination, which will lead to conflicts and frustration sooner or later.

CLASSROOM BEHAVIOR

Children should sit in assigned seats. They should leave their places only with the teacher's consent. They should be required to participate, which means answering in a loud clear voice and generally working hard at the tasks the teacher presents. Toys should not normally be allowed in the classroom. Sometimes, however, they can be allowed if they do not interfere with the proceedings. "Tommy, you can wear your holster, but if you play with it, you'll have to take it off." Children should not be allowed to interrupt the teacher at will. They should be discouraged from relating personal experiences or interjecting ideas that are irrelevant to the teacher's presentation. The teacher should allow relevant ideas and should praise the child for these. The teacher may occasionally allow a minute or two for the children to speak their minds, but this should be at the teacher's discretion, not the children's.

MORAL BEHAVIOR

The question of how vigorously the preschool should pursue the task of changing the child's moral behavior can be viewed as a question of return on investment: how great is the investment, and what is the return? In order to ensure complete cessation of chalk and trinket stealing, extensive policing and searching would often be required. These procedures not only are time-consuming, but also are distasteful because they demonstrate that the authority figures in the school are fundamentally opposed to the children. Preventing lying is even more difficult because the act of lying is probably not understood by the culturally deprived child in the way we think it should be understood. On the other hand, the children should not learn that lying and stealing are condoned. Children should be told that toys, chalk, paper, pencils, etc. belong to the school and must not be taken home. The more serious offenders should be checked from time to time. These children may be told that if they do not stop stealing, they will not receive snacks. To reduce the "value" of the items that are usually stolen, a teacher should give children pieces of chalk, paper, etc., especially during the first two months of school. Perhaps the most expedient way to handle lying is to first define it for the child and to then point out that the punishments for lying are greater than for telling the truth. No punishment should be administered until a child is caught red-handed in a lie. He should then be taken aside and asked the question which he had not answered truthfully. If he lies, he is told "You are lying, Harold." He is asked to "Tell me what really happened, now," and the question is repeated. The questioning continues in this manner until the child realizes that the "lie" will not be accepted. After he tells the truth, he is praised and admonished. "After this, when I ask you what happened, I want you to tell the truth. If you don't tell the truth, you will not get your cookie at juice time." A child should never be questioned in this manner unless the teacher is *positive* that he lied.

What are the principles the teacher should follow in establishing appropriate behavior?

PRINCIPLE 1:
REWARD THE CHILD WHO TRIES.

The primary criterion is not whether the child performs, but whether he tries—whether he tries to attend to the presentation, whether he tries to produce the statements, whether he tries to take the steps that are necessary to arrive at the solution to a given problem, *whether he tries to think.* The child who tries should be rewarded, regardless of whether or not his performance was correct. The child who does not try should have rewards withheld and should be told why.

PRINCIPLE 2:
TRY TO AVOID REWARDING UNDESIRABLE BEHAVIOR.

Sometimes a teacher has a tendency to hold a child who misbehaves during the music period. To her, taking him out of circulation in this way seems to be a way of handling the situation without creating a scene. Sometimes a teacher will take a misbehaving child aside and hold a warm, intimate conversation with him, the rewarding effects of which will far outweigh the reprimand. Sometimes a teacher is eager to reward a child who is a behavior problem, and in her eagerness she rewards him for behavior that would be considered substandard for other members of the group. All of these tendencies are undesirable, because all are obvious demonstrations to the child who misbehaves (and others with tendencies to misbehave) that acting up is rewarded: the child who misbehaves receives special attention and special affection.

PRINCIPLE 3:
AVOID SHAMING AND COAXING.

Rules of behavior should be enforced in a matter-of-fact way. The teacher should tell a child what to do. She should not ask him to participate. Such requests as "Don't you want to work with us, Harold?" and "Can't you talk a little louder, Tommy?" *simply invite the children to have doubts,* to wonder whether they can talk louder or work with the group. These doubts can be avoided by presenting rules in a positive manner. "Harold, you know the rule. You've got to try hard." "Speak up, Tommy. I can't hear you." If the teacher demonstrates through her behavior that the children are stupid or that they really cannot be expected to perform a task without considerable coaxing, the children will reflect her expectations. The teacher should therefore *expect* the children to perform and work hard; she should *expect* them to be "smart"; and she should *expect* to be proud of them most of the time.

PRINCIPLE 4:
PRESERVE THE SPIRIT OF THE GROUP.

The children should understand that the teacher is on their side; however, they should not identify with her values to the extent that they sever allegiance with their peers. After children have been in school for several months, they usually show signs of becoming too teacher-oriented. They now know that the rules are important. When another child breaks one, they therefore tell the teacher. If the teacher acts on what they say, the children will be reinforced for turning on each other, and, before long, tattling will become the standard means by which they vie for the teacher's attention. When this happens, each child's identification with the group is weakened, which is not desirable. *The teacher should never discipline a child unless she personally observes the offense.* If the children report that a certain child misbehaved, she should acknowledge that the behavior went against the rules. "You shouldn't spit in the hall, should you?" She should not act on such reports, however (beyond telling the offender that if he did what had been reported, he broke a rule).

Just as she discourages tattling, the teacher should not turn the group against a child by punishing the entire group for one child's misconduct. The child who misbehaves is the only one who should be punished.

PRINCIPLE 5:
EMPHASIZE THE RULES OF BEHAVIOR THAT MUST BE
MAINTAINED, NOT THE CHILD'S ADEQUACY.

In the permissive nursery school, the rules are not always expressed openly, which leads to undesirable consequences. The child learns that he *must* wash his hands after using the toilet. If he wishes to abstain from playing farmer-in-the-dell, however, he may do so—at least so the rules seem to imply. The teacher usually assures the child "You don't have to play if you don't *want* to," and periodically she inquires "Do you *want* to join us now?" While this approach seems innocent enough, it actually shifts the emphasis from what must be done to the adequacy of the child's *wanting* mechanism. If his wanting mechanism corresponds to that of the other children, he will want to do what they do. If his wanting mechanism is different, he will not. A child who does not want to join the group in farmer-in-the-dell is prompted to conclude that he is different, that something about him is bad.

Stating rules openly not only produces more rapid conformity than the more permissive approach; *the child's conformity is limited to the situation,* so that he does not have to espouse a new value system in order to succeed in the school situation. He is free to dislike the activity if he chooses, and, in other situations, he is free to do as he feels. Openly stated rules, therefore, infringe less on individual freedom.

PRINCIPLE 6:
EXPLOIT WORK MOTIVES RATHER THAN PLAY MOTIVES.

People play because it is fun. People work largely for two reasons: working brings rewards, and it provides a secure routine. People will stop playing when the play ceases to be fun. They will stop working only when the work ceases to bring rewards or when it ceases to provide security. Children can learn a good deal from play, but as soon as the learning becomes difficult or threatening, they will cease to play, as they have every right to do. The things that a culturally deprived child has to learn are difficult, and they often pose a substantial threat. He is expected to abandon responses that have proved to be effective in the past and to speculate on difficult, untried responses. Thus, an educational program that is based on the play motive is always in danger of collapsing at the very moment when the most important steps in learning are being approached.

An educational program based on work motives is designed so that learning is consistently rewarded. The principal rewards are in the form of increased competence and mastery, but when these prove insufficient, other rewards are supplied. The work-oriented program provides a stable routine. The security of the routine counterbalances the threat of the learning situation. Although the child may not know specifically which new responses will be required of him, *he knows generally what to expect.* He knows where he will be, what he will be doing, what kind of behavior will be expected of him, etc. This knowledge serves as a kind of reassuring backdrop for the specific learning tasks with which he will be confronted. Perhaps the most valuable aspect of a work routine, as compared to a play routine, is that a child does not expect to be able to abandon it at a moment's displeasure. He learns, in fact, to expect that it will not always be pleasant or rewarding from moment to moment, but that it will generally pay off in the long run. Thus, motivation becomes less fickle, and the teacher does not have to worry that a single dull lesson will bring a project to ruin. This gives her more freedom to make bold attempts, and allows her to focus more on the content of instruction and less on the tormenting question "Will the children like it?"

Because the work-oriented program makes greater personal demands on the child, it is able to produce faster learning. It transports the child more rapidly through the awkward stage during which he is unfamiliar with the rewarding sense of mastery associated with the work-oriented learning.

PRINCIPLE 7:
PROVIDE THE CHILD WITH A REALISTIC DEFINITION
OF SUCCESS AND FAILURE.

Teachers are sometimes too aware of the need for the disadvantaged child to succeed in the learning situation. In some cases, their attitude about success jeopardizes learning. It must be kept in mind that the teacher's reaction to a child's response has two rather distinct functions. One is to provide the child with *specific information.* The other is to let him know something about *his adequacy.* When the teacher says "No, Tommy, not quite," she is telling Tommy that the conceptual framework used to generate the response needs revision. Tommy needs this *information* if he is to modify his conceptual framework and learn the concept. In addition, the "no" response tells Tommy that perhaps he is not doing a good job, which implies something about his ability. The two functions—that of providing information about the concept and that of providing information about the learner's adequacy—should not be confused. The teacher who tries to convince the child that he is adequate by approving incorrect or inadequate responses is not helping the child. Unless he knows that his response is wrong, he has no basis for changing it in favor of the correct response. In the long run, therefore, the practice of bestowing sham praise becomes very hollow. The child ultimately is faced with the problem of reconciling the idea that he is very smart with the sobering awareness that he does not seem to know anything. At the opposite extreme, the learning situation can proceed so that the child learns a great deal but must reconcile this fact with the fact that he fails quite a bit and does not seem to please his teacher when he is learning. A balance between information and felt adequacy must be maintained, at best a difficult task requiring both a curriculum that produces a relatively high percentage of correct responses and a good teacher.

It is possible to achieve a healthy definition of success in either a permissive or a work-oriented setting, but the definition follows a little more naturally in the work-oriented setting because the emphasis of the program is on *work*. The teacher's interpretation of the child's performance centers around the manner in which he works rather than the outcome. If he apparently works hard, he is rewarded for doing a good job—although he is not misled into thinking that his wrong responses were correct. The work-oriented program, therefore, is able to achieve a rather clean separation of content and personal adequacy.

What are the motivators that should be used to establish appropriate behavior?

Because the culturally deprived child is inexperienced in the rewards associated with mastering new concepts and because he is not strongly motivated to work for praise, it is very difficult for the teacher to reach him through the standard motivational channels. Therefore, a motivational bridge must be built. The child must be initially rewarded in terms that already mean something to him. These rewards serve as a bridge to teach the child the meaning of verbal praise and verbal castigation. If the teacher's warning of punishment is followed by punishment, her warning will soon become "meaningful." Similarly, if her praise is followed with some "proof" of good will, her praise will soon signify something of value. In the work-oriented situation, extrinsic rewards, such as cookie rewards, can be introduced and withdrawn gracefully *by placing the primary emphasis on a situational rule, not on the teacher's feelings.* A rule is defined as something that governs both teacher and children. For this reason, the children *do not tend to hold the teacher responsible for the rule* or for changes in the rule.

THE COOKIE REWARD

Food rewards are sometimes seen as objectionable motivators because they "condition" the child. Actually, this interpretation of the reward as a stimulus does not strike at the core of the problem. The question is not one of conditioning the child to do something blindly but one of defining what it means to work for praise, of demonstrating the emotional import that should be associated with working for praise. The most economical way to achieve such a definition is to find something which functions as praise *should* function in motivating the child and then to substitute praise systematically for other motivators, thereby teaching the child how to react to praise. Since the first step in establishing the praise reaction involves using something which the child already values, the question of selection is an empirical one. What types of rewards is the child willing to work for? It turns out that cookies are effective motivators. They therefore serve as good bridge rewards in establishing the meaning of praise rewards.

1. Teach the rule "If you work hard, you get a cookie. If you don't work hard, you don't get a cookie."

2. Starting from the first day of the program, award a cookie to a child if he tries hard during a reward segment of the study period. Initially, the reward segments should be no more than five minutes. When it begins, the children are told "If you work hard on this next job, you'll get a cookie. If you don't work hard, you won't get a cookie." Questions about this rule are asked. "Are you going to get a cookie if you work hard? . . . Are you going to get a cookie if you don't work?"

3. Issue cookies individually and relate each child's performance to the rule. For the child who has earned a cookie: "If you try hard, you get a cookie. You tried hard, so you get a cookie." For the child who did not earn a cookie: "If you try hard, you get a cookie. You did *not* try hard, so you do not get a cookie."

4. Relate the reward to the appropriate statements of praise and disappointment. "Debby, Harold, and John, I'm very proud of you. You are good workers. Tommy, I'm sorry, you didn't get a cookie, but you didn't work hard." The teacher can help establish the meaning of praise by shaking hands with the children who have earned cookies.

5. Assure children who did not receive cookies that they are not inadequate. "Tommy, you're a very smart boy. But you've got to work harder. You can do it if you put your mind to it."

6. When the children have gotten so that they behave adequately without frequent reminders about the cookie rewards, change the rules so that the children receive their cookies during juice time and not at the end of the period. The change should be handled in a matter-of-fact way, with the emphasis on the rules. "You did a good job today, but you don't get your cookie now. You get it at juice time. That's the rule from now on. Sometimes the rules change."

7. Continue to praise and reprimand the children after the cookie reward has been withdrawn. "I want to shake hands with all of the children who did a good job. I'm very proud of them."

Through experience with the cookies, the children will have learned to appreciate the "value" of the teacher's praise and will be much more strongly motivated than before to work for it. If a child continues to misbehave during the class period, the teacher can withhold his snack-time cookie, but this sanction should be used sparingly.

OTHER REWARDS

Whatever the children like can be used as a reward if it can be quickly given or withdrawn by the teacher—a particular learning game, a look at some fascinating object, a chance to sit on a certain chair. These rewards tend to have a short life-span, but the alert teacher can keep finding new ones.

PUNISHMENT

Especially during the first month of the program, punishment may be necessary to clarify the rules of the school situation. The use of punishment should be viewed as objectively as possible. The purpose of punishment is to deter the child from behaving in an undesirable way. The punishment should therefore be designed to "outweigh" the gratification the child derives from misbehaving. Punishment, in other words, should hurt. What hurts for one child may not hurt for another, so the question of which punishment should be administered is one of discretion. Punishment should not be freely administered. Emphasis should be placed on the positive rewards. Only when these fail should negative sanctions be introduced.

1. Reserve physical punishment for situations in which the child's behavior is unthinking and automatic. Physical punishment is not called for in dealing with most children; however, especially during the first month of the program, physical punishment seems to represent the quickest and most dramatic way of punishing a child for unrestrained, unthinking physical behavior. Some children (most often boys) will not respond to their names during the early part of the program. If the activity in which they are engaged is antisocial, destructive, or possibly dangerous, they must be restrained. Holding them momentarily and admonishing them is often not effective. Upon being released, they may simply return to the activity, giving every indication that the teacher's actions and words meant nothing to them. In such a situation, the meaning of the teacher's words should be made clear by demonstrating the consequences that result when they are ignored. Sometimes the best definition comes in the form of anger—a slap or a good shaking. After physical punishment is administered, the admonishment should again be repeated. "Harold, I told you not to throw blocks. I meant, *do not throw blocks.*"

2. Isolation seems to be more effective in combating behavior that is more "calculated." When children act up by clowning during a study period or the music period or when they pout or refuse to respond—

when their behavior is not unthinking—the punishment should be more calculated. The child should be warned two times about what will happen if he persists in his behavior. "John, if you keep doing that, you're going to be put in the isolation room." After the second warning, the punishment should be executed. The "isolation room," if it is to be effective, should be an unpleasant place, providing an atmosphere that is far less enjoyable than that of the study room. A small, poorly lighted closet with a single chair will serve quite well.

Again it should be remembered that punishment should be used with discretion. Equally important, however, it should be used if it is necessary. The teacher who shows children that she is "soft" in carrying out her warnings will quickly lose not only respect but cooperation. After the first month, punishment usually is rarely needed.

Specific Behavior Problems

Children who present "typical" behavior problems can be roughly classified into three types: the troublesome child, the withdrawn child, and the indifferent child.

The troublesome child.

The troublesome child derives satisfaction from resisting the rules of the preschool. The source of his satisfaction may be the approval of his peers, special attention from his teachers, or a feeling of power. The most expedient way to handle this child is to cut off the source of satisfaction and thereby demonstrate that the child's actions are not effective in producing satisfying results. If the child disrupts classes by showing off, put him in isolation, where showing off is unproductive. If he seems to thrive on "scenes," punish him with a minimum of words or show of emotion. If he seems to enjoy the power associated with manipulating others, show him that he is relatively powerless, that he is able to create only a minor disruption and that the cost of this disruption is rather great. The troublesome child may be persistent, but, in the end, *he will come around if the teacher sticks to her rules*. In many cases, the troublesome child is a very charming child, and when he wishes to take the role of the student seriously, he does a good job.

The withdrawn child.

The teacher should try to make him feel secure in the learning situation and should try to "coax" him toward the standards held up for the other members of the group. Coaxing is generally not a desirable training procedure, but, in the case of the withdrawn child, it may be necessary because it may be impossible for this child to perform in the manner expected of the other members of the group. For example, he may be all but unable to speak when called on to recite alone. He may make wild mistakes that seem to represent a hope for a quick escape from a terrifying situation. And he may sometimes curl into a fetal ball, thumb in mouth, retreating into soft oblivion.

This child should be pushed as hard as possible, but absolute conformity should not be required immediately. At first, the teacher should not call upon the withdrawn child individually. Instead, she should build up a sense of security by requiring him to respond only in unison with the other children. But cooperating in group responses should be a firm requirement. "Tyrone, I want to hear you. Let's say it together one more time. Everybody." Later the teacher should begin calling on him to recite individually from time to time, but only on those tasks that he handles best in unison. As he becomes less reticent and more "thinking," she should expand the scope of tasks he is called upon to handle individually.

Initially, the withdrawn child should not be allowed to suck his thumb or to curl up *during the reward segment of the instruction period.* Later, the ban should apply to the entire study period. If necessary, the teacher should use force to prevent the child from sucking his thumb or curling up. "You must sit up properly, Tyrone." Punishment may include withholding cookies and juice or mild physical punishment, *but not isolation.*

The indifferent child.

The most severe behavior problem the preschool teacher will encounter comes in the form of a cheerful, seemingly well-adjusted child, who is reasonably tractable during the instruction sessions. He says what he is told to say, he gives the appearance of paying attention, but he is not. And because of this sham attention and sham cooperation, he is the most difficult type to handle. This is the kind of child who is often labeled "immature" in the kindergarten and is often retained there for a second year. The label is descriptively accurate, for he often does act like a happy baby, but the label tells us nothing about the nature of his problem. Such a child has failed to grasp what the learning situation is all about, and he is happy not knowing. The tasks of the learning situation are simply motions for him. They represent nothing real, nothing that burns inside, nothing to ruminate over, nothing that should be taken outside of the classroom. He is unaware not only of what is expected of him, but also that *anything important is expected of him.*

The teacher should therefore make a strong attempt to show him that there is something important that he is not doing, and try as best she can to help him see what it is. She can do this most effectively by demonstrating to the child *that she has strong feelings about the material,* that she considers it something important enough to arouse strong emotional reactions. If the teacher does not give the child the advantage of this demonstration and if she reacts to his sham efforts as if they were work-motivated efforts, she is simply reinforcing an extremely dangerous intellectual outlook.

The demonstration of emotion is appropriate because the child is acting out of ignorance, not out of a desire to obstruct or displease. When he learns that his interpretation of the situation does not satisfy the teacher, he will probably change his approach, though it may take him a long time to learn what he is supposed to do. The teacher should not taunt the child throughout the learning process. When his lackadaisical attitude is flagrant, however, she should display anger. She should tell the child that what he is doing is inappropriate; she should tell him how she feels about his behavior; and she should reassure him. "Tommy! You are not thinking. You are not trying. I do not like that one bit. I am very mad at you! Now, you can learn if you work. But you've got to work. You've got to think!" Punishment may be justified as an indicator of how strongly the teacher feels about the behavior, but always with the realization that the child probably does not yet understand what he is supposed to do. She should always be on the alert for evidence that the child is thinking, trying, or paying attention, and should point this out promptly (with praise) so that the child learns to recognize what behavior is expected of him. In short, the teacher must first create a problem for the child through her emotional reaction and punishment and then help him solve it.

Note

The writers are quite aware that their suggestions about behavior, and especially about punishment, represent an unpopular viewpoint. They were tempted, in fact, to do what some others probably do when offering suggestions about handling behavior problems: say what is more popular, even if it is not what they think. However, the issue of rewards and punishment is one that should be brought into the open. The child who acts up in the classroom should not be viewed as the victim of trauma, because trauma most probably has little to do with his condition. Similarly, the "punishment" he receives in the school situation will not be traumatic. The withdrawn child will not break or retreat from reality in the face of effective punishment. He will conform. So will the obstreperous child and the good-natured pretender. Such conformity will not come about if they are unchecked in their maladaptive behavior. Again, the writers are not stipulating a particular kind of punishment to be used in teaching a given preschool group. They are merely stating the belief that if a child indicates through his behavior that he must learn something about how to behave and if punishment seems to be the most effective way to bring about this learning, punishment should be used. The issue of punishment should not be disguised, hushed, or treated in an unrealistic and emotional manner. It should be faced with intellectual honesty. The idea that disadvantaged children should be spared punishment because they get so much at home seems to us fallacious. In the first place, the fact that they are accustomed to harsh treatment ensures that they will not overreact to the comparatively mild forms of punishment discussed here. Secondly, they have learned to use punishment as a source of information. The test of whether an adult means what he says is to ignore him and see whether punishment follows. Finally, in a preschool run according to well-defined rules, the child can learn that punishment can be consistently avoided and that it is not something that occurs periodically regardless of what he does. It is important for him to learn that such situations exist, even if they do not exist at home. A situation that is entirely free of punishment cannot teach this.

Maintaining Favorable Public Relations

The preschool, in most communities, is not immune to the force of public opinion. A program that deviates markedly from traditional practices is especially vulnerable, and so public relations become something more of a concern for an academically oriented preschool. Eventually, the preschool must justify itself through its demonstrated results, but until then it will be judged on issues and impressions. It should be publicized as an experiment, as any new undertaking ought to be. Public pronouncements should be tentative rather than dogmatic.

How should visitors be handled?

The major public relations problem has to do with visitors. No matter how open-minded a visitor may be, he is likely to let his subjective impression based on an hour or two of observation outweigh any arguments that may be put forth. This is unfortunate, because in a program where the entire focus is on changes taking place in the children, the one-time visitor necessarily misses the point. No change of any consequence is likely to take place in an hour. The preschool program described in these pages is likely to create a mistaken impression for the following reasons:

1. The visitor is immediately struck by the fact that what is going on

is not like anything he has seen before. This in itself is likely to produce alarm.

2. The children are working, not playing, which seems unnatural.

3. Having observed traditional nursery schools where activities are not progressively organized, the observer assumes that what he sees happening is repeated in exactly the same way every day. This makes the drill work seem ridiculous. He imagines that the children keep saying the same things over and over indefinitely.

4. Because (contrary to the observer's impression) the children are constantly struggling toward the mastery of new concepts and skills, they frequently make mistakes or demonstrate only a tenuous mastery of the tasks they are working on. The visitor interprets this as failure.

5. The content is uninteresting to the visitor. To an adult, there is nothing particularly interesting about simple arithmetic, reading, and grammar, whereas children at play often do charming or amusing things, and children's art work often appeals to adults. The visitor is likely to project his own disinterest in the subject matter onto the children.

These impressions, coupled with whatever convictions the observer may have about permissiveness, affection, spontaneity, concrete experience, discovery learning, creativity, readiness, etc., are certain to produce a negative reaction in many visitors which can later be translated into rather damaging criticism. No strategies for dealing with visitors will be completely effective, but the following suggestions should help:

1. Explain clearly in advance what you are going to do and why, but do not discuss methods except in response to questions.

2. Schedule the visit to begin during the juice and music period. This part of the program is conventional enough to be reassuring, but contains enough that is different to be interesting. A teacher can also be free during this period to talk to the visitor.

3. Take the visitor to the language class next. Have him follow the same group for the remainder of the visit. In this way, he will become acquainted with the children and see them less as automatons. Also, the children will get used to him and act more normally.

4. Take every opportunity to tell him about individual children—what they were like when they started, the problems they have had, and what they have accomplished. Help him to see the school in terms of what it is doing for the children rather than in terms of what the teachers are making the children do.

5. In discussing a lesson after the visitor has watched it, do not dwell on why you did what or on what went before. Rather, stress what is to follow, where it is going to lead. If the visitor is accustomed to watching traditional nursery-school classes, he will not be used to considering a particular activity as a step on the way to something else, and this point should be brought home to him.

Some other standard bits of advice are worth mentioning: Do not allow too many visitors at one time or on too many days in succession. Do not put on a show, but advise the visitor that what he is seeing is a "slice of life" with all its raw edges. Keep the visitor entirely in the background during instructional sessions; do not introduce him to the children or allow them more than one peek at him. Do not schedule parents to visit at the same time as outsiders; some of the things that you would say to one you would not want heard by the other. If the slice-of-life attitude suggested above cannot be maintained, either because a given group of children is too unruly when visitors are present or because the visitor's biases are too strong, limit observations to the music period and unstructured period (during which the visitors will see activity that is more in accord with the stereotyped beliefs). Encourage the parents to visit the school, but limit each parent to two visits. Presence of parents is often disrupting, and although it is important for the parents to maintain an interest in the school, their presence in school is not the most productive expression of interest. Develop a smooth procedure for handling visitors in the classroom. Never allow visitors to sit next to the children. At the beginning of the period, escort visitors to their chairs, which should be located well behind the children and perhaps to one side. Gracefully indicate that the visitors are expected to remain in their assigned places. "You'll be able to see very well from here." Do not become solicitous or unprofessional in the presence of visitors simply because they represent a potential trouble spot. Unprofessional behavior is not effective for convincing visitors, nor for teaching children.

How should parent meetings be handled?

At least four parent meetings should be staged during the school term. If parents are well informed about the performance of their children, they are not receptive to objections about the preschool. Especially within the Negro community, there are those who will be opposed to the intensive preschool. To them, it seems to treat culturally deprived Negroes as if they are different from other children, implying that there is some basis for segregation. Some preschools may in fact be segregated, not because segregation is consistent with racial beliefs but because it is consistent with the educational needs of the children within a given community.

A preschool may find itself in the midst of touchy issues; however, its best protection is *success* and *parents who know about this success*. Such parents will continue to support the school, and they will help insulate the school from community forces.

1. Schedule parent meetings for evenings (since the parents usually work during the day) and arrange for transporting parents to the meet-

ing. Parents should be contacted in advance, either by phone or in person (if they cannot be reached by phone). The time, place, and purpose of the meeting should be told, and a firm commitment to attend the meeting should be sought. The excuse of "no baby sitter" should not be accepted. There are friends and relatives who have watched the children before and who are willing to do so again. For the three meetings scheduled during the school term, the children should be sent home with notes (pinned to their coats or outer garments) that reiterate—in simple, concise language—the details of the meeting. Notes should be written with the awareness that some of the parents may not be able to read. Below is a good sample note.

PRESCHOOL PARENT MEETING ON FRIDAY, DECEMBER 4

Place: The Preschool, Room A.
Time: Meeting starts at 8:00 PM and lasts about one hour.
Purpose: We will talk about what _____ [child's name]
           is doing in school and the doctor's check-up.
MR. HENDERSON WILL PICK YOU UP AT 7:45.
Please be ready.

[Signed]

2. The first meeting should be held about a week before the school term to explain the details of the program. The pace of this meeting and the others that follow should be fast. If the parents know each other, attention should turn to the business of the day. The children's progress should be reported in a positive manner. For example, instead of complaining about poor attendance, the chairman may phrase the issue as a compliment. "We would like to thank you for your splendid cooperation. Our attendance record is generally good. However, . . ." Similarly, the progress of the children should be phrased positively. Instead of indicating, for example, that the children started out a full year behind the average child and caught up six months of that deficit, emphasis should be placed on the gain. "In only two months, the children have gained over six months in language age. We take these gains to mean that the children have a very good capacity to learn."

3. At each meeting, review the two basic educational requirements the parents are to carry out at home:

a. Require the children to respond with full sentences. Do not let them simply point or nod. Do not give them what they want unless they ask for it properly in complete statements.

b. Do not ridicule or shame children by telling them they are dumb or by comparing them to other children. Let them know that they are smart. Be patient with their mistakes.

4. Devote a part of the meeting to brief individual sessions with the parents. The accent of these sessions should be on each parent's child. Advice should be given, but with a certain amount of humility. Parents of culturally deprived children do not have a great deal of free time to work with their children.

How should the community be informed about the preschool?

Newspaper accounts of any preschool can be damaging if they are not written properly. An article that refers to "culturally deprived children" and describes these children as "having practically no language," elaborating with a host of details, is not going to serve the preschool. It merely singles out the parents of children in the preschool and shames them publicly by calling them and their children bad names. Such articles are not always avoidable, but they are in many cases if the newspaper is made to understand the problem.

1. Explain that statements which can be made about "cultural deprivation" as a national social problem should not be made about particular individuals within the community, especially when young children are involved.

2. Explain that articles about the preschool should not focus on the do-gooder theme ("Isn't it wonderful that someone is doing something for these poor little waifs?"). Rather, the focus should be on the success achieved by the school. This success is measured by comparing the children in the school with *any children their age*. The emphasis should be on their academic achievement, on the skills they are learning.

3. Explain that such expressions as "culturally deprived" and "language deficit" should be avoided.

4. Ask if it would be possible to read the article before it appears in the newspaper.

Program Variations

The preceding sections have dealt with the management problems of a preschool that has a school day of two hours, has three teachers for 15 four-year-old children, and has a duration of one school year. Obviously, a great deal of what has been said, especially about motivation, behavior, and public relations, applies to the various program variations that are possible within the framework of the intensive preschool. However, some program variations imply changes in general procedure. These variations and their resulting modifications are discussed briefly below.

What changes are implied when the school day is longer?

FEWER TEACHERS

If the day length is six hours or more, two teachers can effectively handle 15 children and carry out the study-group assignments.

CHANGES IN SCHEDULING

The manner in which activities are scheduled is different from that used in the two-hour program. Children are divided into three groups as before, but all three groups are never engaged in study-group activity simultaneously (since there are only two teachers). Rather, one group engages in study-group activity, while the other two are combined and are engaged in semistructured activity. A schedule for an eight-hour school day appears below.

	Group 1 5 Children	Group 2 5 Children	Group 3 5 Children
Period 1 (10 minutes)		Unstructured Activity	
Period 2 (20 minutes)	Language	Semistructured Activity	
Period 3 (20 minutes)	Semistructured Activity	Language	Semistructured Activity
Period 4 (20 minutes)	Semistructured Activity		Language
Period 5 (40 minutes)		Toilet, Juice, and Singing	
Period 6 (60 minutes)		Unstructured Activity and Lunch Preparation	
Period 7 (60 minutes)		Lunch, Clean-up, and Toilet	
Period 8 (20 minutes)	Arithmetic	Semistructured Activity	
Period 9 (20 minutes)	Semistructured Activity	Arithmetic	Semistructured Activity
Period 10 (20 minutes)		Semistructured Activity	Arithmetic
Period 11 (60 minutes)		Toilet and Rest	
Period 12 (20 minutes)		Music	
Period 13 (20 minutes)	Reading	Semistructured Activity	
Period 14 (20 minutes)	Semistructured Activity	Reading	Semistructured Activity
Period 15 (20 minutes)		Semistructured Activity	Reading
Period 16 (50 minutes)		Unstructured Activity	

CUSTODIAL FUNCTION

The long-day preschool performs a custodial service that is not provided by the short-day preschool. This function is responsible for three general changes in the long-day preschool program:

1. *Reduced transportation problems.* Car pools are usually not necessary because parents are usually quite willing to take over transportation responsibility in exchange for the custodial service.

2. *Responsibility for meals.* The preschool schedule must be modified

to allow the teachers time to prepare meals. (See the sample schedule above.) Suggestions about diet and preparation may be secured on request by writing to Project Head Start, Office of Economic Opportunity, Washington, D. C.

3. *Accommodations for a greater amount of free time.* Play equipment that should not be found in the short-day program (because there is no available time to use the equipment) can be used to advantage in the long-day program. A list of play equipment is available from the Office of Economic Opportunity. However, the Equipment and Supplies booklet should be viewed as a source for a *few* good equipment ideas. Many of the suggestions contained in it should not be taken seriously, since they are generally premised on the notion that "The provision of a wide variety of the most exciting and stimulating materials is essential, particularly for the child from a low-income family whose home environment may be meager and lacking in stimulation." Much of what follows from this premise is understandably tainted.

GREATER EDUCATIONAL LEVERAGE

The long-day program has a great advantage over the short-day program in that it allows the tasks presented in the study periods to be more a part of the child's day. It enables teachers to integrate these with other activities and give the child much greater practice in using the skills he learns. The long-day program offers a particular advantage in dealing with the child who has learned a nonverbal way of getting along in his home environment. The program can be structured so that the child's general approach to play activity, to mealtime, to semistructured encounters with peers and teachers must change. The program can effectively ply him to use language in these situations. If the increased educational potential of the long-day program is to be realized, however, the routines and content of semistructured activities should dovetail with the material presented during the study periods.

What changes are implied when the day length remains at two hours, but when fewer teachers are available?

The curriculum outlined in this book can be handled quite well by one teacher and two good aides. To use aides effectively, however, the teacher should carefully demonstrate the tasks in the manner she wishes them to be presented. She should remain sensitive to any difficulties the aides encounter in executing these tasks. If only one good aide is available, it may be expedient to drop one of the three study subjects—reading. If no good aides are available, both reading and arithmetic may be dropped. Language should be retained, however, because it is the key subject of the program.

What changes are implied when the school term is less than a school year?

A surprising amount can be done in a short-term program (such as the summer Head-Start programs). Children can be given as much as a full year of "language age" in two months. Also, the fundamentals of counting and identifying symbols can be taught. The short-term program should therefore attempt to give practice in all of the categories outlined in the basic-language program (see Chapter 7) and should present the basic arithmetic tasks (see Chapter 10).

What changes are implied when the children in
attendance are older than four years?

In some communities, the preschool will serve as a substitute for a kindergarten, accepting children who are to go to first grade the following year. These children usually learn faster than four-year-olds. The program can therefore be speeded up. A word of warning however: the child who has developed a basically nonlanguage adjustment will not be substantially ahead of where he had been the year before. He will stand in particularly sharp contrast to the other children. By comparison with the others in the group, his performance will be worse than it would have been at four years. The teacher may therefore find it difficult to work this child into the program. The writers know of no thoroughly practical solution to the problem.

What changes are implied when the children in
attendance are younger than four years?

The entire structure of the preschool should be modified to accommodate the needs of younger children.

SHORTER STUDY PERIODS

Study periods should be shorter (perhaps 10 minutes each), and material to be learned should be presented in smaller chunks. A task should be presented, and then, ideally, some kind of interesting activity that is related to the task should follow. The teacher should place greater emphasis on the child's ability to produce single words and should use a more diffuse "verbal bombardment" approach. The program should be devoted to vocabulary—naming things and actions. The teacher, however, should present rhetorical questions about the various things under consideration, thereby laying the foundation for the structural tasks that are to be introduced when the child becomes more facile with language.

SMALLER GROUPS

Groups should be smaller. The teacher should not work with more than three children at a time in a study group, unless they are exceptionally advanced and well motivated.

REWARDS FOR DIFFERENT BEHAVIOR PROBLEMS

Wetting, crying, aggression, and attention seeking are problems that become increasingly prevalent in the preschool for younger children. Appropriate changes in rewards should be introduced to cope with these problems. The teacher should try to structure tasks so that she is always dangling a carrot in front of the child, so that some kind of very desirable activity is coming up very soon. She should then use these activities as a means of reaching the child and motivating him. "Rodney, if you don't stop fooling around, I'm not going to let you play with the train."

SLOWER PACE

The pace must be altered. In some respects, the three-year-old should be able to progress at least as rapidly as the four-year-old, because the four-year-old must often unlearn rules about handling language before he can learn new ones. The three-year-old is not handicapped to the same degree. However, if the task requires simply learning and not unlearning and relearning, the older child can be expected to proceed more rapidly than the younger child—a tendency that is compounded by the fact that the older child is able to work for longer periods in intensive study and is therefore able to receive more practice during the same period of time. Progress with the younger child is often so slow that the teacher cannot see it, and it becomes evident only when she looks back over the preceding months and notes the progress the children have made in handling various tasks.

What changes are implied when less space is available?

Perhaps the most difficult requirement for the intensive preschool is the space requirement. If three or four rooms are not available, however, the program can still proceed. If two rooms are available, language instruction should be carried out in one of the rooms, reading and arithmetic in the other. If only a single room is available, each group can take up a place along three adjacent walls. The single-room arrangement is well suited to the teacher who is using aides to teach the various subjects. She can watch the aides and help them in the single room. However, under such an arrangement, great emphasis should be placed on chalkboard tasks and on other tasks that force the children to ignore what is going on in the other parts of the room.

Summary

Although the various considerations that come under the heading "Management of the Preschool" may seem diverse, all relate to the operation of the school—to transporting the children, establishing behavior patterns consistent with the goals of the school, grouping children, and dealing with parents and other segments of the community.

In this chapter, the schedule of the school was discussed first. It was noted that the standard preschool is designed to teach four-year-old children for about two hours a day, five days a week. The children are to study three major subjects—language, arithmetic, and reading—with language occupying the focal position. For study sessions, children are divided into groups of about five children. A teacher teaches the same subject to all children. The major staffing problem is finding good teachers. The writers suggested that, as rules of thumb, nursery-school teachers are not well suited to the atmosphere of the intensive preschool; elementary-school teachers generally speak the language of learning and performance used in the intensive preschool; nonprofessionals who are motivated by compassion or guilt are not good candidates; parents of intelligent, well-brought-up children are very good candidates. The parents of children in the school, although they should be educated, should not usually be considered for work in the preschool.

The physical facilities of the preschool call for at least three (and perhaps four) rooms. These should not be overstocked with toys and stimulating material. Toys are simply vehicles for concepts. If a toy is to be a good vehicle, the child must be led past the sensory glitter to the concept, which is not easily achieved when the glitter of one toy is in competition with the glitter of many others. Toys, it was noted, should be limited to form boards, puzzles, and other material that is obviously educational.

The process of getting started poses a number of crucial management questions:

1. How should the program be presented to the parents?
2. How should car pools be organized and handled?
3. How should the children be grouped?
4. How should the teachers be oriented?
5. How should medical examinations be handled?

Brief answers to these questions were provided.

Once the program has been put into action, the primary management problems center around the behavior of the children and the methods that should be used to establish appropriate behavior. Often these issues are glossed over or sugar coated. At the expense of espousing an unpopular view, the writers attempted to give realistic recommendations for establishing appropriate schoolroom behavior. The principles of discipline were first outlined:

1. Reward the child who tries;
2. Try to avoid rewarding undesirable behavior;

3. Avoid shaming and coaxing;

4. Preserve the spirit of the group;

5. Place emphasis on the rules of behavior that must be maintained, not on the child's adequacy;

6. Exploit work motives rather than play motives;

7. Provide the child with a realistic definition of success and failure.

Various motivators were then suggested to shape desired behavior—the cookie reward, praise, and punishment. Since the disadvantaged child does not understand what it means to work for praise or mastery in the way an advantaged child does, the teacher must demonstrate what she means. She does this by selecting reinforcers that work—that function as praise and reprimand should function—and then by systematically associating the motivators with verbal sanction.

Public relations is a management area of particular importance to the intensive preschool. Some in the minority groups will see the intensive preschool as an instrument of segregation, because only deprived children are enrolled in it, thus implying that there is a basis for segregation. Visitors, parents, and the press should therefore be handled carefully. Visitors should be told what to expect; they should begin their tour during the music period; they should learn about the individual children in the group, with strong emphasis placed on what the school is doing for the children. Parents also should be informed about the progress of their children. At least four parent meetings should be scheduled throughout the school year. Newspaper reporters should be acquainted with the problems associated with calling certain people in the community "culturally deprived." Reporters can be extremely useful in informing the community about the program, but their efforts will not be entirely successful unless they understand the problems.

In the final section of the chapter, different program variations were considered—programs in which the day length is longer than two hours, programs in which fewer than three teachers are available, short-term programs, and programs in which the children are either younger or older than four. Each approach implied departures in procedure from the standard program; however, within each, the educational objectives of the preschool could be carried out in a modified form.

basic
teaching strategies

5

Teaching in an academically oriented preschool is a highly skilled, intellectually demanding job, requiring the highest standards of professionalism. There is no use looking around for "wonder" teachers who possess all the requisite skills as natural gifts. Such teachers do not exist. The skills have to be learned, and a reasonably intelligent, open-minded, and determined teacher can learn them.

This chapter presents the basic principles and strategies that are important in teaching all subjects. The remaining chapters present methods applicable to the teaching of specific subjects. There is no intention to rob teachers of their individuality and turn them into carbon copies of one another. The teacher who follows the rules and prescriptions set forth in these chapters will still have ample opportunity to "be herself" and put the stamp of her own personality on her teaching. What is discouraged, however, is a sort of misplaced individualism that is indulged at the expense of the children's learning. We expect a physician to be an individual, but we do not expect the kind of medicine he prescribes or the size of the incision he makes to vary with his mood. Teaching new concepts to naïve children is often as delicate a task as making an incision. Slight variations can make the difference between successful learning and discouraging confusion. This is not to say that there is only one way to present a concept, any more than there is only one way to perform a surgical operation. But it takes a very sophisticated practitioner to know which variations are optional and which are dangerous.

Because we cannot present all possible ways of teaching concepts effectively, and because for a teacher who is new to intensive academic teaching in the preschool it is difficult enough merely to learn one effective way of performing the variety of tasks that face her, this chapter and the ones following are written in a straightforward "how-to-do-it" manner. It is hoped that the teacher will study and use these chapters as she would a detailed cookbook, recognizing that it is possible to be a very good cook without being an expert in the science of cookery, but that when one is not a thorough master of the science of cookery, it is necessary to stay close to the recipes if one is to avoid failures.

It is sometimes difficult for the beginning teacher to appreciate what is demanded of her. She is often used to working on the level of "ideas." A teaching demonstration, for her, is a demonstration of an "idea," which she uses by incorporating it into her own style. A good teaching presentation, however, deals in units far smaller and more intricate than "ideas." It deals both in specific modules of information and in specific devices for getting the information across. For this reason, a detailed set of teaching strategies would involve many demonstrations of the interplay between information, pace, discipline, rewards, and drama as they relate to specific curriculum tasks. Although a full account of this kind is beyond the scope of the present book, a sample presentation appears below. It will provide an idea of the size of units that are used by the polished teacher. On the left are the responses of teacher and children; on the right are the teacher's reasons for doing what she does. The reader will note that the teacher is a true clinician. Her responses are premeditated and purposeful. Her presentation is sensitive to the vicissitudes that present themselves during the teaching situation. The task being presented is that of classifying things as weapons or nonweapons.

Presentation	*Reasons*
TEACHER: [Presents picture of rifle] This is a _____.	She begins with no verbal explanation. Lengthy verbal preambles do not make learning easier or the material more meaningful to naïve children. They simply bore the child or entertain him in a passive nonproductive manner.
CHILD B: Gun. TEACHER: Good. It is a gun.	She would have favored the word *rifle* instead of *gun,* but since *gun* is correct and since the response was apparently the product of thinking, she uses *gun,* and she praises the child.
Let's all say it: This is a gun. This is a gun. Again. This is a gun.	The children seem uninterested. Learning will not proceed smoothly unless the teacher can secure the children's interest. Many motivating devices are possible, but the teacher prefers one that will favor the members of the class who are paying attention.
Let's say it one more time: This is an alligator. CHILD D: It ain't neither. It a *gun.*	This device would not be recommended if the children had only a tenuous grasp of the concept. The teacher feels reasonably sure, however, that every child in the class knows what a gun is. The task, therefore, is a test of their attention, not their knowledge.

Presentation (cont.)	*Reasons (cont.)*
TEACHER: That's what I said. I said "This is a bulldog."	All the children are interested now. They are aware of the sham battle of wits and they enjoy it, because they understand that they usually win.
CHILDREN (*A, B, C, D, E*): No, no. It ain't no bulldog. That a *gun*.	The children are laughing at the teacher. She pretends to be hurt.
TEACHER: Well, what did I say?	She has ordered the task so that the proof hinges on what was said. The children who attended to the presentation are the only ones who are in a position to apply the *coup de grâce*.
CHILDREN: You say that a bulldog.	The teacher apparently wilts, as the children laugh.
TEACHER: You're just too smart for me. You listen so big that I can't get away with a thing.	The moral: knowledge is strength. If one thinks and remembers, he can even "outsmart" his teacher. (Moral 2: Even teachers are wrong sometimes.)
Okay, I'll start again. This is a gun. Is that right?	The children are attentive. Perhaps they are motivated out of a desire to catch the teacher in another mistake, but they are definitely motivated. So the teacher proceeds quickly. The common error beginning teachers make is to win children over and then feel obliged to "talk to them" at length. This technique is poor. The teacher has already spent over a minute winning the children. She does not want to lose them, so she moves very fast.
This is a weapon. This is a gun. This is a weapon. CHILD *D:* No it ain't no weapon.	The teacher realizes that she has made a strategic mistake. She has set the children up to catch her errors. Now when she tries to present a new name, the children suppose that she is still carrying on the game. She realizes that she should have introduced the object as a weapon and not as a gun in the first place. She introduced the gun statement first because she felt it would be better to acknowledge the object by the familiar name before introducing the class name.

Presentation (cont.)	*Reasons (cont.)*

TEACHER: [Presents pictures of knife, cannon, pistol] This is a weapon. This is a weapon. This is a weapon. These are weapons. Say it with me. This is a weapon. This is a weapon. This is a weapon. These are weapons. Let's hear that last one again. Make it buzz. These are weaponzzz.

She does not argue with Child *D* because she feels that little would be gained, and time would be lost. Instead, she resorts to a familiar presentation pattern that has been used in connection with labels. The use of this presentation, she feels, will demonstrate to the children that she is serious, that the game is over.

[Refers to knife] This weapon is a _____. Who knows?
CHILD *E:* A knife.
TEACHER: Yes, a knife. Let's say it. This weapon is a knife. Again. This weapon is a knife.

She beat the children to the punch. Before they could raise the objection that the first picture did not depict a weapon but a knife, the teacher presented a full acknowledgment in one statement. She demonstrated that it is, in fact, a weapon. At the same time, she allowed the children to show off their knowledge about the knife.

[Refers to cannon] This weapon is a _____. Who knows?

She phrases her questions so that the children can answer with a single word. Yet, her questions are phrased so that the single-word answer completes the statement "This weapon is a _____." She reinforces the statement even when she wishes to move fast.

CHILD *C:* Battle.

TEACHER: That's pretty good. You use this thing in a battle, but it's called a cannon. This weapon is a *cannon.* Say it, everybody. This weapon is a cannon.

She wants the child to know that she approves of the manner in which he is thinking, but that his answer is wrong. She rates his answer as a reasonable one, but follows with a clear correction.

Is this a *battle?* . . . No, this is *not* a battle. This weapon is a _____. Come on, tell me.

When a child makes a mistake of this kind, his mistake may be picked up by the other children, and will often be repeated by the child who made it. She therefore labors the identification of the cannon.

CHILDREN *A* AND *D:* Cannon.
CHILD *B:* [Mumble.]

The teacher notices that Child *B* is not forming statements, but is trying to imitate the sounds made by Child *A* and Child *D.*

TEACHER: Boy, I'm really proud of *A* and *D.* Do you hear the way they

The old adage about catching flies with honey applies to the classroom

Presentation (cont.)	*Reasons (cont.)*
are talking up? And are they ever thinking! I'm really proud of them.	situation. The teacher could have put Child *B* on the carpet, which would have taken time and might have disgraced him for only a momentary lapse. If he persists, she will be forced into more direct means, but, for now, she selects the band-wagon motivating technique.
CHILD *B:* I'm thinkin big. CHILDREN *A, C, D, E:* Me too. Me too.	
TEACHER: Okay, just keep it up. Here we go. [Refers to pictures] This is a weapon. This is a weapon. This is a weapon.	She reviews the new statements before introducing the new task.
CHILD *A:* I got a cannon at . . . [stops talking as teacher holds outstretched hand only a few inches in front of child's face].	The summary should be conducted at a fast pace, so that the pieces are brought together and the children see where they are. Interruptions at this point are costly. The child is discouraged when the teacher's hand is placed close to his face—a useful technique.
TEACHER: Here's the rule: [claps rhythmically] If you use it to hurt somebody, then it's a weapon. Again. If you use it to hurt somebody, then it's a weapon. Say it with me. If you use it to hurt somebody, then it's a weapon. One more time. If you use it to hurt somebody, then it's a weapon.	The teacher drills this rule until the children learn it. They have learned in connection with other rules that the teacher will expect them to use the rule in the next set of tasks. They also know that she thinks rules of this kind are important—so important that she will not relent until this one has been learned (assuming that the rule is not beyond them).
And if it's a weapon, what do you do with it? Do you tickle somebody with it? CHILDREN: No. TEACHER: Do you eat with it? CHILDREN: No! TEACHER: Well if it's a weapon, do you use it to hurt somebody? Yes.	The teacher flips the rule so that the child will be prepared to handle task questions of the type "If it's a weapon, what do you do with it?" and "If you use something to hurt somebody, what do you call it?" She presents the *yes-no* questions first because they are the easiest. They represent a simple rephrasing of the question provided by the teacher. The teacher selects interesting examples for this task because interesting examples prompt the children to use the rule.
What do you use a gun for? CHILD *A:* Shoot.	The teacher immediately presents applications of the rule.

Presentation (cont.)

TEACHER: That's good, *A*. And do you hurt somebody when you shoot him?

CHILD *C:* Maybe kill im dead.
CHILD *D:* That hurt.

TEACHER: Yes, you use a gun to hurt somebody. And what's the rule? Come on, think. If you use it to hurt somebody, then it's a _____.
CHILD *E:* [Mumble.]

TEACHER: [Claps and smiles] Oh, it's a tough one. But I can say it. Listen. If you use it to hurt somebody, then it's a weapon. You use a gun to hurt somebody, so what do you know about it? It's a weapon. Because what's the rule? IF YOU USE IT TO HURT SOMEBODY, THEN IT'S A WEAPON. Let's hear it. IF YOU USE IT TO HURT SOMEBODY, _____.
CHILDREN: THEN IT'S A WEAPON.

TEACHER: I'm thinking of a rifle, and what do you use a rifle for? You use it to POW POW—hurt somebody. AND IF YOU USE IT TO HURT SOMEBODY, _____
CHILDREN: THEN IT'S A WEAPON.

TEACHER: So what do you know about a rifle? Is it a peanut?
CHILDREN: No, it's a weapon.

Reasons (cont.)

The response is correct, so the teacher acknowledges it as a correct response, even though she would rather have a child say "To hurt somebody."

The children are quite interested, so the teacher allows them to volunteer information.

The teacher attempts to apply the rule. She structures the task so that the children must supply only a single word. They do not respond, which the teacher takes to mean that her presentation left something to be desired. The children were obviously motivated and interested. Presenting the task at this stage was probably premature. The children did not have sufficient practice in saying either the regular-order or the reverse-order rule. The teacher decides to adopt a more rigid procedure, starting with the rule.

The teacher puts on an act. She becomes entertaining, knowing that the children will need to work with the rule for a few minutes and knowing that such drill can become terribly drab if it is just "Say it after me" activity. She therefore yells and claps and talks as if the rule is *fun*. She encourages the children to shout with her.

The teacher again presents the gun example, but this time in a much more structured manner. She is establishing a presentational format for processing a number of things. The children are familiar with this general approach.

This step in reasoning, the teacher realizes, is quite difficult and probably beyond the ability of some of the children in the class. She therefore amends her *what* question (What do you know about a rifle?) with a more highly structured *yes-no* question. By presenting the *yes-no* question, the

Presentation (cont.)	*Reasons (cont.)*
	teacher can prompt the children and increase the possibility of correct answers.
TEACHER: I'm thinking of a cannon, and what's a cannon for? You use it to CA-POW—hurt somebody. And if you use it to hurt somebody, _____ CHILDREN: Then it's a weapon.	The teacher moves fast. She is using statements that allow her to demonstrate the rule quickly, and she takes advantage of the chance to speed and enliven the presentation.
TEACHER: I'm thinking of a cow, and what is a cow for? Do you use a cow to hurt somebody? No. And if you don't use it to hurt somebody, then it is *NOT* a _____. CHILDREN: Weapon.	The fast, rhythmical presentation tends to encourage repetition, both of tasks and of answers. The children tend to answer every statement with "Then it's a weapon." To prevent this presentation hypnotism, the teacher includes examples of things that are not weapons. These are as useful from a concept-building standpoint as from a presentation standpoint.

The preceding teaching segment lasted about two minutes. A great amount of thinking is packed into those two minutes, and much of the thinking occurs so quickly that the presentation is not interrupted for a moment. The teacher is obviously proficient. She has a number of specific techniques at her disposal, and she knows when to use them. This knowledge did not come overnight. Rather it came a bit at a time—a trick for motivating children, a technique for commanding attention, a way of restructuring tasks in anticipation of trouble, and a thorough knowledge of her subject. This teacher is not the product of magic. She is a good teacher because of what she *does,* not because of what she is. And she does the right things because she has learned the right techniques —sometimes slowly and painfully. Although her presentation may impress a visitor as being perfectly natural, it was at one time anything but natural to her. With practice, however, it became a part of her teaching habit.

On the following pages some of the specific techniques used by the polished teacher are examined in detail. These should be studied by anyone who wishes to teach in the intensive preschool.

Work at different levels of difficulty at different times.

The teacher should present tasks on four levels of difficulty:

1. Require the child to point to or *locate* the instance of the concept nonverbally. "Show me which truck is bigger."

2. Require the child to *answer* (with one word) *yes-no* questions about the presentation. "Is this truck bigger?"

3. Require the child to *repeat* the basic statements; present questions that require these statements as answers. "Tell me, is this truck bigger than this truck? Give me the whole answer. *Yes, this truck is bigger than this truck.*"

4. Require the child to *identify* the relationship by producing the appropriate statement without the support of a directed question. "Tell me about this truck."

The teacher should try to work at Level 4 as much of the time as possible. Her goal and her emphasis are on the production of statements. However, she cannot work on this level all the time, especially during the intial stages of the program. The child may fatigue after two or three minutes of verbal exercises. With fatigue comes an increasing number of mistakes. Mistakes are sometimes valuable in that they point out a weakness to the child, an area that needs work; however, too many mistakes naturally draw the child to the conclusion that he is a failure. *Therefore, when the child starts to show honest signs of fatigue, the teacher backs up to a task that is less difficult (which means less verbal), perhaps to answering simple* yes-no *questions, perhaps (if the child has to exert great effort to produce any kind of verbal response) to pointing tasks.*

As children become more facile in repeating statements and producing them, the teacher shifts the presentation toward the more verbal tasks. Pointing tasks are virtually eliminated, and the *yes-no* answer and statement repetition become the core tasks from which the children must work. To the question "Is this truck red?" they must now answer not simply "Yes," but "Yes, this truck is red." The superior teacher does not require the children to work on Level 4 when they do not have the verbal skills that are necessary to produce the statements. Nor does she make the equally undesirable mistake of requiring skilled children to waste precious time working on the pointing level or nodding their heads to indicate "Yes" and "No."

Adhere to a rigid repetitive presentation pattern.

For the highly verbal teacher, it is a hard job to develop the habit of adhering to memorized statements and a fixed pattern of presentation, because these practices go contrary to one of the major principles of cultivated diction—that of varying sentence structure and word choice to avoid monotony. However, it must be recognized that the culturally deprived child is not a sophisticated adult who is so familiar with basic language structures that these quickly bore him and grate against his sensibilities. He is a language-deprived child, and even the simplest pattern stands as no less than a challenge to him.

The objection may be raised that a child has to learn to understand various types of statements and that some variation is necessary to keep him from being bound like an automaton to only certain forms of expression. This objection certainly is a reasonable one. Ultimately, the child should be expected to handle language in its natural setting, with all of its nuances and irregularities. However, there is no reason to suppose that such language is the logical starting point for a preschool program (any more than to expect a child to distill mathematical principles by attending a college course in which the instructor uses mathematical principles in the way we ultimately expect the child to use them). A far more expedient approach is to work from the crucial core patterns with irregularities and nuances stripped away and to build from this core, in the most systematic manner possible, to the various statement expansions of language.

Initial uniformity is extremely desirable, because the child who is backward in language tends to concentrate on the "key words" in the sentence—usually the nouns. To progress in language, he must learn to attend to the structure words—conjunctions, prepositions, and the like. If the teacher allows sentence patterns to vary freely, the "key words" will become the primary elements that carry over from one variation to another. Therefore, the introduction of variations merely reinforces the false idea that the "key words" are the only important words.

Actually, the introduction of statement variations is not a problem, because, even when the teacher works with what seems to be mechanical perfection, considerable variation creeps into the presentation. The teacher automatically becomes less mechanical when it is apparent that the children have mastered the basic tasks and no longer benefit from a very skeletal presentation. She rarely finds it difficult to amplify and enrich; the difficulty usually comes during the initial stages of the program, when she must streamline her presentation and adhere to "rote" statements.

Use unison responses whenever possible.

As a rule of thumb, the teacher should assume that while she is working with one child individually, the others in the class are not learning anything. Accordingly, she should work with children individually no more than is absolutely necessary. She can avoid individual sessions by introducing unison responses. In a sense, a unison response enables the teacher to work individually with each member of the class throughout the entire period. In another sense, it allows her to work with the entire group, so that the total number of responses produced during a class period is increased many times, and the speed with which concepts are learned is generally increased accordingly. The deprived child's mastery of many fundamental concepts is premised on a certain amount of practice, and the practice is as effective in unison as it is individually.

Never work with a child individually in a study group for more than about 30 seconds.

Sometimes it is expedient to structure tasks so that each child has a turn. If each turn takes more than about 30 seconds, the teacher should restructure the task. Ideally, each turn should take five seconds or less, and ideally each child should not know in advance when he will be called upon to recite. If he knows, he can turn his attention off, waiting for his turn to come. If he does not know, he must remain alert throughout the presentation. If a task, such as reading a simple statement, requires more than 30 seconds to complete, it should be restructured so that different children read different parts of the statement or so that the task is broken by intermittent questions that are directed at other members of the class.

Phrase statements rhythmically.

Rhythm in the classroom situation has nothing to do with the culturally deprived Negro's supposed natural feel for rhythm. Rhythm, rather, is introduced both as a "set" that allows children to produce the desired statements more easily and as a convention that enables the children to say things together when they are producing unison responses. It is very difficult for the teacher to tell whether members of a class are producing the statement properly if each member is speaking at a different speed. On the other hand, when the children are taught to produce the statement in the same tempo with the same accent, the teacher can hear what each child is saying. The rhythmically learned statement is also easier for the children to produce, because a certain amount of "meaningfulness" has been infused into it through a beat. Because the statement has a distinct "personality," the child can more easily put the sound elements in their proper place. For example, in trying to produce the rhythmically phrased statement so that it comes out "Sound sound—[pause]—sound sound," the child immediately recognizes departures from the pattern as mistakes. Thus, the scope of unrecognized mistakes (while certainly not eliminated) is considerably reduced.

Require the children to speak in loud, clear voices.

The measure of a good school is sometimes the noise level. If the children are working "at their own rate," quietly, without disturbing others, the school is sometimes judged to be successful. However, the no-noise axiom has no place in a preschool classroom. Mumbling serves to mask the deprived child's inability to talk properly. Furthermore, when the child mumbles, the teacher is not receiving the information she needs to pace her presentation. The axiom for the preschool classroom should be: *a quiet classroom is an ineffective classroom.* In requiring loud responses, the teacher will encounter a great deal of resistance, because the children often have learned that one speaks in a wee voice around adults. She should be persistent and should not allow wee-voiced responses, perhaps playing deaf. "Tommy, you'll have to speak up. I can't hear what you're saying."

Do not hurry children or encourage them to talk fast.

Often, the deprived child, as pointed out in Chapter 2, has a tendency to amalgamate the parts of sentences and pronounce them so quickly that he has difficulty appreciating them as parts that can be taken out of the sentence, rearranged, and placed in other statements or questions. Therefore, the tempo should always be moderate, with the accent on correct pronunciation. Some children will develop what might be called an "information-processing" language, which seems to function as a second language. Their native language will be fast and sometimes unintelligible. At the same time, their "information-processing" language is slow and distinct. With practice, the child will become increasingly facile at taking statements from his habitual language and rephrasing them in the learned language; however, unless the child is constantly reminded of the learned-language standards, *he will integrate his two languages by reducing statements of his learned language to his natural-language pattern, thus rendering them relatively useless.* This type of reduction is particularly evident during the early stages of instruction, before the children have firmly learned language patterns. The tempo of the lesson should always be mechanical enough to prevent these reductions and to allow the child to proceed from the reduction patterns of his native language to production of the learned language—not in the opposite direction.

Clap to accent basic language patterns and conventions.

As noted earlier, the culturally deprived child is "deaf" to certain words in a sentence. Since he is, it is sometimes difficult to call his attention to the critical sentence elements. It is often even more difficult to make him aware of the element's proper place in the sentence. For example, when trying to repeat the sentence "Push up or push down," the deprived child may be initially unaware of the word *or,* omitting it from his sentence. "Push up push down." After becoming aware of *or,* however, he is faced with the task of placing it in the sentence. At first, he may be so acutely aware of it that he awards it the most prominent position in the sentence. "*Or* push up push down." Next, he may try the "shotgun" approach, using more than one *or.* "Or push up or push down." Finally, after many attempts he may be able to produce the correct sentence.

The teacher can help the child become aware of the critical element and locate it by phrasing the sentence rhythmically and clapping as she says the critical word. The clap functions as an accent that helps place the element more dramatically. "Push up *or* push down." This clapping procedure is also useful in defining the relationship between questions and statements. "There are *how many* days in a week? There are *seven* days in a week." The clap dramatizes the fact that the question and the statement are identical except for the accented elements. The clap also shows specifically how statement and question are different. The clap, therefore, is extremely useful in teaching basic sentence forms, in correcting mistakes, and in calling attention to changes in sentences.

Use questions liberally.

Questions are valuable because they call the child's attention to specific parts of a sentence or process and help define them.

To demonstrate that statements are made up of parts and that each part functions, the teacher should (especially during the first several months of the program) follow every statement with a string of questions that focus on the various parts of the statement. "The book is on the table. Where is the book? . . . What is on the table? . . . Is the book on the floor? . . . Is the book under the table?" In answering these questions, the child learns not only about prepositional concepts, but also, what is equally important, about the structure of the statement "The book is on the table."

When the operation deals with a series of steps, the teacher should use the appropriate question-and-answer series to lead the child to the solution. "What do we know about this thing? . . . Yes, it's a word. And what do we know about words? . . . They have a beginning and an end. And which one do we start out with? . . . So what do we know about this part of the word? . . . Yes, that's where we start out." Many tasks involve question-and-answer series. These are important, but also difficult. Through such series, many of the culturally deprived child's gravest deficiencies are brought to light: his inability to connect language with reality, his unawareness of contradictions, his vocabulary limitation, and his desire to please the teacher rather than seek information.

The teacher should try to appreciate how difficult the task of handling a series of questions is for the child. The assumption behind a series is that for each question in the series, more than one answer is possible. The ultimate answer is discovered not by making a snap decision at the beginning of the series, but by proceeding through the series, a check-point at a time, answering each question before proceeding to the next. The deprived child usually resists, rather effectively, any approach that involves such an "uncertain" answer. He would rather reduce a series of questions to a simple question that can be disposed of with a guess. He can learn a rote rule, such as "If they're not the same, they must be different," much more easily than he can grasp the idea that something should be called "different" only after he has asked himself if the objects are the same and answered "They are not." Taking the extra steps to use the rule requires careful training in how to handle question-and-answer series.

Use repetition.

The culturally advantaged four-year-old child is often capable of learning in minutes what it may take the culturally disadvantaged child of the same age days to master. The teacher should enter the classroom fully aware of this fact. She should plan on going over basic statements perhaps *hundreds of times*. She should further anticipate that the child will tend to forget that which he has a great deal of trouble learning initially—unless the skills are reviewed daily, which is not always practical. There is no substitute for sheer repetition in teaching basic patterns. Interest-arousing devices should certainly be included in the curriculum, but only with the awareness that repetition is the backbone of the program.

Be aware of the cues the child is receiving.

The culturally deprived child will often try to be a "mind reader." Instead of attending to the material that demonstrates the concept, he will watch the teacher's face. If her lips seem to be forming the beginning of a familiar phrase, he will produce that phrase. If she starts to say something, he will try to say it with her, sound for sound, perhaps without understanding what he is saying. If the class is heterogeneous and one of the members knows the answers most of the time, the other children may wait for him to start responding and then try to match his statement. *The purpose of any kind of cue in the learning situation is to introduce an element that is not essential to the understanding of the concept but that makes the processing of the concept easier. Good cues, however, should operate within the minimum-concept framework.* They should involve little that must be unlearned or relearned, and no conventions other than those that are familiar to the child. They should be simply a more dramatic way of approaching the material. A good cue is often nothing more than a distinctive sing-song manner in which a statement is presented.

For cues to be entirely effective, however, the teacher must have them under her control. She must resist the empathy she experiences when a child is searching her face for the answer. She must not let her lips form the word, or the child will probably say the word and learn to focus on her lips instead of on the material from which the response should derive. She should watch for spurious unison responses in which one child is merely trying to imitate what the others say. She should try to remove from the group a child who is substantially ahead of the others. She should avoid telegraphing responses through expression, glance, or word. She should avoid placing materials on the chalkboard or in the room that will cue the child. She should not always present tasks in the same order (so that the child cannot learn to answer by rote order).

The control of cues is quite difficult. Sometimes the teacher gives them unconsciously. For this reason, it is a good practice to have a person sit in periodically and watch for what seem to be unconsciously awarded cues.

Use short explanations.

A verbal explanation assumes a knowledge of the language. Since the deprived child does not have a great deal of language knowledge, explanations that are extended much beyond a single sentence are usually wasted.

Tailor the explanation and rules to what the child knows.

If an explanation or rule assumes more knowledge than the child has, the explanation should either be simplified or, if this is impossible, should be replaced by a demonstration that will show what the teacher is trying to get across. The teacher *could* present the verbal rule for adding zero to another number as "The sum will always be the same as the value of the other number." However, since this rule assumes a sophisticated understanding of addition and of numbers, the teacher should not use it. Instead, she can lead the child to the rule through demonstration. The series $1 + 0 = 1, 2 + 0 = 2, 3 + 0 = 3, \ldots 10 + 0 = 10$ can be taught as a rote unit, as a kind of counting. The series demonstrates that a pattern holds for each number in the familiar 1–10 counting series. With only a slight jump in reasoning, the child can conclude that the pattern should hold for *any number.* Thus, he can learn the rule by being led through a pattern, not by trying to work from a verbal rule that is quite beyond him. This technique has a great deal of application in the preschool.

Use lots of examples.

When teaching a new concept, don't make the mistake of presenting a limited number of objects and then "talking" about these. This approach merely confuses the concept with irrelevant detail. The child has no way of knowing in advance what the concept is, so he must rely on the teacher's presentation to clarify what she means by "long," or "between," or "red." If the teacher presents one example of "long," the child has no way of knowing whether long refers to relative length or to some irrelevant detail, perhaps the shape of the object presented. The best way to rule out irrelevant details is to use many examples. This technique rules out the possibility that *long* is a designation applied to a line of a particular length. The best way to show the child which are the relevant details of the letter *A* is to show him scores of A's—big ones, small ones, thick-lined ones, and thin-lined ones. The best way to show the child that *red* is an absolute, is to show the child through examples that the attributes other than color can change—position, shape, texture, and so on—and the object is still called *red*. Many sources of serious confusion can be eliminated by presenting different examples that show the child how far a concept "stretches."

Prevent incorrect responses whenever possible.

The teacher who anticipates an incorrect response before it occurs and short-circuits it helps the children overcome chronic mistake patterns more quickly.

If the task requires the child to make a visual discrimination and the child has not inspected the material, the teacher can assume that the child is about to make a guessed response. She can prevent it by saying "Now look at it. What is this? What do you know about it?"

If the task requires several steps in reasoning but the child begins to respond immediately, the teacher can assume the child could not have gone through the reasoning process. She can prevent a guess by saying "Now, think. Take it a step at a time. What do you ask yourself first?"

If a child makes a mistake, the teacher should always assume that *he will repeat the mistake the next time the task is presented.* The teacher should anticipate the mistake and handle it in a way that will give the child experience in processing and mastering chronic-mistake material— by pointing out the child's tendency to err. "Tyrone, you want to call this animal a deer as you did last time, but I'll bet if you think big, you can remember what it really is."

Prevention techniques tend to stop the child even though he might have given a correct response by chance. This is important because a child suffers if he makes a correct response by applying an inadequate procedure. He learns to rely on this procedure, which means he learns to rely on a false rule that must be unlearned before he can proceed according to the prescribed learning schedule.

Be completely unambiguous in letting the child know when his response is correct and when it is incorrect.

If the teacher asks the child to "Put the yellow pencil on the book," and the child puts the green pencil on the book, she should not respond in an equivocal way. She should not say "That's good, Tyrone. You put the pencil on the book. Now put the *yellow* pencil on the book." He probably will not understand this subtle correction. This approach provides the child with success experience but at the expense of information. The teacher should give the needed information in a matter-of-fact, non-threatening, and completely unambiguous manner. "No, that's not right," or "Not quite. That is the *green* pencil, not the *yellow* pencil." Only if she constantly directs the child's output by letting him know when his responses are correct can the teacher achieve fast, relatively smooth learning.

Dramatize the use value of learning whenever possible.

The intrinsic value of learning comes from the sense of mastery associated with the use of the concepts. By using the concept, a person can do things he could not have done previously, including showing off and exhibiting his superior knowledge to others. Interpersonal mastery can be handled especially well in the classroom. The teacher can set the situation up so that the children look smarter than she. They can fool her, they will enjoy themselves doing it, and they will learn to appreciate some of the power that comes from thinking and learning. The teacher should not devote the entire lesson to interpersonal mastery. However, she should select certain fairly well-mastered tasks and set herself up as the goat. "Okay, I'll bet nobody remembers how to do this, not even Tyrone." When the children give the correct answer, the teacher should act shocked. Later, she can use a similar technique to challenge children to learn new tasks. "I'm going to try to teach something that's so hard I don't think anybody here will be able to catch on." The challenge is an extremely good incentive, but it should be given only to those children who are ready to accept it. For those who are ready, it provides a slightly simplified experience with the kind of challenge on which academic progress rests.

Encourage thinking behavior.

If the child indicates the green pencil when he is asked to point to the yellow pencil, the teacher should not mislead the child into thinking that his response is correct. However, she should be equally careful to praise the child for trying, if he did try. After correcting the response, she should acknowledge that he is operating in a way that will ultimately lead to success. "Tyrone is trying. He doesn't guess, does he? He'll get it, you'll see. That's because he's trying to think big." *The teacher should let the child know that she approves of his approach, even though it sometimes leads to incorrect responses.* Conversely, nonthinking behavior, even if it leads to the correct answer, should be discouraged. This should be done in a positive way. "Did you try hard today? I don't think so. You fooled around a lot and didn't pay attention. But you're a smart boy and you can get it if you try. You come in tomorrow and really work, okay?"

Summary

This chapter dealt with the basic teaching strategies that have application in the preschool for culturally deprived children. The following specific strategies were explained:

1. Work at different levels of difficulty at different times.
2. Adhere to a rigid, repetitive presentation pattern.
3. Use unison responses whenever possible.
4. Never work with a child individually in a study group for more than about 30 seconds.
5. Phrase statements rhythmically.
6. Require children to speak in a loud, clear voice.
7. Do not hurry children or encourage them to talk fast.
8. Clap to accent basic language patterns and conventions.
9. Use questions liberally.
10. Use repetition.
11. Be aware of the cues the child is receiving.
12. Use short explanations.
13. Tailor the explanations and rules to what the child knows.
14. Use lots of examples.
15. Prevent incorrect responses whenever possible.
16. Be completely unambiguous in letting the child know when his response is correct and when it is incorrect.
17. Dramatize the use value of learning whenever possible.
18. Encourage thinking behavior.

Each of these apparently simple rules requires a considerable amount of skill if it is to be executed successfully. This chapter has provided a number of specific suggestions and examples for putting these rules into practice, but the actual skill can only be acquired through disciplined experience. It was pointed out that no teacher possesses these highly specialized skills as a natural gift but that almost any teacher can acquire them if she works at it. It is hoped that this chapter will have convinced the prospective teacher that she has a good deal to learn, regardless of her previous experience, and that there is no mystery surrounding the skills needed to become an effective teacher in an academically oriented preschool.

language as a **6**
teaching instrument

*L*anguage enters into almost every phase of human activity; a list of possible language uses would be almost as long as a list of possible human activities. Therefore, an immediate problem confronts the person who wishes to construct a program of language training that focuses upon those aspects of language that are of greatest utility for the child. The various linguistic and psychological theories of language do not provide much guidance for focusing and limiting language to the necessary ingredients of communication. The value of these theories is measured by their adequacy in describing a full range of language behavior. Their purpose is not to assign priorities to certain kinds of skills and content. As a result, an educator who seeks guidance from psychological or linguistic theory finds himself with a criterion for selection that remains neutral on most of the important issues of what to select and how to present it. At best, this criterion can refer him back to the language behavior of the language community under consideration, implying some very general remedies.

The problem of prescribing the content of a basic language training program is solved only by looking at language, not in terms of what is normal or expected but in terms of what is necessary. The main question to be dealt with in this chapter is *what is necessary in order for language to function as an adequate communication system between teacher and children in the learning situation.*

In order to appreciate what language must do, we consider first the common properties of all teaching situations. In any teaching situation, the child must learn something. He comes into the situation without an adequate understanding of a certain conceptual dimension. Through verbal or nonverbal means, the teacher demonstrates the concept by presenting examples of what the concept is and what it is not. The teacher then requires the child to respond and demonstrate through either verbal or nonverbal means that he understands the concept as defined. The child may perform in a way that shows his understanding of the concept, or he may not. In either case, the teacher responds by telling him something about his performance. Perhaps this "telling" will come in the form of a nonverbal demonstration of a contradiction in his thinking;

perhaps it will come in the form of a direct "No, that's not right." Regardless of the manner in which the child is told, he must be told whether he is right or wrong.

The minimum teaching language must be sufficient for the two phases of the teaching presentation described above: the phase in which examples of the concept are presented, and the phase in which feedback is provided for the child. Therefore, a minimum teaching language— whether it is phrased in standard English or uses a series of nonverbal symbols—must satisfy two basic requirements:

1. It must be capable of representing reality, of naming or pointing out things (even if the naming is accomplished by a series of grunts), and if the language is to be a full-fledged communication system, it must be capable of creating a symbolic equivalent of what is observable in physical reality.

2. A closely related requirement, it must have provisions for indicating truth and falsity in a relatively unambiguous way.

The learning situation takes place in the world of physical reality. The demonstrations of a concept are demonstrations of what *is*. And the attempt of the child to act consistently with the concept is treated as an instance that either *is* consistent with the concept or is *not* consistent with the concept. From the beginning, the language of the teaching situation must be the language of what is, symbolizing what is presented in some segment of physical reality. The truth and reality-representing requirements of language may be illustrated with the teaching of a concept such as *between*. The presentation begins with a physical reality, and, on this level, the concept is seen as an arrangement of at least three objects in a row. The communication system, to be relevant, must be capable of symbolizing not only the three objects, but also the relationship of the medial object to the other two. Conceivably, the symbolizing could be achieved through a series of gestures, but it is neatly accomplished in ordinary language by the statement form "The *A* is between the *B* and the *C*" which can be varied to accommodate any arrangement of the objects *A, B,* and *C*. When the child attempts to demonstrate his mastery of *between,* the second application of the teaching language comes into play. The child is corrected. Correction is achieved quite easily, and, therefore, the fact that it is a necessary part of the teaching language is not always appreciated. If the teaching language is to be consistent, however, the presentation created by the child must be comparable with the teacher's, which means that it must be expressible in the same language. "No, Harold, the *A* is *not* between the *B* and the *C*."

A final requirement of the minimum teaching language is that it must be shared by the teacher and the child. If the child does not understand the code, he obviously will fail to appreciate how reality is being represented, and he will not benefit from feedback that is designed to bring him closer to the concept.

Language as an Equivalent of Reality

Language, if it is to be adequate in the teaching situation, must be capable of standing for reality. It must be capable of creating a verbal description of reality which may be treated as if it were reality. An adequate teaching language is one structured so that a person familiar with language is able to perform many of the same operations with a physical presentation and a language presentation. For example, if this person is confronted with the statement "All coins are in the box," he can use the statement as if it were a physical presentation. He can draw immediate inferences in response to such questions as "Are some of the coins under the box? No, all coins are in the box"; "Is the box empty? No, because it has all of the coins in it."

Through some kind of experiences, *the child must learn about the substitution property of language.* He must learn, for example, that the statement "All coins are in the box" is something that has a physical counterpart and that this counterpart can be created. Furthermore, he must learn that what is true of the physical presentation (so far as the relationship of the coins and the box is concerned) must also be true of the statement. That he does learn about the substitution property can be demonstrated rather conclusively in many ways. Two such demonstrations are presented below.

Demonstration 1

We ask a culturally advantaged five-year-old to repeat the statement "All gleeps are in the perk." We then ask him the following questions: "Are any gleeps under the perk?" "Is the perk empty?" "Where are all the gleeps?"

We note that the child answers the questions in the same way he would answer analogous questions raised in connection with the analogous statement "All coins are in the box." Although he has never encountered gleeps or a perk, he treats these entities as if they were somehow equivalent to *coins* and *box*. The most reasonable explanation seems to be that the child has generalized a truth about the relationship expressed by the statement form "The *B* is in the *C*." The child has observed many relationships on the order of "The *B* is in the *C*" (hats in boxes, dog food in cans, shirts in drawers, etc.). All instances of this relationship—no matter what *things* were involved—had common characteristics. In all instances, the *C* was not empty. In all instances, no *B* was under the *C*. These and other common characteristics can all be observed by a child who understands the reality represented by the statement. When confronted with an instance of "The *B* is in the *C*" in which *B* and *C* are things never experienced, the child cannot rely on physical experience of *B* and *C*. He must therefore rely on *statement experience*. In order to draw his conclusion about gleeps and perks, he must first appreciate the fact that the statement "All gleeps are in the perk" is analogous to "All horses are in the barn," "All beads are in the box," etc. He can then draw the conclusion that "If there were such things as gleeps and perks and all the gleeps were in the perk, then I would know certain things about them, just as I would know certain things about coins and boxes if all coins were in the box." Clearly, the various *in*-statements in the child's repertoire form the basis for the conclusions. The child understands that these statements imply a certain reality. Therefore, an analogous statement would imply an analogous reality. Conversely, when the child handled analogous statements as if they imply analogous realities, we can conclude that he understands the substitution property of language.

Demonstration 2

We present an advantaged five-year-old with three related tasks that involve constructing a *statement*. For the first task, we present an arrangement of toys, including a doll under a toy bed. We say "Show me: The doll is under the bed." The child points to the doll. Next, we lead the child to a room in which there is a doll and a full-sized bed, but the doll is not under the bed. Again we say "Show me: The doll is under the bed." The child takes the doll and places it under the bed. For the third demonstration, we present a doll that is permanently fixed to a table top, and we present a light toy bed. We repeat "Show me: The doll is under the bed." The child takes the bed and places it over the doll.

The instructions in all cases were identical, and yet the actions were different. How is it possible for the child to arrive at the appropriate outcome by such radically different routes? The only reasonable answer is that the child who understands language works from a knowledge that certain presentations are equivalent to certain statements. In each of the situations above, the child was aware of what presentation was necessary. When he found one that satisfied the requirements, he pointed to it. When it proved expedient to create the presentation in one way, he created it that way. When the situation changed, he changed his approach. But, in each case, he worked toward the equivalent of the statement "The doll is under the bed."

The point of the two demonstrations is that the advantaged child does not simply learn words and concepts. He learns about what language is supposed to do. He learns that he can observe relations on the physical level and translate these into words—or actions—since statement, action, and physical reality are all facets of a total, observable relationship. The observable facts provide the ultimate sanction for language. And the child who learns language under favorable conditions learns this fact early and thoroughly.

Language as a Vehicle for Truth

Closely related to the substitution requirement of the teaching language is the requirement of truth. The teaching language should be designed so that the teacher can monitor the production of the child by letting him know whether his behavior is consistent or inconsistent with the concept being presented. This means that the teaching language must occur in the domain of *yes-no*. The teaching language must be able to let the child know either "Yes, your behavior is consistent with the concept" or "No, your behavior is not consistent." Since this *yes-no* orientation is common to *all* teaching situations, the basic unit of the teaching language must be the statement of fact. Only statements of fact are capable of being submitted to *yes-no* monitoring. And not all sentences satisfy this requirement. We cannot say that the sentence "Look at John run" is either true or false. However, we can submit the idea "THIS *IS* AN EXAMPLE OF RUNNING" to *yes-no* evaluation.

The basic assumption of every teaching situation is that the examples of the concept being presented can be translated into a statement of fact, a statement containing the verb *to be*. Regardless of how un-statement-like the presentation seems, the learner must realize that the presentation is an attempt to convey a fact—*a picture of what is*. When the teacher runs, the assumed translation is "This *is* an example of running." When she says "Give me the ball," the assumed translation is "The act of giving me the ball is what I want you to perform," and the correction "No, no" translates into "The act of giving me the ball is what you are not performing."

The Substandard Language

The teaching language in a given situation may fail for either of two reasons: (1) the language may be inadequate for the task; or (2) the language may be adequate, but the child may not learn that it is. In either case, the net result is the same: *the conventional, basic concepts cannot be effectively taught to the child, because he cannot be corrected in an unambiguous manner.*

Examples of palpably inadequate language which is incapable of teaching the relationships between statements of fact and observations of reality can be found in many residential schools for the deaf. The language instruction provided in these institutions is often characterized by an attempt to create a "natural language" or a kind of grammatical language, and, in pursuit of these goals, the teachers submerge the generalizable truths about language in a mire of idiomatic statements that defy translation. Often the child's first exposure to the verb *is* comes in the idiomatic and structurally useless expression "It is cold outside." Often, half of the *yes-no* equation is not presented, because, according to the assumption of the language program, children should be concerned with the positive, not the negative. Often the child does not receive the basic labeling statement "This is a _____" until he has been exposed to constructions of a much higher order, such as "Give me the ball" (which translates into "The act of giving me the ball is what I want you to perform" and is therefore more complex than the statement "This is a ball," for example).

Often the results of the language instruction received by these children are clearly reflected in their inability to handle language. Below are "stories" written by children who have studied under a substandard language for more than six years. The "stories" were written in response to a picture story. In the first picture of the series, a boy and a girl are preparing to play catch, while a baby, sitting on the grass, looks on. In the second picture, the boy is throwing the ball to the girl. The third picture shows the ball rolling under a house as the boy, the girl, and a dog look on. In the final picture, the dog is bringing the ball to the boy, who is kneeling.

> *Paul (age: 13 years, 8 months):* Boy and girl play a red ball. Boy and girl throw a red ball. The ball has a in house. The ball has a out dog.
> *Linda (age: 13 years, 1 month):* Boy and girl fun baby. Oh baby throw boy and girl. House under ball dog look.
> *Bonnie (15 years, 0 months):* The boy throw ball catch the ball girl. The girl play in house. The ball see boy came dog help walk mouth ball gave boy.

Note that these children are not simply deficient in their use of words; they are deficient in their repertoire of concepts. The teaching language to which they were exposed failed to teach them how to translate reality into statements. It failed to teach them which cues are relevant to a particular situation and which are accidental. It failed in teaching the simplest truths, such as "If the ball is under the house, the house is not under the ball." (House under ball dog look.)

The culturally deprived preschooler shares certain language deficiencies with the deaf child. The profiles of culturally disadvantaged and deaf children are quite similar on the Illinois Test of Psycholinguistic Abilities. The severely deprived preschooler, like the deaf child, can often understand such acceptable commands as "Go put that chair over by the window," but he may be quite unable to do what the culturally advantaged child does—answer a question related to his action, "What are you doing?" Although his reluctance to respond is usually interpreted as "shyness," it is far more often a simple manifestation of his inability to translate actions into statements. He can recognize statements (just as the reader can recognize pictures of many famous Americans), but he cannot produce them in an acceptable fashion (just as the reader may not be able to create an identifiable likeness of George Washington). The culturally deprived child can handle single words that denote obvious actions and things, such as *boy, girl, throw, catch, house.* However, like the deaf child, he flounders when the concept becomes one that is more firmly embedded in connected language, such as the idea represented by "The ball is under the house." The jumble of words that seems to be "meaningful" to the deaf child is often meaningful to the deprived child.

The teaching language used to present concepts to the culturally deprived child *may be adequate.* The writers are of the opinion that generally it is not. However, its adequacy is irrelevant, because, regardless of the caliber of the dialect used by the adults in the community, the children do not have the specific, prerequisite knowledge about their language. They do not have an adequate teaching language. The problem facing the teacher of the culturally deprived preschooler, therefore, is not simply teaching concepts *but teaching the basic and necessary rules of language.* The knowledge of language is crucial, because, without it, the child will be limited in much the same way the deaf child is limited, to the obvious parts of the universe—the things to which one can point and which one can label in a relatively unambiguous way. Such labeling constitutes only a small part of concept learning.

The Statement Hierarchy

Earlier, it was noted that the teaching language must express complete statements which are either true or false. The method used to teach the culturally advantaged child simple labels seems, however, to contradict this requirement. The mother of the advantaged toddler often uses single words, which are apparently quite effective as teaching instruments. Actually, the advantaged mother is creating an illusion. She is using statements, but she presents part of the statement nonverbally. She does this by pointing to the object or calling the child's attention to it in some way. The pointing is part of the statement, and, without it, there would be no true statement. If the mother walked into a room and said "Asphalt tile" without completing the statement by pointing, the child would probably recognize that she was not talking about anything that is true or false. Rather, he would interpret her behavior to mean that she was playing a word game. When she points, however, she completes the statement. She can then say "Yes" and "No" in response to his behavior, and the meaning of the words can be clearly understood. "Cup. . . . Yes. Cup. No, not that. That's a *glass.*"

The one-word-label statement is important because it represents the simplest form of true statement: *Point*—"book." The unfortunate aspect of this statement is that it leads to a dead end quite quickly unless the act of pointing is verbalized. This fact can be demonstrated by replacing the word *book* in the statement above with *a nonverbal signal that is defined to mean book.* For example, the teacher could tap herself on the head instead of saying "book" without altering the kind of information supplied by the statement *Point*—"book." She could then present a series of objects and indicate either by tapping herself on the head or by shaking her head whether the object was a book. Her responses to a series of objects would go something like this: red book, *Point*—*head tap;* little book, *Point*—*head tap;* cup, *Point*—*head shake;* thick book, *Point*—*head tap;* pencil, *Point*—*head shake;* and paper, *Point*—*head shake.*

If language consisted of nothing more than simple label designations, such as "Book," the language above would be quite adequate. But there are very few entirely adequate labels in language. The same object that is called "book" on one occasion is called "reading material" on another and "inanimate object" on still another. The object referred to as "boy" on one occasion may also be referred to as "child," "human," "living thing," "David," etc. The object called "dog" may also be called "big," "brown," "mean," and "mangy." There are few simple labels in language, and, for this reason, the half-verbal statement used to teach simple labels is dangerous. When an attempt is made to modify concepts already mastered—to call attention to a compatible concept that is related in some way—the half-verbal language fails. It does not have the grammar necessary to handle concept modification. Consider the child who learns to identify *book* either through the point-and-tap statement or the point-and-label statement. What happens when the child tries to learn the concept *red?* The teacher wants him to understand that the object is still a book but that attention should now be focused on some aspect of the book. How does she do this? If she proceeds to introduce a word or signal to denote *red,* she will probably convince the child simply that she wants to call the book something new. The child will conclude that she has changed her mind. Instead of being called "book," the object will now be called "red." Instead of calling the object *head tap,* it will now be called *hand clap.* Very simple, and very wrong.

What is needed is some method by which the identity of the object can be held—a method which enables the teacher to suggest "Look. It's still a book. I'm not saying that it isn't a book. I'm just trying to tell you something about this book." One such method would be to call the object by both names, first the originally learned name (book) and then the new name (red). This presentation could also be effective on the nonverbal level: *Point—"book"—"red"*; or *Point—head tap—head clap*.

Two important points emerge from this demonstration:

1. The problems encountered with the half-verbal presentation are precisely the same as those encountered with the nonverbal presentation. Both must reduce ambiguity and direct attention to the concepts in a prescribed way. For this reason, the solutions to the problem are the same. The half-verbal statement is a parallel to the nonverbal statement.

2. Both the half-verbal statement and the nonverbal statement are being forced into the formation of a grammar. Already, conventions for *yes-no* have been introduced, as well as conventions for the order of "words." When the concept to be taught was simple, the grammar was relatively simple (*Point—"book"*). When the concept to be taught was a "second-order" modification, the grammar became more complicated. In order to teach prepositions, the grammar would obviously have to become more complicated, involving at least three content words in addition to the pointing signal.

Whether one uses a half-verbal presentation, a nonverbal presentation, or a fully verbal presentation, *he must teach a language.* He must teach the conventions of *true-false statements,* because, without these, he cannot possibly process the more complicated concepts which the preschooler is expected to learn. However, the fully verbal language has two great advantages over the half-verbal and nonverbal presentations:

1. It represents a minimum learning. Even if a child learned a perfectly adequate nonverbal language, he would be expected to learn the standard, verbal language also. A great deal of time is saved if he does not spend time learning two such languages but concentrates on the one that will ultimately be expected of him.

2. Verbal statements that precisely parallel any half-verbal or nonverbal presentation can easily be created. The teaching language, whether it is completely nonverbal or completely verbal, is the language of *true-false* statements. The statement demands of a given situation are the same for any presentation. Fully verbal language is well designed to handle *true-false* statements. In fact, it is far better designed than the half-verbal or nonverbal language.

To determine the irreducible verbal statement in the teaching situation, we return to the simplest teaching situation, in which a label is attached to a relatively virgin object such as a book. As noted earlier, the problem facing the teacher is that of calling attention to the segment of reality under consideration and then symbolizing it in some way. The act of pointing and naming seemed to satisfy the statement demands of the situation rather well: *Point—"book."*

Using this statement as the model for the fully verbalized statement, we simply verbalize the act of pointing, thereby making the statement fully verbal: "This is—a book."

Statements of this form must represent the irreducible statements of a teaching language. We shall refer to them as first-order or *identity* statements. In one sense, the identity statement does no more than identify, saying in a verbal way what the point-and-word statement said. However, it is a full-blown statement and is therefore capable of being submitted to verbal *yes-no* questions and to other operations that are possible through conventionally defined language.

The *second-order* statement (the statement used to modify some aspect of the concept that has been mastered) again translates rather directly from the half-verbal presentation, *Point—"book"—"red."* The verbal statement: "This book is red."

Statements of this form do, rather gracefully, what the half-verbal and nonverbal presentations could do less efficiently. The first part of the statement, "This *A*," functions as an identity holder. This part of the statement says "Look, it's still an *A*. Nothing has changed here." The second part of the statement, "is *B*," completes the equation and directs attention to something about *A*. In essence, it says "Don't discard *A*; just attend to something about *A*."

The structure of identity statement and modifying statement may seem somewhat arbitrary, but actually they are not. This fact can be demonstrated by changing the second-order statement from "This book is red" to the apparently equivalent statement "This is a red book." These statements are not equivalent in the teaching language because the second one *does not hold the identity of "book."* Therefore, the second one is ambiguous. The *not* statement that is related to the first statement, "This book is not yellow," is quite unambiguous, while the *not* statement related to the second statement, "This is not a yellow book," could apply to buffaloes, blocks, buildings, or bottles, as well as books.

The second-order (modifying) statement is infinitely expandable: "This car is red"; "This red car is an Oldsmobile"; "This red Oldsmobile car is speeding down the road"; "This red Oldsmobile car which is speeding down the road is being driven by a woman"; etc.

The expandable property of the second-order statement is an indication that by using the statement form, it is possible to teach a series of compatible concepts in a completely unambiguous way. First, each concept is established as the predicate in a subject-predicate relationship. "This ball is *blue*." The concept is then moved to the "identity holder" position on the other side of the verb. "This *blue* ball is on the table."

The first-order statement form and the second-order statement form are capable of teaching all the basic concepts—names of things and actions, position, color, class, and relationships in time and space. *They therefore constitute the basic teaching language.* They represent the minimum language needed to assure an unambiguous presentation of those concepts a preschool child is expected to learn. If the two statement forms are to realize their communication potential, however, *the child must understand them.* Token understanding is not sufficient. If the child does not fully understand the two basic statement forms, he must be taught. He must learn the essentials of the teaching language before the teaching language can be used with any certainty.

Language instruction for the culturally deprived child (who may have little more than a token understanding of the two statement forms, the questions related to each, and the *not* statements) is not merely a drill in sounding good. It is instruction in handling a powerful tool. In order to handle this tool, he must learn that

1. Statements have parts.
2. The parts retain their identity even when they appear in different statements.
3. Statements imply questions, and questions can be answered by referring to the original statement.
4. Certain statements contradict other statements.
5. Certain statements are compatible with other statements.
6. A physical presentation is capable of being described with many non-contradictory statements.
7. Relations expressed by statements are generalizable to a range of situations.

The Structure of the Second-order Statement

The second-order statement "This book is _____" can be completed in an infinite number of ways—"This book is big"; "This book is on the table"; "This book is heavier than a mouse"; etc. *Not all of these completions imply the same kind of information processing, however.* In other words, not all of these completions are structurally the same. Consider a specific chair—the one the writers have in mind. What does the person who is knowledgeable in language know about this chair? Does he know where this chair is? No, he does not, because determination of position rests on an empirical investigation. Does he know the color, shape, or relative size of the chair? Again, these determinations require an empirical investigation. Does he know that the chair is not a table, not a book, not a car, or not any other kind of nonchair? He does. This kind of determination does not require empirical investigation. Does he know that the chair is a piece of furniture? He does.

The second-order statement, "This chair is _____," may be completed in a way that requires an empirical investigation or in a way that does not require such an investigation. This difference in information processing *implies a difference in the manner in which the two types of statement completions would be taught.* Obviously, a child should not be led to believe that he can determine whether a chair is a piece of furniture by inspecting the chair and trying to find "furnitureness." Equally obvious, he should not be led to believe that he can specify the size, color, or position of a chair without inspecting it. He must also be aware that both types of information processing may come into play in regard to a given concept. While someone must conduct an empirical investigation to determine that a given object is not hard, no further investigation is needed to determine that the object is soft. The reason is that not-hard = soft. On the other hand, if an investigation has disclosed that an object is not red, no further statement about its color can be provided without further empirical investigation. One cannot conclude that if a chair is not red, it is blue (or that if a chair is not on the table, it must be under the table).

On the basis of structural difference, there are three basic ways in which a second-order statement may be completed:

1. With a polar concept—one that has an opposite (This dog is big)

2. With a nonpolar concept that is shared by only some of the members of the identity class (This dog is white; This dog is in the yard)

3. With a nonpolar concept that is shared by all members of the identity class (This dog is a four-legged creature; This dog is an animal)

Since the concepts within each of these divisions are structurally similar, they raise similar problems and therefore can be taught in a similar manner. All polar concepts, for instance, are based on the same *not* equation:

$$hard = not\text{-}soft \text{ and } not\text{-}hard = soft$$
$$big = not\text{-}little \text{ and } not\text{-}big = little$$
$$loud = not\text{-}soft \text{ and } not\text{-}loud = soft$$

Since all opposites are the same in this structural dimension, the presentations used to teach them are logically the same, even though the concrete objects and the sensory modalities involved may be quite different. After all, the purpose of the teaching presentation is simply to define the structure of the concept for the child.

Therefore, the following set of directions for teaching the polar concept *hard-soft* is actually a kind of prototype that *can be readily adapted to any common polar concept* merely by changing the presentation so that it is consistent with the kind of investigation necessary to appreciate the polar distinction.

1. Present three balls, three lumps of clay, and three crusts of bread. Two of the balls, lumps of clay, and crusts of bread should be identical to each other except in hardness. The third member should be soft and dissimilar to the others in many ways—in color, size, etc.

2. Identify the things that are being presented. Identify each with the statement "This is a ball," "This is a piece of clay," or "This is a piece of bread." Ask the *is* and the *what* questions about each object.

> "Is this a ball? . . . Yes, this is a ball.
>   . . . No, this is *not* a ball."
> "This is a what? . . . This is a ball."

3. Define the concept *soft.* Push against the object and say "This ball is soft. *See how I can push it in?*" Repeat the statement "This ball is soft" and require the child to say the statement after you. Ask the *is* and *what* questions about each of the various objects.

> "Is this ball soft? . . . Yes, this ball is soft.
>   . . . No, this ball is not soft."
> "What can I say about this ball? . . . This ball is soft.
>   . . . This ball is not soft."

4. Introduce the concept *hard.* Refer to an object that is not *soft* and have the child produce the appropriate *not* statement. "This ball is not soft." Follow with the equivalent statement "This ball is hard." Have the child repeat the statement. Demonstrate that every object that is not soft can also be referred to as *hard*

5. Finally, introduce the concept *not hard.* Refer first to the various objects that are *hard* and elicit the appropriate statement. "This ball is hard." Refer then to the objects that are *not* hard. Ask "Is this ball hard? . . . No, this ball is not hard. This ball is soft."

Just as the various polar concepts can be taught by using a variation of the presentation outlined above, the various nonpolar concepts that are shared by all members of an identity class can be taught using a variation of one presentation, and the various nonpolar concepts that are shared by only some members of the identity class can be taught using a variation of another presentation.

The basic teaching language which we set out to establish consists of two basic statement forms:

1. "This is an ___*A*___ ."
2. "This ___*A*___ is ___*B*___ ."

and four basic presentation patterns:

1. The first-order pattern (This is a dog)
2. The second-order pattern for polar concepts (This dog is fat)
3. The second-order pattern for nonpolar concepts that are shared by only some members of the identity class (This dog is brown)

4. The second-order pattern for nonpolar concepts that are shared by all members of the identity class (This dog is an animal)

Summary

To say that the culturally deprived child should learn "language" is perhaps to say a great deal and perhaps very little. Does language learning consist primarily of learning how to sound acceptable? Does language learning consist of building a noun vocabulary to a certain level? Does it consist of experiences with the "natural" and social uses of language? The answers to these questions depend largely on the manner in which language is defined. Unfortunately, the usual definitions of language (in terms of expression or meaning or association) are usually incapable of implying specific learning tasks. At best, some tasks are more consistent with a given interpretation than others, but the range of possible tasks is appallingly broad. The definition of language usually remains neutral on most of the important issues connected with curriculum development. The analysis in this chapter begins, therefore, with a definition of language that cannot be neutral on important issues. The analysis is limited to a consideration of language as a tool for presenting concepts—language as a teaching instrument.

The first question raised about this tool is: What is it? Language, of course, is many things. But so far as the learning situation is concerned, language is a self-consistent representation of reality that deals in true and false statements. There is no way to teach basic concepts without presenting examples of the concepts. Consequently, the language of the teaching situation is primarily a language that is consistent with the show-and-tell presentation.

A teaching language, it was noted, may be ineffective in a given teaching situation for one of two reasons. The language may be inadequate, or the child's understanding of an adequate language may be inadequate. The language used to teach deaf children is often an inadequate language, while the language of the culturally deprived subculture may be adequate, although the understanding of some children within the subculture is definitely inadequate. The situation facing the teacher is the same whether the language is inadequate or the child's understanding of the language is inadequate. The child's understanding of the language must be made adequate. The child must be taught the minimum language skills necessary to process the basic concepts he is expected to learn.

This language, according to the present analysis, consists of two basic statement forms: "This is a $\underline{B}$" and "This $\underline{B}$ is $\underline{C}$." The first of these is the identity statement. It is a fully verbalized statement that corresponds to the act of pointing to an object and indicating the object's name. The modifying or second-order statement form, "This $\underline{B}$ is $\underline{C}$," has no ready counterpart on the level of half-verbal statements (although it would be possible to create some). The first part of the statement functions to hold the identity of the concept already presented through the first-order statement form, "This is a $\underline{B}$." The second part of the statement, "This $\underline{B}$ is $\underline{C}$," introduces a new modifying concept that is compatible with B. These two statement forms are capable of processing all of the basic concepts—up to hypotheticals.

Not all of the modifications that can be processed through the second-order statement form, however, are the same in structure. Basically, they differ according to the kind of information processing upon which they rest. Some concepts, such as color, relative size, position, etc., require an empirical investigation; other concepts, such as class names, do not require an empirical investigation. No contradiction is created by envisioning a barn that is not red; however, a grave contradiction is created by envisioning a barn that is not a building.

There are three structurally similar types of concepts that are processed through the second-order statement form. These are:

1. Polar concepts
2. Nonpolar concepts that are shared by only some of the members of the identity class
3. Nonpolar concepts that are shared by all of the members of the identity class

Since concepts within each of these groups are structurally similar and involve similar inferences and similar types of information processing, *the concepts within each of these groups can be taught in a similar manner.* For example, the presentation that directs learning efforts to an appreciation of *long-short* in the most unambiguous way serves as a prototype for the presentation of any other polar concept.

The language program presented in the following two chapters is based on the nature of the teaching language as it was analyzed in this chapter.

the beginning
language program 7

*A*s nearly as possible, the writers have attempted to make the beginning language program a truly beginning program—one that starts from zero, assuming no prior mastery of English, because even when all the children come from homes where a dialect of English is spoken, the teacher is seldom in a position to ascertain in detail what each child can and cannot do. Therefore, the safest program is one that assumes no prior mastery.

It would be wasteful, of course, to spend a great deal of time teaching children things they already know. The program is designed so that if the children are already able to handle a given task, they can move through it and on to the next in a very short time—in less time, generally, than it would take to find out through individual testing whether or not they possess the skill. Accordingly, the length of time to be devoted to each step in the course sequence is left unspecified. The children work at a task until they have mastered it, whether it takes five minutes or five weeks.

The basic teaching method is "pattern drill," similar to that used in the teaching of foreign languages. However, there are important differences, all of which relate to the emphasis on the cognitive rather than the social aspects of language.

1. The drill does not focus upon idiomatic expressions and irregularities. These are avoided, in fact, as representing the ungeneralizable aspects of a language, whereas what the naïve child needs to grasp is that substantial part of the language that makes sense, that follows consistent rules, that facilitates logical reasoning. Such limited idiomatic expressions as "in a mess," for example, undercut the foundation meaning of *in* and lead the child to false conclusions: The house is in a mess; the woman is in the house; therefore, the woman is in a mess.

2. Whereas linguistic pattern drill is supposed to reinforce natural, colloquial intonation patterns, the intonational patterns suggested in the present program deliberately exaggerate many small words and affixes that are normally slurred over, since these embody the logical distinctions that the children must learn.

3. In this program, sentence patterns are selected and grouped not

on the basis of their frequency of use or grammatical similarity, but on the basis of the rules of inference that apply to them. The sentences "This book is not heavy" and "This book is not green," although they are grammatically identical, are treated differently and appear in different sections of the program, because different deductions can be made from the first sentence than from the second.

4. The most important difference of the present program has to do with the relation between concepts and words. When a child is being taught a foreign language in school, it is assumed that he already has most of the concepts expressed in the foreign language. Modern foreign-language teaching makes use of illustrations and physical props, but these are not generally used to teach new concepts. They are used to eliminate the need for literal translation. In the program that follows, however, the children are learning new concepts—new ways of organizing experience or relating one experience to another. One cannot expose the child to a brief demonstration of the concept *long* and expect him to conclude, either consciously or unconsciously, "I get it. It means _____." For the typical deprived child, there is no way of completing the statement "It means _____." Demonstrations, therefore, play a much more vital role than they do in foreign-language learning. They must be chosen and used with great care, always being closely wedded to the language drill. The child is not merely learning how to express a concept in a new language or dialect. He is learning the concept *through* learning how to make the appropriate statements about illustrations and concrete objects.

All of the beginning language concepts presented in this chapter are to be taught through either first-order statements (This is a _____) or second-order statements (This _____ is _____). These concepts are arranged roughly in order of increasing difficulty, beginning with the first-order labels and then proceeding to the second-order refinements: polar opposites and nonpolar dimensions of color, location, and class name.

First-order Statements

The identity statement—singular.

The identity statement form is the most rudimentary in the language hierarchy. "This is an alligator." "This is a 3." "This is a word." The identity statement is the starting point for the language program. It defines the relationship between language and the child's awareness of the physical world. *It tells him that the statement for the familiar act of pointing at the block is "This is a block."*

The following procedure is recommended for presenting the identity statement form:

1. Adopt a stereotyped procedure.

a. Present an object and give the appropriate identity statement. "This is a ball."

b. Follow the statement with a *yes-no* question. "Is this a ball?"

c. Answer the question. "Yes, this is a ball."

d. Repeat the question and encourage the children to answer it.

e. Introduce *what* questions after the children have begun to respond adequately to the *yes-no* questions.

2. Make up identity statements about those objects you will be talking about in the preschool: boy, girl, piano, book, chalkboard, coat rack, articles of clothing, furniture, fixtures, parts of the body (face, mouth, ears, eyes, hands, fingers, arms, feet, legs, etc.). Avoid proper names and other nouns that do not take articles, such as *sand* and *paint*. Later, expand the list to include words that will be presented in reading and arithmetic classes.

3. Strive for clear pronunciation, but not so insistently that pronunciation becomes the foremost consideration. Typically, deprived children will have a great deal of trouble with the identity statement. For example, in dealing with the statement "This is a table," they may have difficulty with the hard-*s* ending on *this,* the word *is,* and the article, perhaps reducing the statement to something like "Diii table." Call their attention to the omitted parts of the statement. Repeat the statement five to ten times, clapping to accent the missing parts. Repeat the same statement often.

4. Introduce tasks that dramatize the equivalence between the identity statement and the act of pointing at the appropriate object. Present four objects, perhaps a ball, block, cup, and pencil. Have the children point to the appropriate objects as you make the statements "This is a ball," etc. Then point and ask the children to *produce* the statements in answer to "This is a what?"

5. Do not work on identity statements for more than three or four minutes. Make these statements a part of the daily language routine, perhaps at the beginning of the language period.

6. After the children have become reasonably familiar with the presentation that begins with a given identity statement (This is a ball) and then introduces questions (Is this a ball? This is a what?), change the order of presentation so that it opens with a *question*. "This is a what?" After the answer has been produced, have the children repeat it several times in unison.

Modifications for severely deprived children.

The seriously deprived child may not understand what the identity statement, "This is a _____," is actually trying to do. He can best be shown by demonstrating how the statement is related to familiar commands. He has learned that commands call for *specific actions,* "Shut up." "Go outside." "Gimmie da." Therefore, commands can be used as a basis for defining the identity statement. The idea is simply to show him that the statement form, "You are _____ing," is roughly parallel in what is trying to denote to the statement form, "This is a _____." This can be achieved by introducing verb expansions and simple pronoun exercises from the Advanced Language chapter *at the beginning of the program,* and relating these exercises to the identity statement.

First, work on the production of statements related to commands. "Stand up . . . Good. Are you sitting down? . . . Are you running down the street? . . . Are you flying through the air? Are you standing up? . . . Yes, you are standing up." After working on similar statements for a few minutes, present examples of the identity statement, using the most familiar objects, and introduce a similar question set. "This is a nose . . . Is this a train? . . . Is this a baseball? . . . Is this a roller skate? . . . Is this a shoe? . . . Is this a nose? . . . Yes, this is a nose." Such demonstrations show the child that the questions related to both statement forms have the same function and that both statements rest on the same kind of observation of what is.

Adjust the presentation for those children who do not have enough language to handle statements effectively. It may take some severely deprived children three months before they are able to produce even a reasonable semblance of an identity statement. In order for their language learning to proceed, they must be allowed to use one-word and pointing responses. Efforts to get them to repeat statements should continue, however, with the stimulus being presented very rhythmically and slowly.

The identity statement—plural.

The plural identity statement is different from the singular. The singular begins with *this* and has an article before the final word. "This is *a* ball." The plural begins with *these,* has no article, and attaches an *s* to the last word. "These are balls." Initially, the children may have trouble including the article in the singular identity statement; later, they may have trouble omitting it from the plural statement. They may say "These are a balls," which shows that they are transferring what they have learned.

1. Introduce the plural statement only after the children are able to enunciate the singular statement clearly enough so that there will be no trouble in distinguishing the two.

2. Define the changes that occur in the plural statement. Begin with the *s* ending. Present three objects of the same name—three hands, three balls, three lines on the chalkboard. No words with irregular plurals should be presented. Point to each object and identify it. "Ball. Ball. Ball." Embrace all three objects and say "Balls." Repeat the procedure, using the word *this* to apply to each individual object and *these* to apply

to the group of objects. "This. This. This. *These.*" Repeat the exercise until the children are able to place the *s* ending on the noun and to produce the word *these*.

3. Give the children practice in listening to the plural identity statement.

a. Present a statement that implies an action and requires the children to demonstrate the action. "See if you can show me this statement. Listen. This is a hand. . . . Good. These are *hands.*" The basic exercise can be repeated using ears, eyes, legs, arms, fingers, etc. The *s* sound on the plural noun should be grossly exaggerated and accented with a clap. To further sharpen the children's grasp of its function in the statement, introduce songs involving plurals and singulars in the music session.

b. More difficult listening tasks can be introduced after the children have worked on plurals for several weeks. "Touch your ear. . . . Touch your ears." To succeed, the children must be able to hear and understand the function of the *s* ending. No other clues (such as the *are* in the declarative statement "These are ears") are present in sentences of this form.

4. Give the children practice in producing plural identity statements.

a. Hold up an object and ask for the identity statement. "Tell me about this."

b. Pair the object with another of the same kind and ask the children to "Tell me about *these.*"

c. As the children become more familiar with the plural statement, ask a more general question. "What can I say?" To help children with the *s* ending, remind them that it buzzes (as it does in all soft-*s* words). Some children may have a tendency to transfer the ending to other words in the statement, perhaps to *the beginning* of a word. However, the rhythm, the clap, and practice will help them locate it properly. The pronunciation of *are* is a potential source of difficulty, sometimes being confused with *or*. It should be pronounced in an extremely exaggerated way until the children become accustomed to pronouncing it.

5. Use books and pictures to find objects about which singular and plural identity statements can be made. Most Dr. Seuss books contain good illustrations. These books, however, should not be read. The teacher should adopt the procedure of first asking for a statement about each member in an illustrated group, then for a statement about all of the members. She can indicate her desire by pointing or by asking the children to "Tell me . . .": "Tell me about this" (This is a dog.); "Tell me about this" (This is a dog); "Tell me about these" (These are dogs).

The not statement.

The *not* statement is as necessary as the identity statement in defining simple concepts. The identity statement points to instances of the concept in question (providing the *genus*), while the *not* statement indicates those things that are *not* instances of the concept (providing the *differentiation*). "This is a ball. This is not a dish. This is not a coin. This is not a balloon. This is not a globe." Together the identity and *not* statements define the concept.

The children encounter the *not* statement in answering questions about identity statements. However, it is relatively incidental and perhaps meaningless at first. Begin teaching *not* statements as soon as the children have begun giving correct and reasonably articulate affirmative answers to the "Is this a _____?" question.

1. Define the words *yes* and *no*. The children may have only a hazy idea of what the words mean. However, they probably have a good understanding of the meaning of head nods and shakes. Therefore, it is possible to define *yes* and *no* by associating them with the appropriate motions.

a. Point to a child and ask a question that can be answered with yes. "Is this a boy?"

b. Nod your head in an exaggerated fashion and say "Yes. This is a boy."

c. Point to a girl and ask the original question. "Is this a boy?"

d. Shake your head vigorously. "No. This is not a boy." Accent the word *not* with a clap.

e. Repeat this procedure with other familiar objects. Also introduce a variation in which a number of questions are asked about *the same object.* "Is this a pencil? . . . Yes. This is a pencil. Is this a book? . . . Is this a man? . . . Is this a table?"

2. Introduce pointing tasks involving *not.*

a. Present three familiar objects (or pictures of objects) and have the children identify each. "This is a house. This is a tree. This is a girl."

b. Ask members of the class to point to objects that are *not* a house, *not* a tree, and *not* a girl.

c. After the children have located an appropriate object, have them say the *not* statement in unison. "This is *not* a house." Ask the question. "This is not a what? . . . This is not a house." Also introduce the *yes-no* question, and shake your head vigorously to help reinforce the meaning of *no.* "Is this a *house? . . . No,* this is *not* a house." The statement should be repeated four or five times before proceeding to the next.

3. Have the children produce the *not* statements. After they are reasonably proficient at locating the appropriate objects and repeating the *not* statement, make the children responsible for production of the identity statement and different *not* statements.

a. Point to a familiar object and ask the children to "Tell me about this" (This is a pencil).

b. Point to a series of objects that are not pencils and ask about each "Is this a pencil?" The only acceptable answer is "No, this is not a pencil." If a child identifies the particular object (This is a ball) instead of producing the *not* statement, he should be told that he is correct, but that "I didn't ask about a *ball*. I asked about a *pencil,* so you must tell me about a pencil. Is this a pencil? . . . No, this is not a pencil." This convention, although it may seem needlessly rigid, will prove to be quite valuable later in the language course.

c. After the children have worked on *not* statements for several weeks, introduce a task in which they have to make up a *series of not statements* about a single object. This task is the most difficult in the present set of exercises and also the most useful. It helps the children formulate the notion that once something is classified as a pencil, it cannot be classified as something that is not a pencil. After the children identify a familiar object, such as a pencil, ask them to "Tell me what this is not." If they balk, give an exaggerated clue. "Is this thing I'm holding a piano? . . . No, it is *not* a piano. So we can look at it and say 'This is not a piano.' Say it." Before long, the children will learn that there are many "silly" things they can say in describing what an object is not, which they will probably find enjoyable. The task of making series of *not* statements should be presented regularly throughout the basic language program.

Second-order Statements: Polar Attributes

Polar discriminations.

The identity statement links language with the act of pointing at something. "This is a ball." The next step up the ladder of language abstraction deals with statements describing the ball. "This ball is _____." As noted earlier, the second-order statement can be completed in any number of ways. "This ball is red." "This ball is next to the house." "This ball is a football." One way of completing the statement is with a polar element, that is, an element that has an "opposite." "This ball is [hot-cold] [big-little] [fast-slow] [soft-hard]." Through work with polar elements, the children have their first encounter with genuine deduction, inferring something beyond what was explicitly given in a statement. Having been told that a ball is not soft, they can deduce that it must be hard—a small step, but one of the most fundamental operations in reasoning.

The basic statement form of the polar statement is "This _____ is _____." The first blank is filled in with the name of the familiar object. "This *book* is _____." The second blank is filled in with the name of some property of the object *book*. Not any name will do, however, but only a name for which there is a polar opposite, such as *big*. "This *book* is *big*."

1. Introduce polar tasks after the children have become proficient in both the affirmative and *not* forms of the identity statement.

2. Introduce only one of the members in a polar pair. For example,

introduce the concept *long,* but do not introduce its opposite, *short.* Introduce *big,* but do not introduce its opposite, *little.* The children will learn *short* and *little* after they have learned the basic discriminations of *long* and *not long, big* and *not big.*

3. *Initially,* introduce at least three examples of the concept (a soft pillow, a soft rubber ball, a soft part of the body, such as a cheek) and many examples of what the concept is not (many *not*-soft objects). After the children have mastered several polar concepts, they will have learned the general rule that the concepts apply to a range of physical objects and are not limited to the demonstration object. Therefore, after the first several polar concepts have been introduced, the presentation should become less elaborate. Several dramatic instances of the concept usually suffice.

4. At this stage in the program, *never* deviate from the basic statement form—always "This line is long," not "This is a long line" or (much worse) "This is long." These two variations have the form of the identity statement, and so they will encourage the children to believe that "long line" or "long" is the object's name. The basic second-order form, on the other hand, makes it clear that the object is still called a line and that "long" is something additional that is being said about the line.

5. Point out the polar relationship *as a relationship.* An isolated object is not rough or long or big. It is only rough or long or big when compared to another object that is smooth or short or little. To make this point, set up an uncluttered demonstration that makes the comparison as obvious as possible. In teaching *long,* for example, present two horizontal lines of obviously different lengths. Define the concept *long* by

starting at the left and saying "Which of these lines is long?" Trace the lines from left to right, pausing where the top line terminates. "Is this top line long? . . . No, it stopped already. But the other one keeps on going and going and going. It's long."

6. Follow the demonstration with a statement about the concept. "This line is long. Say it with me." The statement may give the children some trouble. They may try to put the verb *is* in the wrong place. "This is line long." To help them hear the difference between the polar and identity statements, present the statements together, accenting the *is* in both statements with a clap. "This *is* a line. This line *is* long." The statements should be repeated in unison four to five times before proceeding; they should be reviewed often.

7. Follow the repetition of the statement with *yes-no* and *what* questions about both of the objects that were used to demonstrate the polar

concept (in the *long-short* example, the two lines). "Is this line long? . . .

[clap]

Yes, this line is long. Is this other line long? . . . No, this line is *not* long. What can we say about this [bottom] line? . . . This line is long." Some children may have initial difficulty in answering the *what* question, but, with practice, they will improve. Some children will already know the opposites of some words. If a child says "No, this line is short," acknowledge that he is correct, but remind him that you are talking about *long* and repeat with emphasis "Is this line *long?*"

8. Introduce polar concepts for the various senses—sight, hearing, touch, etc. For the children to understand the logic of polar concepts, they must know that there are auditory and kinesthetic polar properties, as well as visual properties. Listed below are the primary polar concepts and notations about how to present them.

a. *Long (visual)*. Demonstrate primarily with two pieces of chalk, two lines on the board, two strings, silly illustrations of long dogs, etc. Present the operational definition of *long*, as illustrated above, by demonstrating that the long member is the one that "goes the farthest." The standard *yes-no* and *what* questions should be presented in connection with each object presented in the demonstration.

b. *Big (visual)*. Demonstrate with physical objects, book illustrations, and figures drawn on the board. The figures should be identical except for size. Use your hands expansively and your voice to help show the concept. "This man is big—BIG. This other man is not big." Questions should be introduced.

c. *Fat (visual)*. Draw simple figures of a fat woman and a skinny woman on the board. The figures should be approximately the same height. Identify each as a woman. "This is a woman." Refer then to the drawing of the fat woman and introduce the statement "This woman is fat." The children may be familiar with the opposite of fat, in which case they may point out that the other figure is skinny. "Her skinny." Acknowledge the answer, but remind the children that they were asked about *fat*. Repeat the exercise with men, dogs, trees, etc.

d. *Tall (visual)*. Draw two figures on the board, one tall, the other short. Identify each. "These are men." Then give an operational definition of tallness, which is merely an extension of the definition for *long*. "See how long this man stands. He starts at the ground and he keeps on going. This man is tall. Say it." *Yes-no* questions should be introduced, but the *what* questions should be deferred because several different concepts may apply to the same object—the tall tree may also be big, fat, etc.

e. *Fast (visual)*. Stage a race between two pieces of chalk from left to right on the chalkboard, tracing a path with each piece of chalk. After the winning piece reaches the right side of the board, the other should not be advanced. Since something is fast if it covers a greater distance in the same amount of time, the demonstration nicely isolates the concept. Point out that one piece of chalk is fast. "This chalk got here first." Require the children to repeat the statement "This chalk is fast" and then proceed with the usual *yes-no* and *what* questions. To demonstrate that *fast* does not apply exclusively to pieces of chalk, repeat the exercise with boys, toy cars, etc.

f. *Dark (visual)*. This concept is best demonstrated in a closet or a room with no windows but with lights. The demonstration begins with the identity statement. "This is a closet." The light is then turned off, and the dark statement is presented. "The closet is dark. Say it." The light is turned back on, and the *not-dark* statement is presented. "The closet is *not* dark." The usual *yes-no* and *what* questions follow.

g. *Straight (visual)*. Two lines are drawn on the board—one straight, the other wavy. Both lines are identified, and the polar concept of straight is introduced. "This is a line. This line is straight." *Yes-no* and *what* questions follow.

h. *Smooth (visual-tactile)*.

(1) Present *smooth* first as a visual concept, later as a tactile concept. Demonstrate the concept with a piece of cloth, which is first identified (This is a cloth), and then is smoothed out, perhaps over a chair or table. Introduce the concept statement. "This cloth is *smooth*. Say it." Wrinkle the cloth. "This cloth is not smooth. Is this cloth
[clap]
smooth? . . . No, this cloth is *not* smooth." The concept is expanded by presenting pictures of water and sand, which are identified as being either smooth or not smooth.

(2) Demonstrate the tactile version of smooth by presenting behind the child's back textures which can be felt but not seen. This convention avoids a great deal of confusion because it prevents the child from formulating the concept according to some visual cues. To acquaint the child with the concept, present something smooth, perhaps a piece of paper. "This is paper. This paper is smooth. Say it." Next use something that is not smooth, perhaps a piece of sandpaper. "This is sandpaper. This sandpaper is not smooth. Say it." After the child has been exposed to different smooth and not-smooth things and has mastered the *yes-no* questions, ask the child to produce the concept statement. "What can I say about this piece of wood?"

i. *Heavy (proprioceptive)*. Demonstrate initially with a marble and a ball bearing of about the same size. Identify each as a marble. "This is a marble, and this is a marble." Instruct the child to close his eyes, and place the ball bearing in his hand. "This marble is heavy. Say it." Next, present the marble in the other hand. "This marble is *not* heavy." After the initial demonstration, *heavy* can be demonstrated with various objects, such as rocks, chairs, toys, etc. There is no need to require the child to close his eyes after he demonstrates by answering *yes-no* questions correctly that he understands the concept.

j. *Cold (tactile)*. Use two identical, unopened cans of frozen fruit juice, one of which has been warmed to room temperature and one of which is still in the process of thawing (do not use it straight from the freezer). Identify each as a can. "This is a can. Say it." Present the cold can. "This can is *cold*. Say it." Present the unfrozen can. "Is this can cold?" . . . No, this can is *not* cold." Shift the two cans about and then hand one to a child. "Tell me about this can."

k. *Soft (tactile)*. The concept should be initially demonstrated in such a way that the child cannot see the material. A baseball and a soft rubber ball of about the same size should be presented behind the child's back. After the objects are identified, the concept statements are presented. "This ball is soft. This ball is *not* soft." The concept can be further demonstrated with parts of the body, such as cheeks (soft) and elbows (not soft), and with various objects around the room.

l. *Loud (auditory)*. Instruct the child to close his eyes. Define the word *voice*. "Listen. This is my voice." Ask various members of the class to talk, and provide the appropriate statement about each one. "That is Tyrone's voice." Proceed to introduce *loud* and *not-loud*. Speak in a loud voice and say "THIS VOICE IS LOUD." Resume a normal voice or speak in a whisper, saying "This voice is not loud." Ask the usual questions. "IS THIS VOICE LOUD? . . . Yes, *THIS* VOICE IS LOUD. Say it." In music sessions, children can use their knowledge of this concept to sing in voices that are loud and not loud.

9. Do not overemphasize the demonstrations suggested above. Place primary emphasis on the statements that signify the concepts demonstrated. The demonstrations merely function as guides to an awareness of the concept. But understanding does not automatically accompany awareness. The proof that a child understands is his ability to answer such relatively unstructured questions as "What can you tell me about this marble?" This kind of understanding may come quite slowly at first. Therefore, the presentation should systematically unstructure the tasks, starting with the highly structured, uncluttered initial demonstrations and accompanying statement presentations, and proceeding to less structured tasks as quickly as possible. Protracted demonstrations are neither necessary nor desirable. After the initial demonstration, chalkboard tasks should be introduced. These permit moving rapidly from one concept to another. For instance, after the initial demonstration of *tall* and *not-tall*, work from the chalkboard, introducing three stick figures (two of which are tall and one not tall). Identify the figures. "These are boys." Then point to each figure and ask, "What can I say about this boy?" Chalkboard tasks of this type can be used in connection with *big* (big balls, big boxes), *long* (long trains, long cars), and the other visual polar concepts.

Multiple polar discriminations.

It is very important for the children to see that there are many things one can say about an object. After one identifies it, one can say that it is hard, heavy, blue, hot, etc. However, the axiom that seems to govern the language of some deprived children is that if something is long, it is only long. They tend to believe that *long* is the object's name and that calling it something else is to deny this name. The present exercises are therefore very important. They require the children to use more than one word to describe an object.

1. Present two chalk lines on the board—one short and fat, the other long and thin. After each is identified as a line, refer to the *short line* and ask "What can we say about this line?" If the children do not respond, ask *yes-no* questions. "Is it long? . . . No, it is not long. Is it fat? . . . Yes, it is fat." Then present a summary statement about the line. "This line is *not* long, and this line is fat." Similar demonstrations can be conducted with drawings of trees that are both tall or not tall, and fat or not fat; balls that are both big or not big, heavy or not heavy, and also, possibly, soft or not soft; rocks that are both smooth or not smooth, and big or not big; cans of fruit drinks that are both big or not big, and cold or not cold (which is a good exercise because the child must combine information from sight and touch).

2. Present multiple *not* statements. These are extensions of the *not* tasks used with the identity statement. Present an object and identify it. "This is a ball." Instruct the children to "Tell me what it is not" (This is not a dog; This is not a girl; This is not a house). Then ask "What can I say about this ball?" (This ball is big; This ball is hard). Finally, present a small, soft ball and ask "What is this ball *not?*" (This ball is not big; This ball is not hard). Through this exercise, the children learn that there are *not* statements connected both with the identity of the object and with its characteristics.

3. Introduce *I don't know* statements. These are valuable because they help the children articulate what they know and what they do not know about an object. The *I don't know* statement sets the stage for deductive processes that require more than a single step.

a. Show the children two juice cans, both at room temperature. Hold up one and ask "Is this can cold?" If a child offers an answer, explain "You are guessing. You don't know that this can is cold. How can you tell? You have to touch it." Let the children feel the can and determine that it is not cold. The second can is introduced unopened, and the procedure is repeated. The children are likely to assume that this one must be cold. "You are guessing. Do you know? Did you touch it? . . . No. You don't know. Say 'I DON'T KNOW.' Say it."

b. Draw two figures, one tall and one short, on the chalkboard.

Cover all but their feet and legs with a sheet of paper and ask about each figure. "Is this man tall? . . . I don't know." Then slide the paper up, revealing the figures. "Now I know." This masking technique can be used for all visual discriminations—for long and short cars, big and little dogs, fat and skinny boys, etc.

Polar discriminations—plural.

1. Present two figures that are the same in one polar dimension but different in another, such as two fat dogs, one of which is much bigger than the other. Ask the children to make the appropriate polar statement about the first figure. "This dog is big. This dog is fat." Repeat the procedure for the second figure. "This dog is *not* big. This dog is fat." Point out that the figures share a statement. Do this by pointing to the first figure and saying "This dog is fat" and pointing to the second figure and saying "This dog is fat." Then restate the observation. *"These dogs are fat.* Say it." Since this plural statement is different from the plural identity statement (These are dogs), the children may have some trouble with it initially. The basic exercise should therefore be repeated many times—with long, thin lines and long, fat lines; with smooth, hard rocks and rough, hard rocks; etc. The usual question series should be a part of every presentation.

2. Ask the children to produce the appropriate plural statement after they have mastered the more structured tasks. Present two figures that are the same in one polar dimension *but different in another,* such as two lines, both of which are thick, but only one of which is long. Ask "What can I say about these lines?" If the children have trouble, structure the task by having them first tell about one line and then about the other. Then ask "So what can I say about *these lines?*" If they are unable to give the answer, structure the task further by reminding them of the statement that applies to both lines. "This line is fat. This line is fat. So what can I say about these lines?" As the children become more proficient with these tasks, a variation involving three figures can be intro-

(a)   fat and long

(b)   not fat and long

(c)   fat and not long

duced. Ask "What can I say about these lines [*a* and *b*]?" (These lines are long). Repeat the question for lines *a* and *c* (These lines are fat). Many variations of this exercise should be presented, using straight, fat, and long lines. Through them, the children receive practice in refocusing on an object and classifying it according to different dimensions.

Polar deductions.

The opposites of concepts presented in the preceding section are treated most gracefully as deductions. Since *not-long = short, not-big = little, not-smooth = rough,* etc., equivalent names can be substituted for each other, and nothing is really changed. Substitution works in the other direction, too: *not-short = long; not-little = big; not-rough = smooth.* These equivalences are arbitrary; however, they serve as the basis for the four fundamental deductions that are possible with polar elements:

> If this is short, this is not long.
> If this is long, this is not short.
> If this is not short, this is long.
> If this is not long, this is short.

1. Introduce the new polar terms as equivalents of *not* terms. Require the children to produce a *not* statement involving a polar concept. "This line is not long." Explain that there is another way of saying "not long." "When a line is not long, we say that it is short. This line is short. Say it."

2. Require the children to repeat the statement many times and to answer *yes-no* questions. These are important because they help define the equivalence. "Is this line short? . . . Yes, this line is short. Is this line *long*? . . . No, this line is *not long."*

3. After the children have learned the opposites of the different polar concepts, present exercises in *saying things another way.* These exercises are purely verbal—no demonstrations are used.

    a. "What's another way of saying 'This line is not long'? . . . This line is short. What's another way of saying 'This pencil is not long'? . . . 'This table is not long'?"

    b. Vary the predicate. "What's another way of saying 'This truck is not fast'? . . . This truck is slow. What's another way of saying 'This truck is not big'? . . . 'This truck is not long'? . . . 'This truck is not heavy'?"

    c. Vary both the subject and the predicate. "What's another way of saying 'This rock is not smooth'? . . . This rock is rough. What's another way of saying 'This woman is not fat'? . . . 'This man is not tall'? . . . 'This room is not dark'? . . . 'This voice is not loud'? . . .

'This bar is not heavy'? . . . 'This water is not cold'? . . . 'This ball is not soft'?" The children may already know of the opposites, but phrasing them in this manner helps the children appreciate how the opposites are related to familiar *not* statements.

4. Introduce *yes-no* tasks. These should be introduced while the children are becoming familiar with the new polar words. The tasks do not require the children to produce the word (which may be a difficult thing for them to do during the first few days), and yet they require an understanding of the new word and its function.

a. Present two lines on the board. Ask the children two questions about the first line. "Is this line long? . . . No, this line is not long. Is this line short? . . . Yes, this line is short."

b. Have the children repeat the statements slowly and rhythmically before the same questions about the second line are presented. "Is this line long? . . . Yes, this line is long. Is this line short? . . . No, this line is not short."

c. Shift the responsibility of producing the statements involving the new words to the children as they become more familiar with the words.

d. Use this basic procedure with the other new polar words.

5. Introduce statement-production tasks. These are extensions of tasks outlined in step 4 above. Instead of asking *yes-no* questions about each figure, however, ask "What can I say about this line?"

6. Introduce *not*-statement tasks. Ask the children to tell what each line *is not* after they have told what each line is. "What can I say about this line? . . . Yes, this line is long. What is this line *not*? This line is not what?"

Special polars.

For the children to proceed in both the reading and arithmetic sections, they must have a knowledge of how elements are arranged in a series—a knowledge of *next to* and *before-after*. These concepts should therefore be presented as soon as the children have grasped the fundamentals of polar deductions. The concepts have been simplified somewhat so that early presentation is possible. The *where* question that is usually associated with these concepts (Where is Harold? Next to Tyrone.) has been eliminated, and *before-after* has been reduced to a polar concept (which will be expanded in the advanced language section).

NEXT TO

1. Demonstrate the statement form (which differs from any the children have yet encountered) by drawing two balls on the chalkboard and

identifying each, concluding with the plural statement "These are balls." Point to one of the balls and say "This ball is *next to* [point to the other ball] this ball." Have the children repeat the statement.

2. Define the concept by introducing a third ball, far to the left of the other two. Point to it and say "This ball is not next to [point to the far right ball] this ball."

3. Ask *yes-no* questions. "Is this ball [far left] next to this ball [far right]? . . . No, this ball is not next to this ball."

4. Introduce the *what* question. Refer to the middle ball. "What can I say about this ball? . . . This ball is next to this ball." Do not introduce a *where* question (Where is this ball?).

5. Provide the children with a firm operation for producing the statement. "Ask yourself 'Which one am I talking about?' Put your finger on that one and say '*This one is* _____.' Then move to the other one." Give the children practice in carrying out this operation.

6. As they become familiar with the statement form, introduce series of elements. Have three children stand in front of the chalkboard. Point to the middle one. "I want to know about Harold. So I point to Harold and say 'Harold is [point to one of the other children] next to Linda.'" Refer to one of the end children. "Now, I want to know about Tommy. So I point to Tommy and say 'Tommy is next to Harold.' Say it." Introduce the *not* demonstration. "Tommy is not next to Linda." Repeat the exercise with different children.

7. Introduce the demonstration that *next to* is a reversible concept (If *B* is next to *C*, *C* is next to *B*) only after the children are well grounded in the verbal conventions of the statement. The danger of introducing reversibility tasks too early is that the children will become confused over which element should be mentioned first in the statement. Have two children stand in front of the chalkboard. Ask "What can I say about Debby? . . . Debby is next to Tommy." After the children have repeated the statement, ask "And what can I say about Tommy? . . . Tommy is next to Debby." Combine the statements, touching each child as he is mentioned. "Debby is next to Tommy, and Tommy is next to Debby." Repeat with different children and with chalkboard figures.

8. Introduce more unstructured tasks. Present a series of dots on the chalkboard. Identify each as a dot; then point to one of the middle dots and ask "What can I say about this dot?" Refer to the dots on either side of the original and produce the statement "This dot is next to this dot. This dot is also next to this one." Give the children practice in producing such statement pairs. If the children have trouble producing the second *next-to* statement, prompt by asking a *yes-no* question. "Is this dot also next to this dot? . . . Yes." This task can be used to describe the children as they remain seated in a row. "Tommy is next to Harold. Tommy is next to Linda."

BEFORE-AFTER

The primary difference between *before-after* and *next to* is that *before-after* refers to a one-way direction in either time or space. This difference must be carefully defined, or the child will understandably become confused.

1. Explain the function of the arrow. "The arrow tells us which way to go." Draw a small arrow on the board (pointing right) and have the children take turns at doing what the arrow says. Have each child make a fist with his right hand and place the back of the hand on the shaft of the arrow near the head, so that his extended thumb points toward the head of the arrow. Have him then move his hand in the direction indicated by the arrow (as in thumbing a ride). "Now just make your thumb go this way." After the initial demonstration, give the children practice with arrows that point in different directions. The children should be reminded simply to "Make your thumb go the way the arrow says."

2. Draw a large arrow on the board pointing right. Position two children below the arrow and draw a large dot on the arrow's shaft directly above each child. (The children should stand with their backs to the

board. Do not make the mistake of having them face in the direction the arrow is pointing. The children may have had some experience with "lining up" where the one who was nearest the head of the arrow—the goal—was said to come before the others. This is the reverse of what is to be taught.)

3. Explain "I'm going to follow this arrow. Watch." Pat the first child on the head and say his name. Pat the second child and say his name. "Here I go, following the arrow. Tommy, Harold. Once more. Tommy, Harold." Have the children follow the action by sighting along their arms first at one child and then at the next, with the thumb still indicating direction. Have them say the children's names in unison as they do so. After they have repeated the names in the proper order several times, present the question "Can we do it this way: Harold, Tommy? . . . No. Because the arrow tells us to go this way: Tommy, Harold." Introduce variations of this task with the arrow pointing in different directions and with different subjects.

4. After the children are able to indicate the proper order in which the children standing under an arrow should be named, introduce the *before* statement. Position two children beneath the arrow and draw large dots above each. Have the children produce the pair of names several

times, following the arrow. Have the children produce the first-mentioned name very loudly (TOMMY, Harold) as the children are patted on the head.

5. Introduce the *before* statement, retaining the strong emphasis on the first-mentioned name, which provides an additional cue to help the child arrange the names in the proper order. "TOMMY is before Harold. Say it with me."

6. Ask the usual *yes-no* and *what* questions. At first, the question "Is Harold before Tommy?" should be used only sparingly and should be preceded by a warning. "Careful now, this one is very hard." The questions that should be stressed are: "Is Tommy before Harold? . . . Yes, TOMMY is before Harold"; and "Tommy is what? . . . TOMMY is before Harold."

7. Repeat the procedure above with different children, always making certain that the names are repeated in the proper order quite a few times before the *before* statement is presented. As the children become more facile at following the arrow, discontinue the practice of patting each child on the head and adopt the practice *of touching the dot above each child.* This practice provides a transition between events in time and points on a line—a most important transition.

8. Make the children increasingly responsible for the production of the appropriate statement. After the children in the pair have been named, with the first name emphasized (LINDA, Tyrone), present the leading statement. *"Tell me about LINDA. LINDA is _____."* The children may volunteer a *next-to* statement. "Linda is next to Tyrone." Acknowledge that this statement is true and ask the *yes-no* question. "Is Linda also *before* Tyrone?"

9. Introduce *before* statements that refer only to dots on the arrow shaft. Draw two dots, a big one and a little one. Identify each as a dot and present the appropriate description. "This is a dot; this dot is big. This is a dot; this dot is little." Next, proceed in the direction the arrow indicates, touching the dots and naming them, emphasizing the first dot. "BIG DOT, little dot." After repeating the names several times, present the statement "The BIG DOT is before the little dot." Repeat the exercise with the arrow going in either direction and with different figures representing the points. (Little man, big man; Big dog, little dog; Skinny woman, fat woman).

10. Introduce *after* as meaning *not before.* Conduct the initial demonstration with the two children, placing each beneath a dot. Produce the *before* statement in the usual manner. "Harold, Linda. Harold is before Linda." Next, ask the *yes-no* question. "Is Linda before Harold? . . . No, Linda is not before Harold." Present the *after* statement. "Linda is *after* Harold." Repeat the demonstration with different people, then with different figures on the arrow shaft. The *after* statement is poten-

tially confusing, and should be presented quite carefully during the initial learning stages.

11. Introduce dot tasks in which the children must *produce* the appropriate statements—*before* and *after*. After reminding the children of the direction in which the arrow tells them to proceed, point to one of the dots on the shaft and say "Tell me about this big dot. The big dot is _____." Next, ask them to produce the statement about the other dot. "The little dot is _____." Too much repetition on this task will almost certainly result in confusion and frustration. Rather than push too hard during a single session, plan to present no more than two of these problems every day. If the children have difficulty initially, produce the appropriate statements and then have the children repeat them.

Second-order Statements: Nonpolar Attributes

The only difference between nonpolar and polar elements is the number of members in the set. Polar elements occur in sets of two—hot-cold, big-little, fat-skinny, etc. Nonpolar elements occur in sets of more than two. This basic difference leads to an important conceptual difference. When there are only two elements in the set, it is possible to assign each element a name and to equate this name with the not-name of the other element (short = not long). When there are more than two elements in the set, however, this procedure is no longer possible. Since there are no opposites in nonpolar sets, nonpolar deductions are necessarily more conservative than polar deductions. While we can draw the polar conclusion that if a line is not short, it is long, we cannot conclude that if a color is not blue, it is red, or that if a building is not a house, it is a barn.

The basic statement form for nonpolar attributes is the same as for polar attributes (This _____ is _____). The first blank is filled in with the name of a familiar object (This *house* is _____), and the second blank is filled in with the name of some *changeable* aspect of the subject (This house is *green;* This house is *on the hill.*) Many different attributes could be introduced, such as "This house is made of bricks," but the ones that are of particular interest in training younger disadvantaged children are those of *color* and *location*. Since these are similar to polar attributes *in many respects,* they can be taught in an analogous way.

Color.

1. Introduce three color variations of three sets of objects. A good initial presentation includes three sheets of colored paper (red, yellow, and blue), three colored blocks (red, yellow, and blue), and three identical

glasses of water. (During the demonstration, food dye is dropped into the glasses of water, making them red, yellow, and blue.)

2. Group the objects according to their names and present the plural identity statement for each group. "These are glasses of water. These are blocks. These are papers."

3. Present the statement of color for each of the nine objects, referring to each as either *red* or *not red*. The water glasses should be presented last, the pieces of paper first. The purpose of this part of the demonstration is to point out to the children what is meant by the statement "This paper is red" or "This block is not red." The children can more easily appreciate the idea that color is something that can attach to any familiar object if they see objects that are the same in every respect except color and if they see that color is not a concept that is limited to a particular class of things, such as blocks or pieces of paper. Each object is therefore identified. "This is a block." Then the color statement is provided. "This block is not red." The water glasses are presented, with the water in its natural transparent state. The children's attention is called to the liquid. "This is water." The *not* statement is then provided. "This water is not red." The red dye is placed in one glass, and as the water changes color, the color statement is presented. "Look. This water is red." Blue or yellow dye is added to the other glasses, and the *not* statement is made. "This water is not red."

4. *Regroup the objects according to color* after a color statement has been given for every object. Two groups are thus formed, one of objects that are red and the other of objects that are not red. Identify the objects in the new group as *things*. "These are things." Present the classification statement for the red things. "These things are red. Say it." Finally, present the classification statement for the nonred things. "These things are *not* red."

5. Have the children repeat the color statements and answer questions about the various objects. "Is this block red? . . . No, this block is not red. This [other] block is red." Point out that every object in the red group is called "red." "This block is red. This paper is red. This water is red. These things are red."

6. Repeat the demonstration on three or four consecutive days, placing increasing emphasis on the statements and questions. Variations of the original material can be introduced, such as cut-outs of different animals —red, yellow, and blue rabbits—and cups, instead of glasses of water.

7. Introduce matching tasks. After the demonstrations, present each child with an object that is either red, yellow or blue. Place a red block on the floor and a yellow block about three feet from it. "Let's put all of the red things here [point to the red block]. Put all of the things that are *not* red here." Require each child in turn to stand, identify the object he is holding (This is a paper), place it in the proper pile, and

produce the proper color statement (This paper is red, or This paper is not red). After each child has had his turn, the statement about the two newly formed groups is produced. "These things are red. These things are not red." The usual questions follow.

8. Introduce a variation of the matching task that requires the children to produce the color statement by themselves. Present the children with two groups of objects—one group of red objects, the other group of objects which are not red. Ask them to describe the objects in each pile. "What can I say about *these* things? . . . These things are _____."

9. Point out various red and not-red things. Help the children apply the color concept to things that he comes in contact with every day. "Look at that tree. Is the tree red? . . . Tell me about that car. Is it red?"

10. Repeat the demonstration (steps 1–5 above) for blue and yellow as soon as the children show some proficiency with not-red statements. If the demonstration is delayed too long, the children will begin to think of color in polar terms—red and not red. The purpose of demonstrating the other colors early is to show the children that things which are not red can be either blue or yellow. This convention may give the children some difficulty. If they have trouble, do not hold them responsible for the production of statements involving blue and yellow. They may require a great deal of practice in "reading" the sensation of blue or yellow before they can identify it; yet, they may be able to perform quite well on matching tasks and statement repetition. In demonstrating blue and yellow, begin with the not-red statement. "Is this block red? . . . No, this block is not red. It is *yellow*. Say it. . . . Can you find some others that are yellow?"

11. Give the colors personality by associating them with children in the class. Hang a colored card (red, blue, or yellow) around the neck of each child in the class. Have each child produce the statement about the card he is wearing. Tommy, for example, would say "This card is yellow," and Tyrone would say "This card is red." Ask the other children in the class to remember what Tyrone said. "He said 'This card is red.' Remember that." After the children wearing the cards are able to remember their own color (after perhaps several days), ask questions of the other members of the class. For a clue, urge the children to remember what Tyrone said. "This is Tyrone's card. Look at it and try to remember what Tyrone said. He said 'This card is _____.' " Through this type of primitive association, each color is given something of a personality. After the cards have been fairly well mastered, the task is extended by instructing each child to pick up another object that is the same color as his card. Thus, Tyrone would pick up a red truck. He would then be required to produce the color statement "This truck is red." The next step involves selecting an object that is the same color as another child's card and producing the appropriate color statement. "Who can find a truck that

is the same as Tommy's color? . . . Good. And what color is that?" The final step requires the children to select objects without comparing them to the card. The cards are put away, and the child is asked "What color is your card? . . . Yes, blue. Can you find a truck that is blue?" As the children become increasingly proficient, the statements can be phrased so that the children must work from the color name. "Tommy, give me a red block. Now remember, a red block must look like Tyrone's card."

12. Introduce green, brown, orange, and the other colors in a relatively straightforward manner after the children have mastered red, yellow, and blue. No extensive demonstrations are necessary because the children know what to expect and what color is. Simply present an object and identify it. "This is a shirt." Give the color statement. "This shirt is green." In order to clarify the notion that green is a color, ask "Is this shirt red?" and answer "No, this shirt is not red. This shirt is *green.*"

Prepositions.

Through statements about position, the children learn to describe an object by locating it in relation to other things in its surroundings. The prepositional statement is similar in form to the other second-order statements, "This _____ is _____," with the first blank filled in with the name of a familiar object (This *chair* is _____) and the second filled in with a positional notation (This chair is *under the table*). Prepositions are taught in basically the same way as color, except that there is usually less confusion about positional words than color words. The reason is that it is relatively easy to change the position of a given object to make a point, but it is not easy to change an object's color. If, for example, the children indicate that the chair is *over* the table when in fact it is *on* the table, the teacher can reply "No. The chair is not over the table. The chair is on the table." She can then lift the chair, changing its position so that it is over the table. "Now, the chair is *over* the table." It is not quite so easy to change a particular object from red to blue to make a peda-gogical point.

1. First, introduce the prepositions *on, over,* and *under.* With these three prepositions, a nonpolar set can be created and the basic statement conventions can be introduced.

2. Use three objects to demonstrate the idea of position—a chair, a book, and a table. Use only two of them (book and table) in the first part of the demonstration. After each object is identified and described in all of the detail that the children understand (This is a book; this book is red), place the book on the table and ask the positional question (which is new). *"WHERE IS THE BOOK?* . . . The book is on the table." Ask

the children to repeat the statement; then introduce the various *not* statements as answers to various positional questions. "Is this book *over* the table? . . . No, the book *is not* over the table. Is the book under the table? . . . No, the book *is not* under the table. The book is *on* the table." The book is then moved to a position over the table. "Is the book *on* the table now? . . . No, the book is not on the table now. The book is *over* the table." Repeat the procedure with the book positioned under the table. Repeat the entire demonstration with the chair in place of the book (to make the point that positional references are not limited to books and tables).

3. After the initial demonstration, give the children practice in carrying out instructions, such as "Put your hand on the table." As soon as the children carry out the action, ask *"Where* is your hand?" (or "Where is this hand?"). Follow with questions that lead to *not* statements. All members of the study group can become involved in a variation of this task, the hand-piling task. Instruct one child to put his hand on the table. Ask the *where* question and answer it. "Tyrone's hand is on the table." Another child is required to put his hand on the first child's hand, and he is asked the *where* question. "Mary's hand is on Tyrone's hand." Continue until all the children have hands in the pile. To unpile, the teacher can introduce the idea of *off*. "Tommy, take your hand off."

4. Play positional games in which the emphasis is on statement production. Whisper instructions to a child. "Go sit *under* the table." With eyes closed, tell the other members of the class "Now, I can't see where Harold is, so you'll have to tell me *where* he is. Don't point, because I can't see. Tell me about Harold. Harold is *where?*" A child can often be prompted by being presented with preposterous possibilities. "Tommy, you tell me where Harold is. Is he standing in the middle of the street? . . . Is he flying through the air? . . . Where is he?" Acknowledge correct answers, such as "He's over there," "He's here in the room," etc.

5. Introduce the other prepositions in a straightforward manner after *on, over,* and *under* have been mastered. The other positional concepts that should be taught are *in, in front of, in back of,* and *between.*

  a. A container should be introduced to demonstrate *in* and *not in.* After the initial demonstrations, tasks involving *in* can be created around dog houses, buildings, and pictures in books. "Is this man in the house? . . . Yes, he is in the house."

  b. Before *in front of* and *in back of* are presented, point out that buildings have a front and a back. A picture of a dog house illustrates the point nicely. "See this door? This is the front of the dog house." Questions about *in front of* and *in back of* can be asked about illustrations in books. If there is a picture of a house, present such questions as "Is the boy in front of the house? . . . No. Can you show me where he would be standing if he were in front of the house? . . . Good." Later, the idea of *in back of* and *in front of* can be extended to objects that do not have an identifiable front or back.

c. *Next to,* which has been introduced earlier, can now be treated like the other prepositions and connected with the *where* question "Where is my hand?" (Previously, the concept had been presented only in connection with the *what* question "What can I say about my hand?") Also expand the concept to refer to objects other than dots and children in a line. "Put your hand next to Linda's hand." "Where would the man be standing if he were next to the train?" "Where is the red circle?"

d. *Between* is the last preposition that should be introduced. It is different from the others because its statement form contains the word *and.* The concept can be nicely illustrated with a chalkboard diagram of a house, a man, and a car. After the objects are identified, point to the man, and ask "Where is the man?" and answer "The man is *between* this house [point] and this car [point]." The basic statement is repeated, and questions are asked about house, man, and car. "Is the house between anything? . . . No, it is not between. Is the car between? . . . No. Is the man between? . . . Yes, see where he is? He is between this house and this car." Replace the house with a car and repeat the series of questions and statements. During subsequent exercises, place the house in the middle and flank it with perhaps two men, perhaps two other houses, etc. The teaching of *between,* since it involves a more complicated procedure than that of the other positional words, is best presented as a chalkboard task. The relationship between the three elements on the board and the structure of the statement can be made clear.

6. Introduce plural prepositional statements as a part of each of the tasks described above. After the children have mastered *on, over,* and *under,* freely introduce plurals, for example by placing two hands instead of one hand on the table. "Where are the hand*s*? . . . The hands are on the table."

7. After the children become facile in handling prepositions, ask them to make up *not* statements. Place an object on the table and ask the children to produce the appropriate statement. "The eraser is on the table." Next, ask them to "Tell me where the eraser is *not.* The eraser is not where?" "Creative" answers should be praised. "Come on, give me some silly ones, like 'The eraser is not in the closet.'" Through absurdly obvious examples of this kind, the fundamental assumptions about position are taught, and the children gain an appreciation of the various elements in a statement that can change.

8. Introduce multiple preposition statements. Point out that the eraser can be on the chair and in the room and in the school and in the city. Three or four objects can be positioned so that a variety of statements are possible. For instance, the book may be on the floor, under the table, and next to the eraser.

Second-order Identity Statements

Second-order identity statements take the standard second-order statement form "This _____ is _____," with *both* blanks filled in with names identifying the object under consideration. It is characteristic of this kind of statement that the names can occur in either order: "This house is a building" or "This building is a house." The primary concern here is with statements in which both names refer to categories, *one of which includes the other*.

Because of the inclusion relationship, a strong deductive rule is associated with these categories. If it is true that all houses are buildings, then "This house is a building" is true for every house (and it is true on a purely verbal level; no empirical investigation is necessary). The program concentrates on teaching the use of this powerful deductive rule with a number of common categories: plants, animals, letters, numbers, geometric shapes, vehicles, buildings, tools, weapons, things to read, parts, toys, food, and clothing.

1. Demonstrate with one of the less familiar categories. It is easier for the children to grasp the relationship between the more general and more specific categories referred to in the statement if they are unfamiliar with the categories and perhaps unaccustomed to misinterpreting them.

2. Present pictures of three wild animals (zebra, elephant, and lion) and identify each *as an animal,* not as a lion, a zebra, or an elephant. Use the plural identity statement to describe the group. "These are animals." Present the standard questions. The larger class name (animal) should be introduced before the subclass names (zebra, elephant, and lion) so that the statements used in the present task are consistent with those introduced earlier. In the statement "This animal is an elephant," as in the statements "This animal is big" and "This animal is on the floor," the predicate distinguishes a particular animal from other animals. If the order of presentation is reversed (This elephant is an animal), the statement no longer functions in the way to which the children have been accustomed, since the predicate no longer refers to anything distinctive about the particular elephant that is being considered.

3. Introduce examples of not-animals, such as plants and a variety of objects that are not alive. From this presentation, the children should distill the working rule that an animal is something that is alive and mobile, although the rule should probably not be presented verbally because it does not lend itself well to verbal presentation.

4. Introduce the different subclass names (elephant, lion, and zebra) after the children can accurately identify animals and not-animals. Present at least three different pictures of each animal so that the children are forced to attend to the distinguishing characteristics of each animal

and not the accidental features presented in a particular illustration. One prominent distinguishing characteristic should be pointed out for each animal—stripes for the zebra, the trunk for the elephant, and the mane for the lion. Also, a brief statement about the size of each animal should be given. Later, when other animals are introduced, additional distinguishing characteristics will have to be pointed out, but initially the method of identification should be as simple as possible. Present animal names in the familiar second-order statement form. "This animal is an elephant. This animal is a zebra. This animal is a lion."

5. Introduce a variation of the *what* question: the *what-kind* question, which applies to any class in the present category. "*What kind* of animal is this?" "*What kind* of vehicle is this?" "*What kind* of building is this?" During the initial presentation, exaggerate the question and answer it. Repetition is important because the children must learn that the *what-kind* question calls for an object name, whereas the *what-color* question calls for a description and the *where* question calls for a statement of position. Such knowledge comes only from a great deal of practice with questions and answers.

6. Introduce *not* statements. After a given animal is identified, ask three questions. "Is this animal a zebra? . . . Is this animal a lion? . . . Is this animal an elephant?" Through this pattern, the children learn that they are not dealing with concepts that are opposites. The task can be later expanded so that the children identify a given animal by telling what it is and what it is not. "Tell us what this animal is not. This animal is not a _____."

7. Introduce *I don't know* tasks. Display pictures of two animals and explain "I'm thinking of one of these animals, and it is *not* an elephant. What do I know about it?" If the children have trouble, have them identify the one that is not an elephant. "Find out the one that is not an elephant. . . . Yes, that's the one. What do you know about it? . . . This animal is a zebra." Next, introduce pictures of three different animals and repeat the procedure above. "I'm thinking of an animal, and it is not an elephant. What do you know about it?" The children must conclude "I don't know." (This task is quite difficult. It is expanded in Chapter 8.)

8. Introduce purely conjectural tasks. "I'm thinking about a zebra. Is this zebra an animal?" (Yes.) "Is this zebra an elephant?" (No.) "Is this zebra little?" (I don't know. It might be a baby zebra.) "Is this zebra sitting down?" (I don't know.) "Is this zebra sitting down next to Harold?" (No.) These tasks should demonstrate that certain questions can be answered "Yes" or "No" solely on the basis of language rules, others can be answered on the basis of information immediately available (e.g., that there are no zebras in the room), but many others cannot be answered at all without additional information.

9. After the children can handle the above operations with three animals, introduce other members of the animal class in a straightforward manner. The presentation involves a statement of the class name (This is an animal), a statement of the animal's name (This animal is a horse), and a reference to the animal's distinguishing characteristics (He looks like a zebra without the stripes). No more than three new animals should be introduced during a session.

10. After some of the more familiar animals (dog, cat, horse) have been introduced, clarify the notion of size (which has been handled only casually). Relate the pictures of dogs to the children's experience by (a) placing a child in the picture and (b) bringing the animal from the picture into the classroom. Point to the illustration and ask "How big would Tommy be standing next to this dog in the picture? . . . Would he be this big? . . . This big? . . . Or this big?" To bring the dog out of the picture, ask "How big would this dog be if he came into this room and stood next to us? . . . Would he be as big as he is in the picture, like this? . . . Would he be this big?" A similar procedure should be adopted to relate the children to other types of illustrations.

11. Arrange a field trip after the animal names have been mastered. A trip to the farm or zoo will be "meaningful" for the children who know what they will find there. It is not nearly so meaningful to the children who have not learned the names and therefore must somehow "experience" the animals nonverbally.

12. After animals have been presented, use basically the same approach to introduce all other categories.

   a. Present the group names in the plural identity statement. "These are plants." "These are vehicles." "These are tools."

   b. If the group characteristic can be described in a simple statement, present the statement. "Do you do work with it? . . . Then it is a tool." Not all groups lend themselves to a verbal rule, however.

   c. Identify each individual in the group. "This tool is a screwdriver." "This plant is a rose." "This vehicle is a bicycle."

   d. Present the tasks that dramatize the fact that all members with a certain subclass name (screwdriver or rose or bicycle) are called also by the class name (tool or plant or vehicle).

13. After the animals have been introduced, work on more than one class at a time. Below are some general suggestions for presenting the different classes.

   a. *Plants.* The children may not know the names for grass, flowers, trees, bushes, etc. Since these objects (unlike lions and elephants) are readily available, actual examples should be presented during the initial exercises. After the initial demonstration, work from books. Verbal rules for identifying plants and plant groups tend to be too difficult for children to grasp, but they can learn the discrimination readily from examples.

b. *Buildings.* The procedure is the same as for plants. During the introduction stage, the presentation should refer as much as possible to actual buildings that can be seen from the window—houses, garages, schools, churches. The emphasis should then switch to pictures of buildings—barns, silos, skyscrapers, etc. The children should be constantly reminded of each building's size. The statement presentation can probably be more condensed than the animal and plant presentation, because the children by now have a fair understanding that they are dealing with a two-name task. Therefore, instead of introducing the class name first and deferring the names of the individual members until later, both names can be introduced at the same time. "This is a building. Say it. . . . This building is a garage. What kind of building is this?" This abbreviated presentation can be used on all of the following classes.

c. *Parts.* The category *part* always implies part *of* something, so that it involves the concept of possession. Accordingly, this topic serves the auxiliary purpose of introducing the use of possessives. The initial presentation should limit the notion of *part* to parts of the body. The concept should later be expanded to include parts of rooms, houses, appliances, plants, etc. In defining the body parts, start with a familiar person and identify him. "This is Tyrone." Present the part statement, which involves the word *of.* Hold up the child's hand and say "This is a part of Tyrone." Repeat the statement while indicating the child's ear, foot, nose, etc. No further verbal explanation is necessary. To introduce the *names* of the body parts, present another statement variation. "This part of Tyrone is a nose. This is Tyrone's nose." To demonstrate the meaning of the possessive statement, ask "Is this Debby's nose? . . . Is this Tommy's nose? . . . No, this is Tyrone's nose." Statements of this form should be repeated by the children until they are mastered. In expanding the notion of part, follow the rule of limiting *part* to a part that can be given a name. Introduce windows, corners, doors, and other parts of a room; chimneys, roofs, and other parts of a house; leaves, branches, and other parts of a tree; legs, tops, handles, and other parts of household appliances; etc. The concept *part* should again be presented with the basic statement form that applies to body part. "This is a part of _____. This part of _____ is a _____." "This is a part of a frying pan. This part of a frying pan is a handle." "This is a part of a room. This part of a room is a floor."

d. *Furniture.* The statement form is similar to that for parts, in that the statement contains the word *of.* It is different, however, in that every piece is a piece *of furniture.* The class designation (piece of furniture) is first applied to chairs, tables, and beds (either the actual physical object or a picture of the object). "This is a piece of furniture." Give some indication of what furniture is by asking the question "Where do we find this piece of furniture? . . . In the house." The names of the member pieces are introduced in the usual manner after the class name has been mastered. "This piece of furniture is a bed."

e. *Vehicles.* This class and those that follow differ from the ones presented above in that the basis for classification can be made explicit through a verbal rule. These rules are not necessary, nor are they even very precise (adequate dictionary-type rules would be too complicated for the children to grasp). However, they are useful in teaching the children how to use verbal rules as a basis for classification rather than to rely on crude impressions. Ultimately, the term *vehicle,* for instance, must be applicable to any objects that can be described by a particular defining statement and not merely to objects that have some impressionistic resemblance. In this and the following classes, the verbal rule is conveyed through a simple question that expresses the criterion of classification. The question for vehicles is "Does it take you places?" If the question is answered affirmatively, the thing is a vehicle; if negatively, the thing is not a vehicle. This basis for classification should be presented in an explicit manner. Three different vehicles (perhaps a wagon, automobile, and bicycle) should be presented, along with various non-vehicles. Begin with a question about the purpose of each object. "What is this thing for? . . . Is it for cooking eggs? . . . Is it for eating? . . . No. It is for taking you places. This is a vehicle." After the name *vehicle* has been applied to various objects, direct the children in the mechanics of classifying things as vehicles. "Ask yourself 'Does it take you places?' If it does, it is a vehicle." The presentation should be handled very mechanically. Introduce different vehicles (boats, trains, airplanes, etc.) and require the children to ask themselves the classification question aloud and to answer it. Then, identify each vehicle. "This vehicle is a ship. Say it." Later, after the children have clearly mastered the routine, the procedure can be relaxed.

f. *Weapons.* The classification question for weapons is "Is it used to hurt someone?" Present pictures of different weapons (guns, knives, cannons, swords, etc.) and pictures of nonweapons. Ask about each object "Is it used to hurt someone? . . . Yes, then it is a weapon." Identify each weapon. "This weapon is a knife."

g. *Toys.* The classification question: "Do you play with it?" The presentation should be the same as for weapons.

h. *Tools.* The classification question: "Do you use it to do work?" The various tools can be demonstrated. "Look. I'm using this hammer to do work. It helps me put these boards together." The demonstrations should not be labored, however. The emphasis should be on the statement.

i. *Food.* The classification question: "Do you eat it?" The answer is of a different form from those of the preceding categories. Instead of saying "This is a food," we say "This is food." The statement that follows the class statement may also be different. Instead of saying "This food is a meat," we say "This food is meat" or "This food is a piece of meat." In other cases, a more conventional (although awkward) statement is indicated. "This food is a turnip. This food is a steak." Various vegetables, fruits, and staples should be introduced under the heading "food."

j. *Clothing.* The classification question: "Do you wear it?" The affirmative answer to the question indicates that it is *an article of clothing.* Initially, the presentation should be confined to real physical objects, but should quickly be expanded to include illustrative material. The statement presentation is similar to that of furniture, with the addition of the classification question. "Do you wear it? . . . Yes? . . . Then this is an article of clothing. This article of clothing is a coat." Some of the statements can become rather long. "This article of clothing is a pair of pants."

k. *Things to read.* The classification question: "Do you read it?" The category of things to read (newspapers, signs, magazines, books) should be introduced after the child has a fair understanding of reading. The presentation: "Do you read it? . . . Yes. Then this is a thing to read. This thing to read is a newspaper. Say it."

l. *Other classes.* Fruits and vegetables are categories often introduced in nursery schools. Actually, these categories are so poorly defined that they invite confusion. However, a few of the common fruits and vegetables may be classified by rote, with no attempts to extend the class concept. Classes which the children have already encountered in other school contexts should be introduced, if only to demonstrate that they can be handled in the same manner as the classes listed above. Class names can be reviewed for *numbers* and *letters.* The standard procedure is used. A series of objects to be classified is presented with others that are to be excluded. Those to be included are identified with the class name. "These are numbers." The subclass name is then applied to the various individuals presented. "This number is seven." In a similar fashion, the children in the study group can be grouped under the class name *children,* and the adults can be grouped as *adults* or *teachers.*

14. Introduce polar subclasses. Divide the class *children* into the subclasses *boys* and *girls,* and the class *teachers* (or *adults*) into the subclasses *men* and *women.* Demonstrate that the statement "This child is a boy" is polar by introducing the standard polar tasks, especially those involving *not* statements. "What's another way of saying 'This child is not a girl'?" Present verbal tasks, such as "I'm thinking of a child that is not a girl. What do you know about that child?" To help clarify the inclusion rela-

tionship (Boys and girls are children), present exercises in which the statements are reversed and are no longer polar. "I'm thinking about a boy. What do you know about him? . . . He's a child."

15. Ask classification questions while reading stories and engaging in other activities outside the language class. When applying language questions and answers to stories and songs, demonstrate that these questions are not limited to language drill but can be asked about objects which are encountered in everyday life. Furthermore, the questions are more interesting and dynamic when they become part of a "story line" or engrossing activity. Therefore, when reading stories, seize on every opportunity to ask about newly learned classifications. "And what is the bear sitting on? . . . Yes, this is a chair. What do I know about chairs? . . . What can I say about this chair? . . . This chair is a piece of furniture." Similarly, during music and free time, remain alert and capitalize on situations that arise. "Yes, those are nice new shoes, Tyrone. What do you know about shoes? . . . What do you do with them? . . . So what can you say about them? . . . Shoes are articles of _____."

16. Introduce multiple-category exercises to demonstrate that an object can be in more than one class at the same time. Tools and weapons or plants and food provide the best examples. Present a picture of a carrot and identify it as a plant. Present the question "What do we do with a carrot?" to point out that a carrot can be classified as food. Then ask "Does a carrot grow and turn green? . . . Yes, a carrot is a plant." Similarly, an ax is both a tool and a weapon, depending upon the intention of the user.

Beginning Language Summary

The basic language skills described in the preceding pages represent the rock-bottom foundation of language.

All the tasks in the basic language program revolve around two simple statement forms: "This is a _____" and "This _____ is _____." Yet, these two forms become the media for transmitting a wide range of language and thinking skills. Through these two forms, the child learns first how to identify the things in his world and how to ask questions about them. He then learns how to compare one thing with another, referring to size, texture, and sound. The two basic statement forms then transport him to the level of more sophisticated comparisons, where many things are grouped together according to a certain conceptual dimension, such as position or color or shared characteristics. In working with the two basic statement forms, he learns the rudiments of empirical investigation. He learns to ask himself certain questions and proceed according to the way he answers them after investigating the material before him. In other words, he learns the basis of *if-then* reasoning.

Through the basic statement forms, he learns the fundamental conceptual framework of logical thought—along with the not-so-logical conventions that sometimes accompany these. He learns to unscramble experience in a very mechanical and stereotyped manner—a very accurate manner—and reduce it to relevant questions and answers that express what something is and what additional statements can be made about it.

In the next section, the operations that have been obliquely introduced in connection with the basic language tasks are expanded. These include the use of *and, or* and *if-then*. In the expansion process, some of the tasks presented in the basic language section are rephrased to refine them and make them more flexible conceptually.

advanced
language

8

*T*he preceding chapter built a kind of language skeleton. The skeleton satisfied the communication requirements necessary to teach first-order and second-order concepts. The purpose of the present chapter is to fill in parts of the language skeleton. During arithmetic instruction, reading instruction, and even the beginning language instruction, the children have obliquely encountered the concepts of *and, or,* and *if-then.* However, these concepts need further clarification, especially *or* and *if-then,* which are based on the assumption that a conclusion is reached by answering more than one question about the presentation. Typically, culturally deprived children operate according to the principle that the answer to any question should be something that can be given immediately without proceeding from one point to another. The present chapter teaches the skills necessary to handle chain reasoning.

The two basic statement forms presented in the preceding chapter are here expanded. A variety of new verbs are introduced. With these, various expanded statements are presented, including past-tense constructions. A series of exercises deals with expanding polar pairs into a nonpolar set (big, bigger, bigger, etc., instead of simply big-little). Finally, logical problems involving polar changes are introduced. These represent a culmination of the language program because they require integration of virtually all the skills presented in the program.

The Five-element Model

The concepts *and, only, or, all, some,* and *if-then* are sometimes difficult to teach and sometimes difficult to verify without resorting to rather sophisticated verbal arguments. Often, these verbal arguments do not serve the needs of the teacher very well because they do not lend themselves to a dramatic demonstration of validity. For example, there is no very intuitively compelling way to demonstrate that the following argument is not valid: If it rains, he stays inside; he stayed inside; therefore, it rained.

To attack the argument, one must rely on the listener's ability to see that there are other possible reasons why a person may stay inside. Perhaps he is sick; perhaps he does not feel like going outside. Yet, pleas to the listener's understanding uncover no obvious contradiction.

The solution to the problem offered here is a five-element model (five circles, five squares, five triangles, etc.) which does for such concepts as *or* and *if-then* what the two basic statement forms did for the first-order and second-order concepts. The model refines, simplifies, and allows presentations that are more dramatic than those encountered in everyday situations. An argument that is analogous to the one above can be shown to be obviously false by using the five-element model.

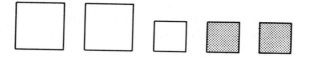

If it rains, he stays inside.	If squares are black [find all the black ones], squares are little.
He stayed inside.	These squares are little [find all the little ones].
Therefore, it rained.	Therefore, these squares are black.

The argument is obviously not valid because it is possible to find a square that is little but not black. This square provides, in a very graphic manner, the contradiction that was only nebulously suggested in the other argument.

The concepts of *and* and *or* sometimes appear easy to present through highly verbal demonstrations and concrete grouping tasks. However, these concepts are deceptive, and the usual presentations run the risk of teaching the children that *or* means "Take one of them" while *and* means "Take all of them." The children may therefore be able to perform adequately such tasks as "Pick up the eraser and the book" without understanding that the book is red *and* black—that *and* is a way of joining certain kinds of statements together. Although the "Take all of them" reduction of *and* is sometimes adequate, the concept *or* is severely violated by the "Take one" reduction. Unless *or* is seen as a concept that conveys a possibility, *or* is not seen at all. When we say that there is a fly in the kitchen or the living room, we mean that possibly the fly is in the kitchen and possibly it is in the living room.

All and *some* are words that are very useful in describing a group. "All of the big squares are red" tells us that if a square is big, a square is red. "Some of the big squares are red," on the other hand, tells us that if a square is big, it *may be red*. One of the reasons *all* and *some* should be defined for the children is that the teacher will probably find herself using them in explanations. They become much more potent ingredients in an explanation if the children understand what they mean.

One problem connected with the five-element presentation is that it may not feel natural to the teacher. For her, the concepts of *and, only, or,* and *if-then* are natural when used in certain "natural" contexts. She may find the context of the five-element model intuitively awkward and not particularly meaningful. She must recognize, however, that her intuitive feeling is the product of her experiences and that naïve children do not—cannot—share her intuitive feelings, since they have not shared her experiences. The teacher is urged to appreciate the fact that the five-element model presents the core of the concepts *and, only, or,* and *if-then.* Although the tasks associated with it may sometimes seem awkward, they satisfy the children's need for a core understanding, which can be gracefully generalized to the entire range of situations that are meaningful to the teacher.

And.

1. Review *and* as it is used in describing an object. The children have already encountered the concept *and* in the beginning language program, when they were required to describe different objects according to more than one dimension. "This line is long *and* red." The present set of exercises reviews this application of the concept and then introduces new tasks.

a. Present the five-square model on the chalkboard, coloring the shaded squares red and the unshaded squares white.

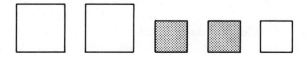

b. Identify the objects. "These are squares."

c. Further describe the left square, referring to size and color. "This square is big. This square is white."

d. Present the *and* statement about the left square. "This square is big *and* white."

e. Ask the appropriate *is* questions. "Is this square big? . . . Yes, this square is big. Is this square white? . . . Yes, this square is white."

f. Conclude with the *and* statement. "This square is big and white."

g. Refer to the far-right square. "Is this square big and white? . . . No, because this square is not *big.*" Refer to one of the red squares. "Is this square big and white? . . . No, because this square is not *white.*" Refer to the other big square. "Is this square big and white? . . . Yes, this square is big and white."

h. Repeat the procedure with the other combinations. "This square is little and red." "This square is little and white."

i. After the children are able to answer the *yes-no* questions, introduce *what* questions. Refer to a given square and ask "What can I say about this square? . . . This square is what?" If the children answer by indicating that the square is big, ask "What else can I say about this square? . . . This square is big and what? . . . Yes, this square is big and *white*. Say it."

j. After working with the five-square model shown on page 174, introduce variations such as those below. The formula for making different variations is: Make two pairs of figures that are the same in both color and size. Ask the *what* question about each object. "What can I

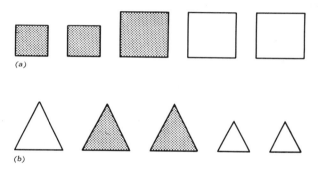

(a)

(b)

say about this triangle? . . . What else can I say?" Answer with the *and* statement. "This triangle is white and little."

k. Introduce *not* tasks after the children have become reasonably proficient at phrasing the appropriate *and* statements that describe a given square or triangle. The *not* variations should be introduced in the following order:

(1) In variation (a) above, find a square that is black and *not* little. Have the children first locate all of the squares that are black, using the statement "This square is black" and then concluding "These squares are black." Have the children then examine these to find one about which they can also say "This square is not little." The presentation should become less mechanical after the children begin to appreciate the function of the *and-not* statement. Variations of the form "Find the square that is _____ and not _____" should be introduced, with increasing emphasis on production of the statement.

(2) Find a square that is *not* black and *not* little. The procedure outlined in step (1) above should be repeated to demonstrate that there is a square about which it is possible to say "This square is *not* black. This square is *not* little." Various statements of the form "Find a square that is not _____ and not _____" should be introduced. A leading

what question can be introduced to help phrase the appropriate state-ments. "What can I say about this square?" The children may need reminders about which dimensions they are using. They may call a square little when they are asked to find a square that is *not big.* "Re-member, the words you have to use are *not little* and *not white.* That's what you have to talk about."

l. Present combination *not* and *what* tasks. Using the five-square model below, say "I'm thinking about a square that is not little. What can I say about it?" The solution is arrived at by first finding the squares

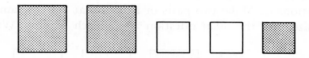

that are *not* little and then noting what can be said about them. "They are big [by polar definition]. They are red. They are big *and* red." The children will learn to answer the first part of the *and* statement quite quickly. Encourage them by pointing out that "If it's not little, it must be *big.*"

m. Use compound *and* statements in a variety of situations after the children have mastered the various five-square model tasks. The children must learn that the procedures used to work out conclusions with the model are not limited to the model but apply to a host of every-day situations. When reading to the children, phrase *and* statements. "Look at this truck. It's not little, and it's not red. What can we say about it? . . . Yes, it's big, and it's green." Also, use *and* statements to describe clothing, furniture, actions, etc.

2. Introduce *and* as it is used *in enumerating different objects.*

a. Present the statement "I'm thinking about *all* of these squares." Ask "Which squares am I thinking about?" Proceed from left to right. "I'm thinking about this one, *and* this one, *and* this one." After all of the squares have been considered, embrace the entire group and define the meaning of *all.* "Yes, I'm thinking about *all* of these squares." Point to any square. "Am I thinking about this square? . . . Yes, because I'm thinking about *all* of the squares." Repeat with other squares and repeat the entire exercise often.

b. Introduce variations that deal with particular types of squares. "I'm thinking about *all* of the white squares. Which squares am I thinking about?" Clarify the basis of selection. Refer to each square and ask "Is this square white?" If it is, conclude "Then I'm thinking about this square." If it is not white, conclude "Then I'm *not* thinking about this one." After considering each square, refer to the white ones and phrase the appropriate *and* statement. "I'm thinking about this square, *and* this square, *and* this square." Repeat the demonstration, referring to the different possible dimensions of the squares. "I'm thinking about all of the little squares." "I'm thinking about all of the big squares." "I'm thinking about all of the red squares." "I'm thinking about all of the white squares." Make the children increasingly responsible for the production of the appropriate *and* statements.

c. Use *not* variations of the basic task. "I'm thinking about all of the squares that are *not* red. Which squares am I thinking about? . . . This square, *and* this square, *and* this square."

3. Introduce *reversible-elements* tasks. In some situations, it is possible to transpose the parts of a statement that are connected by *and*. For example, the statement "Tom and Harry went to the store" is logically the same statement as "Harry and Tom went to the store." This point is certainly one of the most difficult for culturally deprived children to appreciate, partly because the concept is rather sophisticated and partly because they have trouble hearing any difference between the two statements. Their inability to hear the difference is perhaps the key symptom of their intellectual deficiency. It points out rather graphically that their understanding of language is premised on repeating, not on understanding, what is heard. Typically, therefore, when presented with the task of transposing "Tom and Harry," they are unable to do anything but repeat "Tom and Harry," even after the answer has been told to them many, many times.

a. To introduce the concept, present two squares, one little, one big, and both white. Identify the squares and present the plural statement. "These squares are white." Follow with the question "Which squares are white?" Answer it by touching first the left square and then the right square and saying "The little square and the big square are white." *This question and answer are new to the children.* Previous questions were answered by supplying the *predicate* of a *statement*. "What can I say about these squares? . . . These squares *are white*." The new question is answered by supplying the *subject* of a statement. "Which squares are white? . . . *This square and this square* are white." Because the statement form is different, the children may have some trouble with it initially.

b. After they become proficient at producing the correct statements about different pairs (two big squares of different colors, two little squares of different colors, two red squares of different sizes), draw an arrow going from left to right beneath a four-square model. Ask the *which*

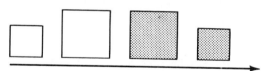

question. "Which squares are white?" Point out a new convention. "I'm going to answer the question by following the arrow. I start over here [left], and I say 'This little one and this big one are white.' "

c. Introduce the alternative way of identifying the members in these groups. "This time I'm not going to go the way the arrow says; I'm going to go *the other way*. Which squares are white? . . . I'm going to go the other way and say 'This big square and this little square are white.' "

d. Speed up the procedure after various examples have been demonstrated. "I can name the ones that are red by going the way the arrow says or going the other way. I can go with the arrow and say 'This big one and this little one are red.' I can go the other way and say 'This little one and this big one are red.' " Present many examples and give the children a great deal of practice in going both ways. They should not be hurried during their initial attempts.

e. Finally, eliminate the arrow and present the task as another way of phrasing a statement. Select a pair of squares and ask "What's another way of saying 'This red square and this white square'? . . . 'This white square and this red square.' " Point to the squares as they are mentioned in the question and statement. Give the children a great deal of practice with this exercise—preferably two to three minutes of practice at the beginning of each language session until they become proficient at producing the appropriate statements.

f. Introduce the reversible *and* to describe a particular square. Point to a big red square and describe it. "This square is big [touch the sides of the square to indicate bigness] *and* red [rub finger over the colored surface]." After repeating the statement several times, ask the question "What's another way of saying 'This square is big and red'? . . . We go the other way and say 'This square is *red* and big.' " Call attention to the original order in which you described the square and refer specifically to actions associated with the statement. It helps to accent one of the elements to be reversed. The children can then hear what is happening. "I said it was big, and I did this. Then I said it was red, and I did this. Big and *red*. Let's say it another way. *Red* and big." Use plural statement variations to describe a group of similar squares. "What's another way of saying '*These squares are* white and little'?" Also introduce *not* statements. "Tell me what this square is *not*. . . . It is not big and *not* white. Let's say it another way. . . . It is *not white* and not big."

g. Introduce the *Turn It Around* song in the music period. It provides a slightly different kind of demonstration of how elements connected by *and* can be reversed.

Only.

The concept *only* can be presented quite easily by presenting a new question, which is similar to the *which* question presented in the preceding section in that it is answered by supplying the subject, or beginning part of the statement.

1. Present a regular five-square model and ask a *what-kind* question.

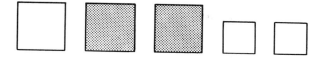

"What kind of squares are white? . . . *Big squares and little squares* are white."

2. Ask "What kind of squares are red?" After the children indicate that big squares are red, ask "What other kind of squares are red? Are little squares red?" Answer the question, using the word *only.* "No, *only big squares are red."* Have the children repeat the statement, exaggerating the word *only.*

3. Repeat the basic procedure, asking "What kind of squares are little?" Instruct the children to "Find the ones that are little. Now, look at them and tell me what color they are. These squares are _____." Continue as in step 2 above. "What other kind of squares are little? . . . Are black squares little? . . . No, *only white squares are little."* The rule the children should learn is that *only* is a kind of opposite of *and.* If it is true that the big squares *and* little squares are white, then it cannot be true that *only* big squares are white.

4. Extend the concept to situations outside of the language session. Questions that call for *only* can be phrased by asking "What kind?" "What kind of children go to the girl's bathroom? . . . *Only* girls." "What kind of cups are on the table? . . . *Only* white cups."

Or.

The procedure for teaching *or* is similar to that suggested for teaching *and.*

1. Begin by showing how *or* is used *to enumerate the candidates in a group.*

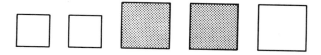

a. Draw a five-square model and define *or.* "I'm thinking of one of these squares—not all of them, just one. Which one is it?" The children will probably claim that they know which one you are thinking of. Tell them emphatically that they *do not know.* Have them repeat "I do not know." Point to each square in turn. "Am I thinking about this square?

. . . Maybe. Am I thinking about this square? *. . . Maybe.*" After going through all of the squares in this manner, introduce the *or* statement, Proceed from left to right again and say "I am thinking about this square, *or* this square, *or* this square." Introduce a variation of the task above. "I'm thinking about *some* of these squares—not all, just some." The procedure is the same as it is for locating one square. "I'm thinking of this one, *or* this one, *or* this one."

b. Extend the *or* concept. Refer to the five-square model above and indicate "I'm thinking about one of the red squares, not all of the red squares, not all of the squares. Just one red square. Which one is it?" Consider every square, beginning with the far-left square. "Am I thinking about this square? *. . .* No. Because it is *not red.*" Cross out the square and advance to the next one, asking "Am I thinking about this square? *. . .* No, because it is *not red.*" After all of the squares have been considered in this manner, only the red ones will remain. The others will have been crossed out. Explain "I'm thinking about one of these red squares—only one. Do you know which one? *. . .* No, you do not. Say 'I don't know.' Maybe it's this one. And maybe it's this one." Restate the original question and answer it with an *or* statement. "I'm thinking about a square that is red. Which one is it? *. . .* It is this one *or* this one." Have the children repeat the statement at least five times. Introduce the other tasks that derive from the model above. "I'm thinking about a square that is little. Which one is it?" "I'm thinking about a square that is white. Which one is it?" "I'm thinking about a square that is big. Which one is it?"

c. Demonstrate the critical difference between the *or* group and the *and* group. Present a familiar *and* task, stressing the key words that indicate an *and* response—*all* and *squares*. "I'm thinking about *all* of the red *squares*. Which squares am I thinking about? *. . .* This square *and* this square." Ask about each red square "Am I thinking about this square?" and answer "Yes, I'm thinking about this square. I'm thinking about *all* of the red squares." Next, form an *or* group of red squares, again stressing the key words, *a* and *square*. "I'm thinking about *a* red *square*—only *one* red *square*. Which square is it? *. . .* It is this square *or* this square." Ask about each red square "Am I thinking about this square? *. . . Maybe.* You don't know." The critical difference between the *and* and *or* groups is that if the question can be answered "Yes," the members are linked together with *and;* if the question can be answered only with "Maybe," the members are linked together with *or*. With practice on tasks similar to those described above, the children will become familiar with this rule.

d. Introduce *not* statements. "I am thinking about *a square* that is not little. Which one am I thinking about?" The procedure is the same as in the tasks above. The group of squares that are not little is assembled, and the plural statement is used to describe the group. "These squares are not little." The *or* statement is then presented, referring to each square in turn. "I am thinking about this one, *or* this one, *or* this one." The children should have a great deal of practice with statements of this type.

2. Demonstrate how *or* can be used *to describe group characteristics.*
   a. Introduce a regular five-square model and pose the problem. "I'm

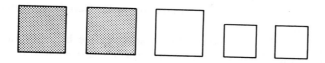

thinking about a big square. What color is it?" The procedure involves first locating all big squares and applying the plural statement "These squares are big." The color question is then asked about each of the big squares. "What color is this square? . . . Red. What color is this square? . . . Red. What color is this square? . . . White." The original problem is restated and answered, using an *or* statement. "I'm thinking about a big square. What color is it? . . . It is red [point to the red squares] *or* white [point to the white square]."

b. Introduce *not* statements. "I'm thinking about a square that is not little. What color is it?" The not-little squares are assembled and then connected with the *or* statement. "This square is red. This other square is white. So a square that is not little is red *or* white." The presentation can become increasingly flexible as the children become increasingly proficient at handling the basic statement form. "What color is it? . . . It is either red or white."

If-then.

The *if-then* tasks suggested here are certainly the most difficult in the present series. But they are also among the most important. The *if-then* line of reasoning is the tie between the *and* statement, the *or* statement, and the *only* statement. It is the common denominator that enables us to talk intelligently in terms of *and, or,* and *only;* it is the link between the conditional situation found in an *or* group and the concrete certainty of an *and* group; and it is a kind of magnificent detection kit that allows one to look over what happened, proceeding first forward and then backward, pausing, supposing, considering, learning.

1. Present a regular five-square model and demonstrate how to form the basic *if-then* statement.

a. Embrace the big squares and ask "What can I say about these squares that I cannot say about any of the other squares?" If the children volunteer that they are white, point to the little square. "I can say 'This square is white.'" Return to the original group of big squares. "What can I say about these squares that I cannot say about any of the other squares? . . . Yes, these squares are big." Demonstrate that it is not possible to make this statement about any but the two squares in the group. Point to each little square and ask "Can I say 'This square is big'? . . . No."

b. Repeat the statement "These squares are big" several times before introducing the first part of the *if-then* statement "If squares are big, _____." Explain briefly what the condition means. "If squares are big, *what else can I say about them?* Tell me." Prompt if necessary. "Are they red? . . . Are they brown?" After the children supply the answer (They are white), present the entire *if-then* statement. "If squares are big [embrace the big squares], squares are white [point to the color surface of each big square]."

c. Introduce a singular variation after step *b* has been mastered. Ask about the red squares "What can I say about these squares that I cannot say about any of the others? . . . These squares are red. Say it. . . . If *a square* is red, what else can I say about it? . . . It is little. If a square is red, a square is little." Repeat with different examples. The procedure is relatively easy. First, assemble a group according to either size or color. Then, examine the members of the group and make a further statement that applies to all the members of the group. Make certain that such a further statement can be made.

2. Introduce basic *if-then* problems. Have the children form an *if-then* statement, such as "If a square is red, a square is little." After they have repeated the statement several times, present the problem. "I'm thinking about a square that is red. What do you know about it? . . . It is little." Repeat the *if-then*. "If a square is red, a square is little." Demonstrate the meaning of the statement with the model. "If a square is red, it must be this one or this one. So what do you know about these? . . . These squares are little. The square I'm thinking about is little." Give the children a great deal of practice with basic *if-thens* of this kind.

3. Introduce *not* statements. "If a square is *not white* it is _____." The children may suggest that it is red. Acknowledge that their suggestion is correct, but add "And what else about it?" From this point, work the problem in the usual manner. "If a square is not white, a square is little. I'm thinking about a square that is not white. What do you know about it? . . . Yes, it is little." The "proof" of the problem can be provided by referring to the squares.

4. Introduce problems involving *or*. These have a dual purpose. They extend the operation outlined in the basic *if-then* procedure, and they

also help define *or* more clearly than was possible without using *if-then* terminology.

a. Draw a five-square model similar to the one at the beginning of this section and present the first part of an *if-then* statement. "If a square is red, _____." Ask "Which one is it?" The children may insist that it is a particular square. Correct them by pointing out "You know that the square is red, but you don't know anything else. So, if a square is red, maybe it is this one, *or* maybe it is this one." Present a variety of these *if* questions. "If a square is big, which one is it?" "If a square is black, which square is it?" "If a square is little, which one is it?" The answer should be expressed with an *or* connecting each element.

b. Introduce a *compound group*. Embrace the little squares and have the children produce the appropriate statement. "These squares are little." Introduce the *if-then*. "If a square is little, a square is what?" Examination of the group of little squares (in the model in step 1 above) discloses that there are both red and white squares in the group. After the children draw this conclusion, relate it to the *if-then* pattern by referring first to the left little square and saying "If a square is little, it may be this one. Then it would be white." Point to the middle square. "If a square is little, it may be this one, and it would be red." Repeat the sequence with the right square and conclude "If a square is little, it is white [point to the white square], *or* it is red [point to the red square]." After the children have gone through the procedure several times, the approach can be speeded up. "If a square is little—find the little ones—a square is white [point], *or* a square is red [point]." Give the children practice with various *or* groups.

c. Referring to the five-square model at the beginning of this section, embrace the white squares and have the children produce the statement "These squares are white." Have them then produce the *if-then* statement. "If a square is white, a square is big or a square is little." Have them repeat it several times. Explain "I'm thinking about a square that is white. What do you know about it?" If the children have trouble, repeat the *if-then*. "If a square is white, a square is big, or a square is little. So if it's white, you know that it is _____." After they have produced the appropriate *or* statement, ask "Do you know if it is big? . . . No, because you don't know which one it is. If it is this one [point to a big one], it is big. If it is this one [point to a little one], it is not big." The children should have enough practice with this exercise so that they can produce the appropriate statements without referring to the model.

5. Introduce the *not if-then*. While this *if-then* can be demonstrated with the five-square model, it should be taught primarily as a verbal convention. The demonstration should be used merely to reinforce the verbal pattern. The children will probably have some initial difficulty hearing how the *not if-then* is derived. Referring to the model at the begin-

ning of this section, present the basic *if-then.* "If a square is big [find the big ones], a square is white." Have the children repeat the statement several times before introducing the *not* convention, which involves flipping the original *if-then* around. "If a square is *not white* [find the ones that are not white], then a square is *not big."* The verbal explanation should be kept short. *"Only* white ones are big, so if a square is *not white,* it cannot be big." The word *only* serves to flip the original *if-then.* "If squares are big, squares are white; *only white squares are big."* The primary emphasis on producing the *not if-then* should be on the verbal production. The verbal presentation should be rhythmical, so that changes in statements are easier to hear. "If a square is big, a square is white. If a square is *not white,* a square is *not big."* The children should work on tasks similar to the one above until they can handle them verbally without looking at the model.

6. Introduce the undetermined *if-then.* This one is very important in logical thinking. Refer to the big squares of the model presented at the beginning of this section. Present the appropriate *if-then.* "If a square is big, a square is white." Then pose the problem. "I'm thinking about a square that is not big. What do you know about it?" The children may indicate that it is not white. Correct them. Point out "You don't know. Maybe it's not white, and maybe it is white. If it's not big, it's little. And if it's little, it's white, *or* it's red."

7. Demonstrate that the *if-thens* learned with the five-element model apply to a range of situations and that everyday *if-thens* present nothing that is really new.

a. Present action pictures that lead naturally to some kind of causal conclusion—a man aiming a gun, aiming a bow, striking a match, preparing to throw a ball, jumping from a high place, dropping something, etc. Have the children predict what will happen, and phrase the situation as an *if-then.* "If he pulls the trigger, his gun will go off." "If he throws the ball, it will fly through the air." "If he jumps from the cliff, he will fall into the water." After the children repeat the *if-thens,* present first the basic *if-then.* "If he lets go of the bow string, his arrow will fly through the air. Let's pretend that he lets go of his bow string. What happens?" Next, present the *not if-then.* "If he let's go of the string, his arrow will fly through the air. If an arrow does not fly through the air, what happened? . . . He did not let go of his bow string." Finally, present the undetermined *if-then.* "If he lets go of the string, his arrow will fly through the air. What will happen if he doesn't let go of his string? . . . We don't know. Maybe it will fly through the air, and maybe it won't. Maybe his string will break. Maybe some other arrow will fly through the air. We don't know." Give the children plenty of practice in applying *if-then* reasoning to a host of situations. The five-element model has no advantage beyond being a graphic device for teaching the basic patterns of *if-then* reasoning. Once these patterns have been mastered in connection with the model, however, they should be extended to the range of experience for which they are intended, namely everyday causal experiences.

b. Phrase rules as *if-thens*. "If you do a good job, I'll shake your hand. You did a good job. So what's going to happen?" "If you stand behind the swing, you'll get hit. You're standing behind the swing, Tommy."

c. Use the *if-then* to express the relationship between classes that are formed on the basis of defining characteristics. "If it's a chair, what do we know about it? . . . It's a piece of furniture. I'm thinking of a chair. What do you know about that chair?" "If something is a hammer, it's a what? . . . It's a tool." "If something is a shotgun, it's a what? . . . It's a weapon." "If something is a tricycle, it's a what? . . . It's a vehicle."

d. Use the *if-then* to point out characteristics of figures. "If a figure looks like this, it is an *oval*. Here's a figure that looks like this one. What do you know about it? . . . Here's another figure that does *not* look like this one. What is it? . . . Actually, we don't know. Maybe it's an oval, and maybe it isn't."

e. Introduce the *If Song* in the music period (see page 222). This song can be used to give the child practice in using *if-thens* to classify names. "If it's a bike, then it's a vehicle"; "If it's a bike, then it's not a tricycle"; "If it's a bike, then it's not a horse"; "If it's a bike, then it's not a building"; "If it's a bike, then it's not a tool"; "If it's a bike, then it's not a bug." This song is extremely useful and should be sung often.

Verb Expansions

The verb *is* has been employed exclusively in the preceding exercises, because the most certain way to "define" a concept is to point out what the concept is and what it is not. The verb *is* provides the perfect basis for such definitions. However, the children, in addition to learning nouns and the descriptive words, should learn something about common action verbs. These can be taught as a simple extension of what they already know.

1. Present intransitive verbs first. These verbs involve the fewest additional words, and when they are phrased in the progressive (*ing* ending), they take the familiar statement form "This _____ is _____." "This boy is jumping." "This man is smiling." "This baby is crying."

a. Have a member of the class stand up and identify him. "This is a boy. This boy is John."

b. Ask the *what* question, and answer it. "What is John do*ing*? . . . John is stand*ing*. Say it." Accentuate the *ing* ending on the words *doing* and *standing*.

c. Ask various *is* questions that are answerable with a *not* statement. "Is John walking? . . . Is John sitting? . . . Is John running?" Repeat the *what* question. "What is John doing?"

d. Introduce *and* statements. Instruct the child who is standing to clap. Ask "Is John clapping? . . . Yes, John is clapping. Is John standing? . . . Yes, John is standing. *John is clapping and standing.*" A variety of *and* statements can be constructed by combining the actions of walking, running, smiling, jumping, frowning, stretching, yawning, sleeping, eating, squatting, falling, etc. For example, a child can stand, smile, and clap, all at the same time. "What is Harold doing? . . . What else? . . . What else?" After the children have repeated the appropriate *and* statement several times, instruct the child who is demonstrating to discontinue *one* of the actions. "Stop clapping, Harold." Then ask "Is Harold standing and smiling and clapping? . . . No. Harold is standing and smiling. But he's not standing and smiling and clapping."

e. Introduce pictures that depict different intransitive actions, such as kittens sleeping, boys running, people dancing, men diving, etc.

f. After the children have learned how to answer the *what* question (properly identifying the various actions and articulating the *ing* ending), expand the task to include modifiers that generate an additional question. For instance, expand "The boy is laughing" to "The boy is laughing *at the clown.*" In addition to generating the question "What is the boy doing?" this statement generates the question "What is the boy laughing at?" To introduce the expanded verb statement, present the familiar statement-question series. "This is a boy. This boy is Tyrone. Is Tyrone standing? . . . Yes. What is Tyrone doing? . . . Tyrone is standing."

Next, introduce the second verb question "*Where* is Tyrone standing?" and provide a few clues. "Is Tyrone standing on the wall? . . . Is Tyrone standing on the ceiling? . . . Well, where is Tyrone standing?" Conclude "Tyrone is standing on the floor." Introduce a variety of similar expanded-verb statements. "The boy is running. *Where* is the boy running? . . . The boy is running *on the street.*" "The man is talking. *Who* is he talking to? . . . The man is talking *to a boy.*" "The kitten is sleeping. *Where* is the kitten sleeping? . . . The kitten is sleeping *under the table.*" Concentrate primarily on *where* questions. "What is he doing?" "*Where is he doing it?*" This is a simple extension of the work with prepositions introduced in the preceding section, and should provide a thorough review of that work.

2. Introduce transitive verbs. The difference between transitive verbs and intransitive verbs from an educational standpoint is trivial. The important similarity is that both the transitive and expanded-intransitive statements generate two questions.

Intransitive: The man is eating at the table.
What is the man doing? Where is the man eating?

Transitive: The man is eating a steak.
What is the man doing? What is the man eating?

Because of this similarity, transitive verbs can be taught in much the same way as expanded intransitive verbs:

a. Continue to phrase statements in the present progressive. "The man is throwing a ball"—not "The man throws the ball."

b. Continue to "derive" the statement by first asking the *what-doing* question. "What is the man doing?" Then ask the second verb question. "What is the man eating?" Partial answers are acceptable (eating a steak), but if there is any doubt about whether the children understand the statement or are shying away from it, they should be required to produce the entire statement. "What is the man eating? . . . The man is eating *a steak.*"

c. Present pictures that can generate such statements as "The boys are throwing stones"; "The man is climbing a rope"; "The girl is painting a picture"; "The soldier is aiming his gun"; and "The man is building a house." Confine the presentation to statements that generate two *what* questions. *"What is the man doing?" "What is the man building?"* When the presentation is so confined, the children will learn something about how transitive and intransitive constructions differ. *What* questions are answered with nouns. "The boy is singing *a song.*" *Where* questions are answered with prepositional phrases. "The boy is singing *in the classroom.*"

d. Expand the transitive-verb statement. After the basic statement "The boys are throwing stones," introduce a question that will further expand the statement. "The boys are throwing stones where? . . . The boys are throwing stones into the water." Many of the statements presented in step *c* above can be expanded. "The man is climbing a rope. *Where* is the man climbing a rope? . . . The man is climbing a rope in the gym." "The girl is painting a picture. The girl is painting a picture *with what?* . . . The girl is painting a picture with a paint brush." "The soldier is aiming his gun. The soldier is aiming his gun *at what?* . . . The soldier is aiming his gun at the tank." "The man is building a house. The man is building a house *with what?* . . . The man is building a house with a hammer, and nails, and boards."

3. Introduce *because* statements as an extension of the preceding tasks. *Because* statements can be treated as two-question statements, the second question of which is "Why?"

a. Begin with such statements as "The boy is crying," "The woman is eating a pie," or "The man is running."

b. Ask the *why* question, and complete the original statement with *because*. "Why is the boy crying? . . . The boy is crying *because* he is hurt." "Why is the woman eating a pie? . . . The woman is eating a pie *because* she is hungry." "Why is the man running? . . . The man is running *because* the dog is chasing him." The form of these statements is obviously comparable to the other two-question verb statements. The only difference is that the *because* statements are produced in response to a special question—the *why* question. The children should be drilled on this point.

c. Ask series of *why* questions about expressive pictures. The pictures should be "action pictures," and the cues that generate the story should be rather bold and obvious—for example, pictures of firemen at work, dogs chasing a rabbit, men felling a tree, etc. (Photography magazines often provide the "clearest" pictures, though good ones are easily found in other pictorial magazines.) Ask "What is *happening* in this picture?" After the action has been described, present a series of *why* questions about those elements in the picture that are *acting* and those that are the *object of the action*. "Why are the dogs chasing the rabbit? . . . Why is the rabbit running?" "Why are the firemen shooting water at this building? . . . Why is the building burning?" Answers that begin with *because* are acceptable. However, rephrase them as complete statements. "Yes, the rabbit is running *because* he does not want the dogs to hurt him."

d. Use *why* questions liberally throughout the preschool day. "Why is Harold crying? . . . Harold is crying because he fell down and hurt his knee." "Why did Linda know the answer? . . . Linda knew the answer because she's thinking big." "Why do you like this kind of juice, Tommy? . . . You like this kind of juice because it's good."

4. Introduce statements containing verbs referring to the senses. These statements provide a logical transition from the familiar statements containing the verb *is* (John is running) to statements that do not contain *is* (John runs). They bridge the gap nicely because they can be directly substituted for *is* in any second-order statement involving attributes. "This wood is rough," for instance, can become "This wood *feels* rough" without changing the primary questions and answers implied by the statement.

a. Present statements for familiar polar concepts, especially those that deal with the sense verbs *feel, smell, taste,* and *sound.* Begin with the familiar statement that describes the object. "This marble is heavy." "This room is dark." "His voice is loud." "This pie is good." "This pan is hot."

b. Rephrase each statement, using the appropriate verb of the senses. "This marble is heavy. This marble *feels* heavy." "This room is dark. This room *looks* dark." "His voice is loud. His voice *sounds* loud."

"This pie is good. This pie *tastes* good." "This pan is hot. This pan *feels* hot." Have the children repeat the new statements several times.

c. In defining each verb, show that it can be substituted for *is*. Place a rock or other relatively heavy object in the child's hand and produce the appropriate statement. "This rock *feels* heavy." Give the child a light rock and say "This rock *does not feel* heavy." Use the same substitution technique to define the other verbs of the senses. "This room looks light. [Turn light off.] This room does not look light." "This record sounds loud. [Turn volume down.] This record does not sound loud." "This flower smells good. [Offer wax flower.] This flower does not smell good."

d. Introduce the *does* question. This question is the counterpart of the *is* question, but it is more difficult because the pieces of the question do not tie together with the statement as nicely as the pieces of the *is* question do.

Is	*Does*
This hat is red.	This hat looks red.
Is this hat red?	*Does* this hat *look* red?
Yes, this hat is red.	Yes, this hat looks red.

e. The verbs of the senses should be differentiated from each other in the different kinds of experience they describe. "Does this hat *sound* red? . . . No, this hat does not *sound* red; this hat *looks* red. Does this hat *smell* red? . . . [Etc.]" These distinctions may be further dramatized by objects that elicit contradictory sense impressions—things that look heavy but feel light or vice versa, that look hard but feel soft, that smell good but taste bad, etc.

f. Introduce plural statements and questions for the various verbs of the senses. These involve a new word, *do,* but no new problems. "These rocks feel heavy. *Do* these rocks feel heavy? . . . Yes, these rocks *do* feel heavy." "These trucks sound loud. Do the trucks sound loud? . . . Yes, the trucks *do* sound loud."

5. Introduce the past-tense statement containing *was*.

a. For the initial demonstration, present three objects—an animal made of modeling clay, an inflated balloon, and a red triangle drawn on the chalkboard.

b. Provide the appropriate statements. "This is a horse." "This balloon is big." "This triangle is red."

c. Squash the horse, deflate the balloon, and color the interior of the triangle white. Provide the appropriate *not* statements. "This is *not* a horse." "This balloon is *not* big." "This triangle is *not* red."

d. Present the past-tense statements, which are identical to the original statements *except for the verb.* "This *was* a horse." "This balloon *was* big." "This triangle *was* red."

e. Repeat the procedure with various examples, such as a figure on the chalkboard that starts out as a minus sign or letter *n* and then becomes a plus sign or letter *h*. The presentation should be so pointed that the children appreciate the fact that the present tense statement (This is a minus sign) *must become false* (This is *not* a minus sign) *before the past tense statement* (This was a minus sign) *can be true.* The presentation suggested above is designed to lead the children to this awareness.

f. Introduce the plural past-tense statements. Conduct the demonstration by referring to a series of squares on the chalkboard. "These squares are white." Change the color of the squares from white to red. Provide the *not* statement. "These squares are *not* white." Then provide the past-tense statement. "These squares *were* white."

g. Introduce past-tense variations of intransitive-verb statements. Have a member of the class stand. Ask "What is Tyrone doing? . . . Tyrone is standing." Instruct the child to sit down. Ask the question "Is Tyrone standing? . . . No, Tyrone is not standing." Ask the *was* question. "Was Tyrone standing? . . . Yes, Tyrone *was* standing." Repeat this kind of task often, introducing plural variations.

6. Introduce the past-tense statement containing verbs of the senses.

a. Review the progressive statements. "This triangle is red." "This triangle is not red." "This triangle was red."

b. Repeat the presentation, this time using the verb of the sense, *look.* "This triangle looks red." "This triangle does not look red." "This triangle *looked* red." This demonstartion points out that the word *looked* functions precisely as the word *was.* Both denote past action.

c. Present examples involving different objects. Confine the verbs to *look, smell, sound,* and *taste.* Since the past tense of *feel* is *felt* (not feeled), the introduction of this ·verb may confuse the children and obscure the general convention of placing the *ed* (or *tt* as in *looked*) sound after the verb.

d. After the children are able to handle the past tense of verbs of the senses, introduce variations with *intransitive verbs.*

(1) Present the statement series. "Harold is walking." "Harold is not walking." "Harold was walking."

(2) Introduce the equivalent past-tense statement. "Harold *walked.*" Explain "This is another way of saying Harold was walking. Harold walk*ed.*"

(3) Introduce the *what did* question. "What did Harold do?" Answer it. "Harold *walked.*" Have the children repeat the statement and pay special attention to the *ed* ending.

(4) Present two-question statements involving intransitive verbs and transitive verb statements. "This squirrel jumped *from the tree.*

What did the squirrel do? . . . From where did the squirrel jump?"
"Tommy pushed *the door*. What did Tommy do? . . . What did Tommy
push?" "They stamped *their feet*. What did they do? . . . What did they
stamp?"

Pronouns

Exercises with pronouns are not so crucial as many of the previous
exercises; however, they acquaint the children with some of the more
arbitrary conventions of language and perhaps help them develop a dialect that sounds more socially acceptable.

1. Define *I* and *you* through structured exchanges. Have the children
describe your action after you describe it. "Look. I made a four on the
board. What did I do?" (You made a four on the board.) These statements should be phrased in the *simple past tense*—not "I was making
a four."

2. Define *we* as the plural of *I*.

a. Walk across the room alone. Describe the action. "I walked
across the room." Ask "What did I do?" (You walked across the room.)

b. Walk across the room holding the hand of a child. *"We* walked
across the room. What did we do?"

c. Introduce a variety of similar past-tense action statements.

3. Define *he, she,* and *it* as substitute words for names of males, fe-
males, and things.

a. Assemble a series of at least ten pictures or objects that can be
classified as male, female, and thing.

b. Identify each object in the series and describe it in some way.
"This is a boy. This boy is running." "This is a block. This block is blue."

c. Rephrase the second statement in the pair, substituting the appropriate pronoun for the name. "This boy is running. *He* is running."
"This block is blue. *It* is blue." Have the children repeat the pronoun
statements.

d. Present a quick rule for using each pronoun. "If it is a man (or
boy), it is a *he*." "If it is a woman (or girl), it is a *she*." "If it is not a *he*
or *she*, it is an *it*."

e. Play a game in which you point to an object and the children
identify it by using the word *he, she,* or *it*. The objects should be presented rapid-fire.

f. Play a game in which the children rephrase statements presented
by you. "Harold is wearing a blue shirt. Say it another way." (*He* is wearing a blue shirt.) "The ball is big. Say it another way." (*It is big*.)

4. Define *they* as the plural of he-she-it.

a. Group a boy, a girl, and a chair together in a corner of the room.

Produce the singular statements about each object. "Tyrone is in the corner. Linda is in the corner. This chair is in the corner."

b. Produce the pronoun statement for each object (pointing to the object under consideration). "He is in the corner. She is in the corner. It is in the corner."

c. Produce the plural statement, embracing all three objects. *"They are in the corner."*

d. Introduce different combinations—one boy and one chair, two girls, three boys and a girl, three chairs, etc. Demonstrate that so long as more than one object is being considered, the word *they* applies.

5. Introduce statements that contain a pronoun and describe an action. Although the children are familiar with some of the statements in the series below, there are some that are irregular and have been withheld for this reason. The irregular statements (those that have not been covered by the statement patterns previously studied) are italic.

I am jumping.	I was jumping.
You are jumping.	*You were jumping.*
He (she, it) is jumping.	He (she, it) was jumping.
We are jumping.	We were jumping.
They are jumping.	They were jumping.

a. Engage in an action such as clapping and ask "What am I doing?"

b. After the children indicate "You are clapping" (perhaps with some prompting), stop clapping and ask "Am I clapping?" (No, you are not clapping.) *"Was I clapping?"* (Yes, you *were* clapping.) The exchange is difficult because of the unfamiliar connections between "I *am*—you *are*" and "I *was*—you *were*." The connections are best taught in a total conversational exchange such as suggested here.

c. Introduce variations of the exchange. Separate the boys and girls into two groups. Have one group describe an action in which they are engaged. "We are sitting." Have the other group phrase the statement from their viewpoint. "They are sitting." Have the first group stand up and say "We are not sitting. We were sitting." The second group then rephrases this statement pair. "They are not sitting. They were sitting." Many interesting variations of this task can be introduced.

d. Instruct one person or a group to carry out several actions simultaneously and to describe the action using *and*. "I am sitting and smiling and clapping." The other children rephrase the statement. "She is sitting and smiling and clapping." In the usual manner, the action is suspended, and the *not* statement and past-tense statements follow. Both of these are rephrased by the other children. "I was sitting and smiling and clapping." "She was sitting and smiling and clapping." The other children can also "Tell her—*talk to her* and tell her what she was doing." (*You* were sitting and smiling and clapping.)

6. Introduce possessive pronouns in a manner similar to that described in step 5-*d*.

a. Form two groups of children, one sitting and one standing.

b. Have each group make a statement about what they are doing. "We are sitting." "We are standing."

c. Have the first group describe some possession common to all of them. First group: "Our chairs are red." Teacher: "Whose chairs are red?" First group: "*Our* chairs are red." Second group: "*Their* chairs are red."

d. Use a similar two-group exchange to define *his, her,* and *my*. Single child: "My shoes are red." Teacher: "Whose shoes are red?" Other children: "*Her* shoes are red." Different children can take turns in producing the *my* statement.

Expanded Polar Concepts

Sometimes we do not consider polar elements as strict "opposites." We may, for example, speak of something that is bigger than something else. By referring to the object in this manner, we are implying that there is a continuum of bigness (along which objects are arranged) rather than simply a category, *big,* to which an object either does or does not belong. An understanding of these "expanded polar classes" is important to logical thinking.

1. Present three squares of different sizes on the board, arranged in order of increasing size.

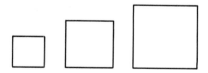

2. At first, limit the presentation to a consideration of bigness.

a. Point to the right square and indicate "This square is the biggest. Say it."

b. Ask the question "How do I know it is the biggest? . . . Because it is bigger than this one [middle square] and bigger than this one [left square]."

c. Introduce a fourth square, bigger than any of the others. Ask "Now which is the biggest? . . . This one is the biggest. Why? . . . Because it is bigger than this one, and bigger than this one, and bigger than this one."

d. Erase all but the smallest square and draw two new squares smaller than it. "Now which one is the biggest? . . . Why?"

3. After the children have caught onto the idea that the *biggest* square is the one about which one can say "It is bigger than this one, and this one, [etc.]," present the concept *littlest* in the same way *biggest* was presented. "This one is the littlest. How do I know? . . . Because it is littler than this one and littler than this one." Through this exercise, the children will learn that the familiar words *big* and *little* are slightly changed to *biggest* and *littlest* to *apply to the extreme examples* (which is not an entirely new concept for the children). The middle members of the series, however, remain relatively undefined.

4. Adopt the procedure outlined for *biggest* to define *hottest-coldest, heaviest-lightest, fattest-skinniest, fastest-slowest,* and perhaps *lightest-darkest* and *loudest-quietest.* In each case, introduce three objects from which the children identify the extremes as hottest-coldest, etc. Introduce additional objects to demonstrate that such words as *hottest* do not belong to a particular pan or a particular ball bearing but are arrived at by comparing the members of a group. The word attaches to different members of the group as the composition of the group changes. The object that may have been the coldest may become the hottest in a different group. As the children become familiar with this point, the presentation can be made more verbal.

5. Have the children imagine extremes of bigness, fatness, and length. "I want you to think about the biggest dog you ever saw." Indicate with the hands something the size of a horse. "Was it this big?" Indicate progressively smaller sizes—"Was it this big? . . . Was it this big?"—until a reasonable size is reached. Repeat for littlest dog and biggest cat, rat, book, and bottle; fattest man, woman, sandwich, and dog; longest pencil, knife, hair, and cat's tail.

6. Classify all the members of the group. The preceding exercise teaches the children that if something is the biggest, it is possible to say about that object "This tree is bigger than _____" and to complete the statement by referring to *any* other object in the group. However, the members of the group that are not at the extremes are not bigger than *all* other members or smaller than *all* other members. Rather, they are bigger than some and smaller than others. To teach this notion:

    a. Present three squares in order of increasing size from left to right. Have the children identify the extremes as *biggest* and *smallest.*

    b. Refer to the middle square and ask "What about this square? Is it the biggest? . . . No. Is it the smallest? . . . No. It is not the biggest, and it is not the smallest."

    c. Explain that it is possible to figure out what the middle square is by asking the right questions. Point to it and say "Take a good look at it and think while I talk. Is this square bigger than this square? . . . Yes, it is bigger than this square." Point again to the middle square and ask if it is bigger than the biggest square. "No, it is not bigger than this square." Limit the presentation to one dimension, in this case *bigness.*

d. Summarize with the statement "This square [the middle square] is bigger than this square and *not* bigger than this square."

e. Introduce three or four new squares into the group so that the size progression from left to right is still maintained. Demonstrate that by using the procedure outlined above, it is possible to produce the proper statements about *any member of the group.* Point to one of the squares and make the point that one can find out about this square by asking the proper questions. Point to the square and say "This square is bigger than" and complete the statement by pointing in turn to each of the other squares. After all of the squares have been considered in this manner, produce the summary statement, which would be on the order of "This square is bigger than this square and this square; this square is *not bigger* than this square, this square, this square, and this square."

f. Present exercises involving the various polar concepts dealt with in step 4 above—hotness, fatness, lightness, etc.

g. After the children have mastered the preceding tasks, introduce the other polar dimension—smallness, coldness, skinniness, etc., using the same question pattern to formulate the appropriate statement for each object. "Is this square smaller than this square? . . . This square? . . . This square?"

h. Have the children arrange objects using a verbal approach. Present six rectangular cards of different sizes. Do not present the cards in the usual order of increasing size. Instead lay them out randomly. Explain "I want to put these cards in order. *I start with any card.* Then I put the smaller ones on this side [left] and the bigger ones on this side [right]." Pick up all the cards. Lay down a middle-sized card and mark it with an *X*. Hold each card that is to be fitted into the series next to the card with an *X* and say *about the new card* "This card is what? . . . Smaller than this [*X* card]. So where does it go? . . . On the smaller side [left]." The process is continued until all of the cards are in their proper order. A card is properly positioned when it is possible to say about it "This card is bigger than this card [the card to the left] and smaller than this card [the one to the right]."

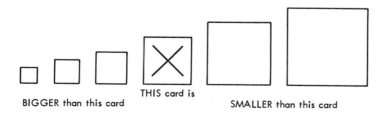

THIS card is

BIGGER than this card   SMALLER than this card

i. Present variations of this task. Cards ranging in color from red to white can be introduced and treated in the same way as cards of different sizes. A card is in place when it is "Redder than this [left] card and whiter than this [right] card."

5. Expand the concept of *before-after*. The concept has been previously presented as a polar concept; however, it can be expanded in much the same way as any of the other polar concepts discussed above. Because *before-after* is a comparison according to time or position and not strictly according to any physical characteristics, the basic presentation must be modified somewhat.

a. Position two children under an arrow that points to the right (see page 154). Review the *before* statements. "Tyrone is before Harold. Harold is not before Tyrone."

b. Introduce a third child to the right (Tyrone, Harold, Tommy) and have the children produce the *before* statement about the child at the *left*. "What can I say about Tyrone? . . . Tyrone is before Harold. Is Tyrone before Tommy? . . . Yes, Tyrone is also before Tommy." Refer to the middle child. "What can I say about Harold? . . . Harold is before Tommy. Is Harold before Tyrone? . . . No, Harold is not before Tyrone." Refer to the last child. "What can I say about Tommy? . . . Tommy is not before Tyrone. Tommy is not before Harold."

c. Review the concept *after* and introduce it into the present task framework. Position three children under the arrow and make two *after* statements about each child. "Linda is after Debby. Linda is not after Tommy. Tommy is after Linda. Tommy is after Linda and Debby." If the children become confused, remind them of the relationship between *before* and *after*. "Ask yourself 'Is Linda before Debby?' She is not before. So she is after."

d. Draw an arrow pointing right on the board. On its shaft write the numbers 1, 2, 3, 4, 5, 6, 7, in that order. Remind the children of the instructions indicated by the arrow. "Remember, the arrow tells me to go this way, starting with one and going through seven." Refer to the first number and ask "What do we know about this number? It is before two. It is before three. It is before four. It is before five. [Etc.] After all of the possible *before* statements have been produced, ask "Can you find a number that one is *not* before? . . . No, one is before all of these other numbers."

e. Proceed to the other numbers on the arrow shaft, producing first the *before* statements and then the *after* statements. This exercise demonstrates the similarity between *before-after* and other expanded polar concepts. The numbers 1 and 7 are the extremes, the beforest and the afterest. The members in the middle of the series are relatively before and after.

f. Repeat the basic exercise, using, instead of numbers, letters, stick figures (each of which can be identified with a different name, such as *house, dog, man, boy*), etc.

g. Present the arrow with the numbers on the shaft and introduce a more difficult task, that of limiting statements to two members of the group. Point to two numbers that are next to each other, such as 3 and 4, and say "I want to know about these numbers." Call attention to the order in which the numbers are introduced when one proceeds in the direction indicated by the arrow. "Listen. *Three, four.*" Have the children repeat the numbers in that order; then introduce a convention for formulating the statement. Repeat the numbers slowly and touch them on the line as each is said. "Three, four. I am going with the arrow, so three is before four." Quite a few demonstrations of the operation may be necessary. The point is not an easy one.

h. Present the concept *after* by proceeding through the series in the direction contrary to that shown by the arrow. "Three, two. I am not going with the arrow. So three is *not before* two. Three is *after* two." Each problem should be presented unhurriedly, and the first statement should always be in terms of *before*. If the numbers are presented in the order indicated by the arrow, the first number is *before* the second number. If the order is not in the direction of the arrow, the first number is *not before* the second number. Therefore, the first number is *after* the second number.

i. Present the arrow with numbers from 1 through 7 in order from left to right. Beneath the numbers print the names of the days in the week, beginning with Monday under 1 and ending with Sunday under 7. Teach the order of the days in the week by reciting the series at the beginning and end of the language session for a week or more. After the children have become fairly familiar with the series, introduce tasks similar to those above. Identify two adjacent days, "Thursday, Friday," touching each name as it is said; then, call attention to the direction of the names. "I'm going with the arrow, so Thursday is before Friday."

j. For the next series of tasks, require the children to make up the statement. Merely select the name of a day and say "Tell me about Thursday." Touch the name Thursday and say "Thursday. What comes next if we follow the arrow? . . . Friday. Thursday, Friday. So Thursday is before Friday." Demonstrate the *after* statement in a similar manner. Returning to Thursday, say "Thursday. What happens if I go the way the arrow says not to go? . . . Wednesday. Thursday, Wednesday. Thursday is *not before* Wednesday (because I'm not going the way the arrow says). Thursday is *after* Wednesday."

k. Repeat the approach outlined to teach the relation of the months in the year. Make permanent "arrow" charts which display the days of the week and months of the year.

l. Introduce the songs *There are Twelve Months in the Year* and *Here We Go Round the Mulberry Bush* in the music period. The introduction of these songs should not necessarily be delayed until the children are studying *before-after* as expanded polars. The more familiar the children are with the order of the days and months, the more smoothly the present tasks will proceed.

Polar Changes

Sometimes the most intuitively obvious tasks are among the most difficult for children who are not broadly grounded in the logic of language. An example of such an intuitively obvious problem is one in which a person leaves a white ball in a room with a freshly painted floor. Upon returning, he discovers that the ball is covered with wet paint. He quickly concludes that the ball rolled across the freshly painted floor. To check out his conclusion, he scans the floor for the track the ball must have left. The reasoning process is quite simple—or at least so it seems. Actually, however, it involves three steps, each of which depends on the possession of language skills that culturally deprived children are unlikely to possess. Consequently, culturally deprived children typically find themselves completely baffled by such a problem—unable to begin solving it.

The three major steps, which the sophisticated adult takes so quickly and naturally that he may be unaware of them, are:

1. Construct two sets of statements, one set describing the possible outcomes and one set describing the possible causes. Each of these is a polar set; that is, there are only two possible outcomes and two possible causes (excluding extraneous possibilities that would render the problem unsolvable), and these are opposites. Condition a = not-b. Condition not-a = b.

Possible outcomes:

a. The ball turned blue.   b. The ball remained white.

Possible causes:

a. The ball rolled across the floor.   b. The ball did not roll across the floor.

2. Establish some connection between the two sets of statements. There is nothing in the two sets of statements themselves that tells the solver how they are connected. It may be that "The ball turned blue" is connected with "The ball did not roll across the floor," or it may be that either cause can lead to either outcome, in which case the problem cannot be solved. Some appeal to the physical world is required. Observation of the physical world discloses that the four statements above describe two sets of circumstances associated with the ball and the floor: one set in which nothing happens and the other in which something does happen. Two of the statements are consistent with the nothing-happened circumstances: "The ball remained white" and "The ball did not roll across the floor." The other two statements are consistent with the something-

happened circumstances: "The ball turned blue" and "The ball rolled across the floor." By grouping the statements according to the circumstances with which they are associated, we see that both a statements go together and both b statements go together.

Something happened:	*Nothing happened:*
a. The ball turned blue.	b. The ball remained white.
a. The ball rolled across the floor.	b. The ball did not roll across the floor.

Since the a statements go together, they are in a sense equivalent; it is therefore possible to substitute one a statement for another (and one b statement for another). Through this substitution process, the outcome statements a and b are connected with the causal statements a and b.

3. Use substitution to proceed from one set of statements to the other and thereby solve the problem. According to the rules for deduction with polar statements (as taught in this chapter), one can conclude "If the ball did not remain white, the ball turned blue." But now, taking advantage of the equivalence established in step 2, the solver can substitute "The ball rolled across the floor" for "The ball turned blue" and arrive at the deduction "If the ball did not remain white, the ball rolled across the floor." In the same way, he can take any possible outcome statement and, by using substitution, arrive at a valid causal statement.

Consider the demands put upon language abilities by this seemingly simple task: the solver must be able to *construct* exhaustive sets of statements to cover all possible outcomes and causes; from the statements, he must be able to construct combinations of statements that are compatible with physical reality; and, finally, he must be able to substitute equivalent statements for one another freely and accurately. Is it any wonder that children who are naïve in basic language skills have trouble with a problem that requires them to see the supposedly obvious fact that "If the ball remained white, it did not roll across the floor"?

The double-H model.

The double-H provides a good introduction to polar change reasoning because it is simple and because it shows the nature of the different changes very neatly. The double-H is simply an H with two horizontal bars. The pair of "opposites" from which the conclusions of change follow are:

Possible outcomes:

a. The top line is longer.   b. The top line is shorter.

Possible causes:

a. The bottom line is shorter.   b. The bottom line is longer.

1. Draw a double-H on the board, no bigger than a chalkboard eraser. Identify the figure. "This is a double-H. We're going to use it to play thinking games."

2. Demonstrate the four primary *if-thens*, in each case beginning with the double-H and changing only one horizontal line, making it longer or shorter. The four *if-thens* implied in the pattern of opposites are thereby demonstrated.

   a. "If the top line is longer, what can I say about the bottom line? . . . It's shorter."

   b. "If the top line is shorter, what can I say about the bottom line? . . . It's longer."

   c. "If the bottom line is longer, what can I say about the top line? . . . It's shorter."

   d. "If the bottom line is shorter, what can I say about the top line? . . . It's longer."

Demonstrate each *if-then* by *changing the line that is mentioned first.*
"If the bottom line is longer [make the bottom line longer], the top line
is shorter."

3. After the statements of change have been demonstrated, introduce
a game in which conclusions about changes can be drawn without looking at the model.

a. Present a double-H and instruct the children to close their eyes
while a horizontal line is changed on the double-H.

b. Cover the double-H with an eraser and instruct the children
to open their eyes.

c. *Tell them which line has been changed and the nature of the
change. Ask them about the other line.* "The top line is now shorter.
What can you say about the bottom line? . . . Yes, it's longer."

d. Uncover the double-H and verify the conclusion, pointing out
that the children had reached it without seeing the model. "See how
well you can think. You don't even have to look at the double-H to figure
out the answer."

e. Present a variety of problems similar to the one outlined here.

4. Introduce a variation of step 3 in which the children are required
to inspect the model and formulate part of the information necessary
to draw a firm conclusion.

a. Show the children a double-H and say "Now close your eyes.
I'm going to do something to one of these lines, but I'm not going to
tell you what I do. You'll have to figure it out." Erase part of the bottom
line, and then cover it with the eraser so that the children can still see
the top line.

b. Provide information about the nature of the change as it relates
to the visible line. "Look at the top line. Now, here's what you can say
about it. *The top line is longer.* What do you know about the bottom
line?"

c. After the children indicate that the bottom line is shorter, ask "Well, what did I do? . . . Did I make the top line longer or the bottom line shorter?" At first, the children may have trouble with this question. The idea can be rephrased by referring to the top line and asking "Did I do anything to this line? . . . No. So I must have done something to the other line. What happened to the other line? . . . Remember, it's shorter. So I must have made it shorter." After the children have worked with a few examples, they will grasp the idea that the line which is not visible is the one that has changed. They will then begin to handle these deductions quickly.

d. Uncover the double-H and show that the conclusion is sound, pointing out again that the children had "figured it out."

5. Introduce an *or* variation.

a. Change one line of the model and cover the entire model with an eraser.

b. Provide information about the nature of the change, but *do not indicate which line has been changed.* "The top line is shorter." After the children indicate that the bottom line is longer, ask "Well, what did I do? . . . Did I make the top line shorter or did I make the bottom line longer? . . . *YOU DON'T KNOW.* Maybe I made the top line shorter. Maybe I made the bottom line longer." (In step 4 above, the conclusion about which line had been changed could be reached by inspecting the model. In the present problem, however, no part of the model is visible.)

c. Have the children repeat the *or* statement. "You made the top line shorter *or* the bottom line longer."

d. Provide the missing information. "I changed the top line. What did I do?" (You made it shorter.)

e. Introduce a variation of the problem after the children are reasonably adept at handling examples like the one described above. Instead of indicating which line has been changed, indicate which line has *not* been changed. "I *did not change the bottom line.*" The children conclude "You changed the top line. The top line is shorter. So you made the top line shorter."

f. Make the presentation less detailed and mechanical after the children have worked many problems and have become more "intuitive" in their approach. The condensed presentation should consist of only a few key statements. "The top line is shorter." (So the bottom line is longer.) "Well, what did I do?" (You made the top line shorter *or* the bottom line longer.) "I did not change the bottom line." (You changed the top line. You made the top line shorter.) "Very good. See? That's just what I did."

Warm water.

This series of problems extends the *or* statements presented in connection with the double-H. The problems are generated from the following pairing of opposites:

Possible outcomes:

a. The water from the faucet got colder.

b. The water from the faucet got hotter.

Possible causes:

a. The hot water was turned down, or the cold water was turned up.

b. The hot water was turned up, or the cold water was turned down.

1. Demonstrate the *if-thens* with a mixer faucet, which is adjusted so that a stream of moderately warm water is being discharged. Point out which handle controls the hot water and which the cold water. Also show what is meant by "turning the water *up* and *down.*" "When I turn the cold water *up,* more cold water comes out. See?" When making the water hotter, be very careful to avoid making it too hot.

a. "How can I make this warm water hotter? . . . I can turn the hot water up like this, or [return to the original warm discharge] I can turn the cold water *down.* Watch."

b. "If I turn the hot water up or turn the cold water down, what will happen? . . . The water will get hotter."

c. "How can I make this warm water colder? . . . By turning the cold water up or the hot water down."

d. "If I turn the cold water up or the hot water down, what will happen? . . . The water will get _____."

2. Present tasks which require the children to provide the *or* statement. "If the water got colder, what did I do?" (You turned the cold up or turned the hot down.) "If the water got hotter what did I do?" (You turned the hot water up or the cold water down.)

3. Introduce the information needed to draw a firm conclusion, as either an affirmative or a *not* statement. "The water got colder. What did I do? . . . Yes, I either turned up the cold or turned down the hot. Now listen big. I did not touch the hot-water handle. (You touched the cold-water handle; so you turned the cold water up.)

The see-saw.

A series similar to the warm-water series can be presented in connection with a see-saw.

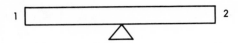

1. Work from a diagram on the board.

2. Present the basic *if-thens*. These are generated from the conditions.

Possible outcomes:

a. Side one goes down.   b. Side one goes up.

Possible causes:

a. Side one is pushed down, or   b. Side one is pushed up, or side
side two is pushed up.   two is pushed down.

    a. "If side one goes down, I pushed down side one *or* pushed up on side two."

    b. "If I push down on side one or up on side two, what happens to side one? . . . It goes down."

3. Present the *or* tasks and give the information needed to draw a conclusion in the manner outlined for the warm-water series.

The silly room.

This is a room with a glass divider in the middle, a pocket on either side, and a freshly painted floor. The ball, which is placed in the pocket

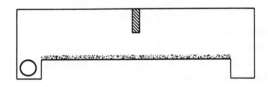

on the left side of the room can go to the other pocket, either by crashing through the glass or by rolling across the freshly painted floor under the divider. In either case, a clue will be left. If the ball breaks the glass, broken glass will be found on the *right side* of the glass divider.

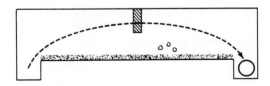

If the ball rolls through the fresh paint (under the glass), the ball will be covered with paint.

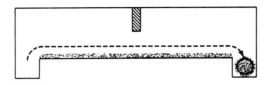

1. Draw the silly room on the chalkboard (using red chalk for the floor) and show the two possible ways the ball can move from one side to the other. Present the *if-thens*. These are generated from *two* sets of conditions, one dealing with the glass, the other dealing with the fresh paint.

Possible outcomes:

a. The broken glass goes this way →

b. The broken glass goes this way ←

Possible causes:

a. The ball goes through the glass this way →

b. The ball goes through the glass this way ←

and

Possible outcomes:

a. The ball turns red.

b. The ball remains white.

Possible causes:

a. The ball goes through the paint.

b. The ball does not go through the paint.

Stress the *if-thens* that go from outcome to cause. "If the glass went this way [→], what do we know about the ball? . . . It went this way, too [→]." "If the ball is covered with red paint, what do we know? . . . The ball went through the wet paint."

2. Present the basic problem. "I put the ball over here [left pocket], and I go out of the room. While I'm gone, somebody comes into the room. I don't know what he does, but when I come back, the ball is over

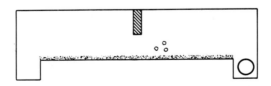

on this side [right], and look on the floor—broken glass. Notice also that there is no red paint on the ball." Call attention to the position of the broken glass. "Which way did the glass go? . . . It started out up here [We're looking at the glass from the side], and it went this way. What's

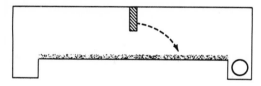

the rule? If the glass goes this way, the _____." Conclude "So the guy that came into the room threw the ball through the glass. We didn't see him do it, but we figured it out." Present a similar problem in which the ball moves from the left to the right pocket and is covered with red paint. "What's this on the ball? . . . And what's the rule about red paint? . . . If the ball turns red, the ball _____."

3. Present various two-step problems. For example, upon returning to the room, one finds the ball in the left pocket where it was originally, but it is covered with red paint, and there is broken glass on the left side of the glass plate.

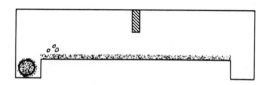

   a. Call attention to the clues. "This room is not the same. What's different? . . . Was there glass on the floor here? . . . Was that ball red when I went out of the room?

   b. Ask leading questions about the broken glass and the ball. "Well, where is the glass? . . . That tells you something. That tells you which way the glass went. Now you know which way the ball went through the glass. But how did the ball get over there in the first place? . . . Look at the ball. It tells a story. Yes, it rolled through the paint."

   c. Draw arrows to show what happened.

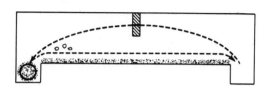

   d. Introduce problems in which broken glass is on both sides of the plate and the ball is not painted, broken glass is on neither side of the plate and the ball is painted, and broken glass is on one side of the plate and the ball is painted.

Other problems.

Various other problems can be introduced. Among the favorites are:

1. "A chicken was stolen from the chicken coop. We don't know whether a man or a wolf took the chicken, but outside, in the snow we see these tracks."

2. "We see footprints of a fox and a man in the snow. The fox prints are sometimes on top of the man's prints. Who was doing the chasing?" (If a print is on top, the top print came *after* the other one.)

3. "A man's footprints go into the house and come out again. When they come out, they are deeper than they were when he went in. Why?" (If you are heavier, you make deeper prints.)

4. "A pie is missing, shortly before supper, and everybody is hungry at suppertime except Tyrone." (If you eat a whole pie before supper, you won't be hungry at supper time.)

5. "We come home from school and find a window of our house broken and a stone lying inside, on the floor, in the middle of broken glass. What happened? . . . What's the rule about broken glass?"

Also, action pictures can be presented, with emphasis on the rules of outcome and cause.

Summary

The advanced language program outlined in this chapter extended the basic language skills that were taught through the first-order and second-order statement forms. The first extension had to do with refinements in grouping things according to what is known and not known about them. The five-element model was introduced to simplify these tasks and make the basis for classification as obvious as possible in teaching the concepts, *and, only, or, some, all,* and *if-then.* The model served to demonstrate the "proofs" and contradictions associated with these concepts. It also helped establish the basis for the *I don't know* response, which is so crucial in processing problems that involve more than one possible condition.

Next, new verbs were systematically introduced—first, intransitive verbs with *is* (He is walking); then, transitive verbs with *is* (The boy is throwing stones); then, verbs of the senses without *is* (This hat looks red); then, past-tense verbs with *was* (He was walking); finally, action **verbs** without *is* (He walked).

Exercises were presented to clarify the use of pronouns and to expand polar opposites—from hot-cold to coldest, warmer, warmest, hotter, hottest. The concept *before-after* was also expanded to a nonpolar concept.

The final series of tasks in the chapter were concerned with polar changes. It was pointed out that the seemingly obvious nature of situations involving polar changes is illusory. The process of reasoning in a polar change situation is circumscribed by a strange set of supposed equivalences between the conditions of change and the possible outcomes. Polar-change problems were presented in such a way that these equivalences were stated as concisely as possible. The series of polar-change problems presented represent the culmination of the language program, because they require integration of the various language skills outlined in both this chapter and Chapter 7.

music for
the preschool

9

Music can be used as a very effective language builder. Songs present statements; songs usually provide a great deal of repetition of these statements; and songs have a distinctive rhythm, which means that the statements are made easier for the child to process. The tempo of most songs is slow enough that the parts of the statement are distinct and that the child is able to become aware of words and their proper pronunciation.

All songs provide good exercise for the disadvantaged child; however, some songs are better than others. In the preschool, tasks must be measured by their relative educational value. Songs are therefore judged according to how much they contribute to the language development of the child. Do they give him practice in reciting archaic phrases and learning rather trivial routines, or do they reinforce the more important language skills? To apply the criterion of educational value to songs is not to say that the music period should become a grim exercise. The child should enjoy music. If he does not, its intrinsic motivating value will be lost.

The songs presented on the following pages provide the child with practice in many language skills—naming objects, translating statements into actions, classifying, reversing important statement elements, forming rhymes, counting, handling plurals, and making up verses. Many of the songs are "rewrites"—new words attached to such familiar tunes as *The Old Grey Mare* and *Twinkle Twinkle, Little Star.* Others, such as *Ten Little Indians,* remain unchanged.

The Music Period

The music period should last 15 or 20 minutes. It should neither drag nor become frustratingly long. The teacher who directs activities during the period should probably be someone other than the piano accompanist, unless the accompanist is experienced in directing from the piano. Ideally, the director should be seated in a position that allows her to watch the children throughout the song and enlist their interest.

1. Present a variety of songs during each period—perhaps one that

requires the children to act something out, another that involves a newly-learned skill such as counting, and another that allows the children to express themselves creatively by making up verses.

2. Set a fast pace. When a song is finished, begin the next without delay. Too many interruptions should not be allowed, and the practice of letting children select songs should not be adopted. Allow the children to choose one song during the period but not all of them. They should understand that, as a rule, the teacher selects the songs.

3. Maintain a rotation schedule. When a new song is introduced, it should be sung every day for perhaps a week or until the children either begin to master it or show signs of becoming bored with it. (Usually the boredom will occur before the song is learned—during the first two or three exposures.) After the introduction period, the song should be presented perhaps once a week. If the children do not like a particular song and if their feelings do not seem to stem from an inability to handle the operations presented, the song should be dropped from the regular schedule and should be tried several weeks later. On the other hand, if a song is exceedingly popular with the children, it should be sung more often than less popular songs.

4. Ask questions dealing with the statements of each song. The statements contained in a song are merely rote elements unless the children are shown that the statements can be pulled out of the song and treated as statements of everyday language. Therefore, preface each song with a series of questions. If the song has to do with riding on a horse to nursery school, ask "What are we riding on? . . . And where are we going?" Through such questions, the promise of the song as a language builder is fulfilled.

5. Adjust the level of the music period to the level of the children's ability. Songs that involve sophisticated statements should not be introduced when the children are grappling with the basics of language. Basic language songs should be presented at this time. As the children improve in language skills, these basic songs should be dropped from the rotation schedule in favor of more sophisticated songs. It is as much a mistake to have the children dwell on songs after their educational value has been exhausted as it is to present songs which the children are not equipped to handle.

6. Systematically withdraw cues so that the children learn to initiate the action and the words of a song and not to simply follow your actions. Initially, show the children precisely what to do. Lead them. As the children become familiar with the statements and actions of the song, however, cease to lead and progressively force the children to be independent. Drop out cues, sing less forcefully, and refrain from joining in the actions associated with the song. Unless songs are de-cued in this manner, the children may grow completely dependent. As a result, they

may never learn to produce the statements of the song properly or to initiate the appropriate actions.

7. Require every child to participate during the music period. Require the children to sit in their place, either on the floor or in a chair, pay attention, sing, and carry out any actions that are associated with the song. There should be times during the music period when they can express themselves by making up verses or offering suggestions. Good suggestions should be praised. But do not be led into the trap of supposing that since music is expressive behavior, bars on misbehavior should be lifted. Unless behavioral rules are maintained, the music session will quickly degenerate into a fiasco. The children will tend to perform adequately on songs that are already mastered, but they will probably resist learning new songs.

Clap Your Hands

(Tune: *Hey, Betty Martin*)

Hey every-body, clap your hands, clap your hands,
A G F D C D F C D F C
Hey every-body, clap your hands.
A G F D C A F G
Hey every-body, clap your hands, clap your hands,
A G F D C D F C D F C
Hey every-body, clap your hands.
A G F D C D E F

This song gives the children practice in translating words into actions, and it can be used to create an awareness that the various children in the preschool have names. The song should be introduced during the first or second music period and retained as a daily song for at least two months.

1. Introduce a variety of actions: "Hey everybody, touch your nose [head, hand, ear, leg, arm]"; "Hey everybody, close your eyes"; "Hey everybody, stand up tall"; "Hey everybody, jump up high"; "Hey everybody, turn around [walk around, skip around]"; "Hey everybody, bend your arm."

2. Introduce verses that are directed at one child, giving a statement of their purpose. "We're going to tell Harold Davis what to do. We're going to tell Harold David to stand up tall. Tell him! Hey Harold Davis, stand up tall, stand up tall." These verses can be used to stimulate children to remember their own names. "Okay, who knows his *full name?* If you can tell me your full name, we can sing about you. Debby Warner, good. Let's tell her to close her eyes. Hey, Debby Warner, close your eyes."

London Bridge

Lon-don bridge is fall-ing down, fall-ing down, fall-ing down.
G   A   G   F   E   F   G   D   E   F   E   F   G
Lon-don bridge is fall-ing down; *all fall down.*
G   A   G   F   E   F   G   D   G   E-C
Lon-don bridge is build-ing up [pointing up], build-ing up, build-ing up.
G   A   G   F   E   F   G   D   E   F   E   F   G
Lon-don bridge is build-ing up; *all stand up.*
G   A   G   F   E   F   G   D   G   E-C

There are two important reasons for including this song in the music program: it is a good disciplining song that requires the children to translate words into action and respond on cue; and it reinforces the basic concepts of *down* and *up*. It should not be kept too long in the active song file, however. It is quite useful during the early stages of training, when the children are learning basic language skills and the rules about how to behave in school, but after the first several months, it teaches nothing new and should be dropped.

1. Before beginning the song, ask the children "Which way is down? . . . Good. Which way is up?"

2. Form a circle and walk—*walk*—in a clockwise direction, falling down on cue.

3. Join hands again while kneeling. Sing the second verse and stand up on cue.

Riding in a Car to Nursery School

Rid-ing in a car to nurs-ery school,
E   E   E E   E   E   G# G#   G#
To nurs-ery school, to nurs-ery school.
G# F# F#   F#   F# G# G#   G#
Rid-ing in a car to nurs-ery school,
E   E   E E   E   E   G# G#   G#
I'm a long way from home.
G# G# G# F#   G#   E

This song is valuable because (1) it acquaints the children with the names of different vehicles and places, (2) it gives the children practice in changing the tempo of the song, and (3) it gives the children practice in pretending.

1. Introduce the song early in the preschool year and use it on a fairly regular basis throughout the year.

2. Introduce each verse with questions about the name of the vehicle and its destination. "We are riding in a what? . . . Riding *in a car.* Where are we riding to? . . . Riding a car *to nursery school."*

3. Introduce different vehicles: "Riding on a horse to nursery school [holding reins and bouncing]"; "Riding in a truck to nursery school [bouncing]"; "Riding on a bike to nursery school [holding handle bars and pedaling]."

4. Introduce different destinations: "Riding in a car to the farm"; "Riding in a car down south"; "Riding in a car to Chicago."

5. Introduce different speeds. "Okay, let's ride on a very, very slow old horse. Here we go, sing slow. . . . Now, let's ride a fast race horse. Go."

I'm Going to Sing

I'm go-ing to sing when the teach-er says "Sing."
C   C   C   F   F   F   F   F   A

I'm go-ing to sing when the teach-er says "Sing."
C   C   C   F   F   F   F   F   D-C

I'm go-ing to sing when the teach-er says "Sing."
C   C   C   F   F   F   F   F   A

And think when the teach-er says "Think."
B♭ A   A   A   G   G   F

I'm Going to Sing acquaints the children with statements about what is expected of them in the preschool. It also gives them practice in acting out different types of behavior.

1. Introduce the song early in the year and continue to use it once a week after it has been learned. Add verses to include such activities as clapping, yelling, whispering, etc.: "I'm going to sing when the teacher says 'Sing' "; "I'm going to think when the teacher says 'Think' [touching forehead]"; "I'm going to clap when the teacher says 'Clap' [clapping]"; "I'm going to stand when the teacher says 'Stand' [standing]"; "I'm going to jump when the teacher says 'Jump' [jumping]"; "I'm going to yell when the teacher says 'Yell' [yelling]"; "I'm going to whisper when the teacher says 'Whisper' [whispering]"; "I'm going to sit when the teacher says 'Sit' [sitting]"; (Last line) "And sing when the teacher says 'Sing.' "

2. Ask questions, such as "What are you going to do when the teacher says 'Sing'? . . . Are you going to jump when the teacher says 'Sing'?"

3. Let the children make up verses. As the children become familiar with the rules of the school, they will probably volunteer such verses as "I'm going to walk when the teacher says 'Walk.' "

Skip to My Lou

Cows in the pas-ture; moo, moo, moo.
F#   F# F# D   D   F#   F#   A

Cows in the pas-ture; moo, moo, moo.
E   E   E   C#   C#   E   E   G

Cows in the pas-ture; moo, moo, moo.
F# F# F# D   D   F#   F#   A

Skip to my Lou, my darl-ing.
E   G G   F#   E   D   D

This is a good creative song that is instructional about plural endings (which typically give culturally deprived children trouble).

1. Introduce basic plural verses: "Cows in the pasture; moo, moo, moo"; "Flies in the sugar bowl; shoo, shoo, shoo [gesturing 'shoo' with hand]"; "Pigs in the living room; what'll I do [throwing hands up in despair]?" "Dogs in the bathtub; splash, splash, splash [making pawing motions with hands]"; "Ghosts in the closet; boo, boo, boo [directing *boo* at each other]."

2. Stress the plural endings. "Now we're talking about cow-zzzz. Not cow, but cow-zzzz. Let's make it buzz. . . . Yes, many cows and many moos."

3. Introduce a singular variation of each verse after the plurals have been fairly well mastered: "Cow in the pasture, moo [pause, pause]"; "Fly in the sugar bowl; shoo [pause, pause]"; "Dog in the bathtub; splash [pause, pause]."

4. Mix up singular and plural verses. Initially, hold up one finger and say "Okay, one cow" to indicate a singlar verse. To indicate plural, say "Many cows." Have the children first sing about "One cow," then perhaps "One ghost," and then "Many dogs." After the children have learned to handle the "One cow; many cows" instruction, the cue words *one* and *many* should be omitted. "Listen big—sing about cow-zzzz." The children will probably have trouble with this task at first.

5. Let the children make up verses. The best verses are usually produced in response to specific directions. Instead of asking the children simply to make up a verse, instruct them to make up a verse about flies or cows. "Today we're going to sing a new verse about flies, and you're going to make up the words." In addition to making up verses about dogs, ghosts, pigs, flies, etc., the children can make up verses about the rooms of the house—the living room, the bathroom, the kitchen. "Let's make up verses about the kitchen. What would we find in the kitchen?"

Put Your Finger in the Air

(Tune: *Oats, Peas, Beans, and Barley Grow*)

Put your fin-ger in the air.
E   E   E   D   C   C

Put your fin-ger in the air.
F   F   F   E   D   D

Put your fin-ger in the air.
E   F   G   F   E   F   G
Put your fin-ger in the air.
D   F   E   D   C   C   C

This is an extremely useful song. It is probably not so enjoyable for the children as some of the others, but it can be used to teach a wide range of language skills.

1. Introduce the song early to teach simple action instructions about parts of the body: "Put your finger on your nose [mouth, eye, ear, foot, hand, neck, head, etc.]"; "Put your hand upon your hand"; "Put your foot upon the floor."

2. Later introduce more difficult tasks: "Put your elbows on your knees"; "Put your wrists upon your ankles"; "Put your fists upon your knees"; "Put your hands upon your shoulders."

3. Give exercises in discriminating between singular-plural variations. The instructions in the song are well suited to teach plurals because they provide *no clue other than the ending on the noun to let the children know whether they should put their hand or their hands upon their knees or their knee.* "Close your eyes. Now listen big. Put your handzzz—HAND-ZZZ—upon your knee. Everybody do it. Okay, let's sing about it." Do not expect the more severely deprived children to learn the significance of the plural ending immediately.

4. Use the song to teach right-left discriminations. The children should not be in a circle for right-left exercises, because if they try to do what the person across the circle from them is doing, they will use the wrong hand. The children should line up behind the teacher. The initial right-left verses should mention only one hand—the right: "Put your right hand on the floor"; "Put your right hand on your head"; "Put your right foot out in front." Later the right hand motion can be extended to turning right. This is handled in steps. First the children sing "Put your right hand to the side" and extend their right arm horizontally. Then the children sing "Chase your right hand round and round" and turn to the right. After the children are very secure in the knowledge of their right hand, verses involving the left hand can be introduced.

5. Ask appropriate questions. "Where are you going to put your finger? . . . Which hand are you going to put to the side?"

Ten Little Indians

One lit-tle, two lit-tle, three lit-tle In-di-ans;
F   F   F   F   F   A   C   C   A   A   F
Four lit-tle, five lit-tle, six lit-tle In-di-ans;
G   G   G   G   G   E   G   G   E   E   C
Sev-en lit-tle, eight lit-tle, nine lit-tle In-di-ans;
F   F   F   F   F   F   A   C   C   A   A   F
Ten lit-tle In-di-an boys.
C   Bb   Bb   A   A   G   F

This song helps the children learn the numbers in the counting order. It is also useful in relating the idea of "how many" to counting. And it gives the children practice in performing a rather difficult finger exercise.

1. Introduce the song during the third week of the term, after the children have had practice with easier songs.

2. Preface the singing with a statement and questions. "We're going to sing about ten little Indian boys. What kind of boys? . . . Yes, Indian boys. What kind of Indian boys? . . . Big tall ones? . . . No, little Indian boys. How many little Indian boys? . . . Ten little Indian boys."

3. Have the children hold up the appropriate number of fingers as they sing.

4. Reverse the operation and count backwards after the children have mastered the forward operation. The finger operation is quite difficult in reverse. Also, the children will probably tend to say "One little Indian boys." They should be reminded "One cow—many cows; one ghost—many ghosts; one boy—many boys."

Ten Little Angels

There was one, there were two, there were three lit-tle an-gels;
C   D   F   C   D   F   C   D   F   A   A   G

There were four, there were five, there were six lit-tle an-gels;
C   D   F   C   D   F   C   D   F   A   A   G

There were sev-en, there were eight, there were nine lit-tle an-gels;
C   D   F F   C   D   F   C   D   F   A   A   G

Ten lit-tle an-gels in that band.
A   C A-G   A   F   D   C   F

Oh, wasn't that a band, Sun-day morn-ing, Sun-day morn-ing, Sun-day
A   A   G   A   G   F   A   G   A-G   F   G   F   G-F   G   A   G

morn-ing.
A-G   F

Wasn't that a band, Sun-day morn-ing, Sun-day morn-ing soon.
A   G   A   G   F   A   G   A-G   F   G   G   A   G   F

This counting song gives the children practice in working on a difficult aspect of language—the use of the past-tense verbs *was* and *were*.

1. Have the children say the first line several times before singing, with emphasis on the words *was* and *were*. Typically, deprived children will say "They wu one, they wu two," and it will take them some time to say "There were." Pronunciation should be exaggerated.

2. Ask questions about the song. Use the same questions presented for *Ten Little Indians*—questions about who, what kind, and how many. "Are we going to sing about a hundred angels? . . . No? *How many* angels are we going to sing about?"

3. Have the children hold up fingers as they sing.

4. Later, introduce counting backwards. In counting backwards, the

children may make the mistake of saying "One little *angels* in the band."
The mistake should be anticipated. "Now remember, it's one little *angel*.
Say it."

The Beginning Says

(Tune: *Twinkle, Twinkle, Little Star*)

The be-gin-ning says *sss*,
D   D   D   D   D   A

And the end-ing says *it*.
A   A   B   B   B   A

Put them to-geth-er,
G   G   G   F# F#

And they make *sit*.
F#   E   E   D

The children who know how to rhyme will have an easier time sounding out words than the children who do not. The reason is that the
word rhymes with the ending. *Sit* rhymes with *it; fat* rhymes with *at;* and
so forth. *The Beginning Says* dramatizes this point by making the
rhyming process explicit.

1. Introduce the song after the children have been in school for at
least a month. Do not introduce it until the children have had practice
with other songs.

2. Make up series of verses. Present two types of series—those in
which the beginning is repeated and those in which the ending is
repeated. An example of the former type would be: "The beginning says
sss, and the ending says *and*"; "The beginning says *sss* and the ending
says *un*"; "The beginning says *sss* and the ending says *at*"; "The beginning says *sss* and the ending says *uperman*."

An example of a series in which the same ending is repeated would
be: "The beginning says *bbb* and the ending says *it*"; "The beginning
says *fff,* and the ending says *it*"; "The beginning says *ppp* and the ending
says *it*"; "The beginning says *mmm* and the ending says *it*."

3. Make up verses about the children's names. These can be fun,
especially when silly variations are introduced: "The beginning says *ddd,*
and the ending says *avid*"; "The beginning says *mmm,* and the ending
says *avid*"; "The beginning says *sh,* and the ending says *avid*"; "The
beginning says *ppp,* and the ending says *avid*."

The Alphabet Song

A, B, C, D, E, F, G,
C   C   G   G   A   A   G

H, I, J, K, L-M-N-O-P,
F   F   E   E   D   D   D D C

Q, R, S and T, U, V,
G G F F E E D
W, X, and Y, and Z.
GGG F F E E D

Now I know my A,B,C's,
C C G G A A G
Tell me what you think of me.
F F E E D D C

The Alphabet Song provides children with an economical set of cues for remembering the names of the letters in the alphabet. The melody and rhythm of the song give the various letters some individuality and personality. The children can therefore learn the letter series with relatively little effort in far less time than an unpersonalized presentation demands.

1. Introduce the song after the children have developed some facility with songs that involve statements and after they have worked with parts of the alphabet in their reading class—perhaps after the second or third week. Use the song daily until most of the children can recite the entire series; then review the song once a week for the remainder of the school year.

2. At first, sing only the first two lines of the song. Sing each line four or five times, and then combine them and attempt to sing both. Do not introduce the remainder of the song until the children can sing through P relatively well.

3. *Sing the song extremely slowly.* The usual pace is far too fast, especially for L-M-N-O-P. Unless the pace is slowed, this part of the song will become an amalgamated five-syllable word.

Turn It Around

(Tune: *Old MacDonald*)

Tom-my and Deb-by turn it a-round;
F F F F C D DD C
It says Deb-bie and Tom-my.
A A G G G F F

Perhaps the key language deficiency of culturally deprived children is the inability to reverse logically reversible elements in a statement. *Turn It Around* is designed to give the children patterned practice in producing reversals.

1. Introduce the song only after the children have been in school for at least a month. Retain it throughout the year.

2. During the initial presentation, have two children stand facing the class. The first-mentioned child should stand to the class's left. When the children sing the words "turn it around," the two children should

trade places, so that the one who was originally mentioned second is now to the left.

3. Introduce a variation. "Boy and girl, turn it around; it says girl and boy."

4. Sing about objects in the room. As someone holds up jam in one hand and crackers in the other, for example, the children can sing "Jam and crackers, turn it around; it says crackers and jam." Many combinations are possible: "Books and crayons, turn it around"; "Chalk and blackboard, turn it around"; "Chair and table, turn it around."

5. Introduce *or* using the same technique. "Books or crayons, turn it around."

6. Introduce various arithmetic facts: "One plus zero, turn it around"; "Six plus two, turn it around." Initially, the numbers can be displayed individually on cards, which can be moved on cue.

Here We Go Round the Mulberry Bush

This is the way we wash our clothes [washing pantomime],
F   F   F   F   A   C   A   F
Wash our clothes, wash our clothes.
G   G   G   G   E   C
This is the way we wash our clothes, so ear-ly Mon-day morn-ing.
F   F   F   F   A   C   A   F   F G G   C-D E   F   F

[Tuesday] This is the way we iron our clothes [ironing pantomime].
[Wednesday] This is the way we scrub the floor [scrubbing pantomime].
[Thursday] This is the way we mend our clothes [stitching pantomime].
[Friday] This is the way we go to school [driving pantomime].
[Saturday] This is the way we play at home [happy, dancing pantomime].
[Sunday] This is the way we go to church [serious head-nodding].

1. Sing the song every day for at least a month. Always introduce it by indicating what today is. "Today is Thursday. Say it. . . . Yesterday was Wednesday."

2. Ask the questions "What *is* today?" and "What was yesterday?" The children should be required to answer with complete statements and to pronounce the words *is* and *was* clearly. "Today *is* Thursday. Say it." Learning *yesterday* is difficult for the children because it is a "reversal" task. It requires the children to think backwards. Learning *tomorrow* is much easier for them. In stating the tomorrow question, use the verb *will be*. "What day *will* tomorrow *be*? . . . Tomorrow *will be* _____."

3. After working on the song for about a week, name the days of the week in unison before singing. "We're going to sing about the days in the week. First, let's say them. Monday, Tuesday, Wednesday, [etc.]." Since the song begins with Monday, the recitation should also begin with Monday.

4. Later, teach a statement about the days of the week. "There are seven days in a week." Then ask the questions "How many days in a week are there? . . . There are seven *whats* in a week?" and so forth. These questions will help the children later when they learn a statement about months in a year. The children who do not learn some of the possible variations of the statement have trouble when they encounter statements that deal with days in a month, weeks in a year, etc.

5. Drop the song from the daily schedule after the children have worked on it for about a month. Present it only occasionally for the remainder of the term. However, continue to recite the names of the days of the week and to present the questions regularly.

There are Twelve Months in the Year

(Tune: *The Bear Went Over the Mountain*)

There are twelve months in a year,
G   E   E   E   D E F-E
There are twelve months in a year,
E   D   D   D   C C E-C
There are twelve months in a year,
C   E   E   E   D E F-G-A
and I will say them now.
A G G F D C
And I will say them now,
G G G A A G
And I will say them now,
E E E F F E
There are twelve months in a year,
G   E   E   E   D E F-E
There are twelve months in a year,
E   D   D   D   C C E-C
There are twelve months in a year,
C   E   E   E   D E F-G-A
And I will say them now.
A G G F D C

[Chanting in unison:]
January, February, March, April,
May, June, July, August,
September, October, November, December.

This song should be introduced after *Here We Go Round the Mulberry Bush* and handled in basically the same manner.

1. Sing the song every day for at least a month. Introduce it by identifying the month. "What month is it now? . . . It's February. What was last month? . . . What will the next month be?"

2. Ask questions about the statement in the song. "How many months

are in a year? . . . Are there seven months in a year? . . . Are there twelve months in a week?" and so forth.

The If Song

(Tune: *The Old Grey Mare*)

If he's a boy, then he's a child,
A D D D   E F# E F#-E-D
He's a child, he's a child.
E   D E-D-C# F# E F#-E-D
If he's a boy, then he's a child,
A D D D   E F# E F#-E-D
He is a child.
E F# E D

The If Song is designed to give the children practice in phrasing *if-then* statements, to give them practice in using *is not* instead of *ain't* or *ain't not*, and to acquaint them with different class names, such as *tool, furniture, building,* etc.

1. Introduce the song after the children have been in school for at least a month. Sing it regularly for the remainder of the year.

2. Sing about what something is and what it is not. Questions should be used to help define what the *if-then* statement in the song is meant to convey. "Let's sing about Tommy. Is Tommy a boy? . . . Sure. Is Tommy a child? . . . Yes. Every boy is a child. If he's a boy, then he's a child." Use the same approach to define the *not* statements. "Is he a boy? . . . Is he a girl? . . . No. If he's a boy, then he's *not* a girl. Say it." The following verses are examples that may be introduced in singing about Tommy: "If he's a boy, then he's a child"; "If he's a boy, then he's not a man"; "If he's a boy, then he's not a table." The first verse of the song should establish what the subject is; those that follow should give examples of what it *is not*.

3. Let the children make up verses. They especially enjoy telling what something is not once they learn that silly suggestions are acceptable.

What Will We Do With the Baby?

What will we do with the ba-by?
D   D   D F# D   D   E F#
What will we do with the ba-by?
D   D   D F# D   D   E D
What will we do with the ba-by? Oh,
D   D   D F# D   D   E E   F#
We'll wrap him up in cal-i-co
A   A   F# A F# E D D

Wrap him up in cal-i-co,
F#   A   A   A   B   A   A

And send him to his Pap-py-o.
A   F#   A   A   F#   E   D   D

The song presents a good exercise in coding by demonstrating to the children that an *o* ending can be attached to any name. Thus, the song helps the children become more part-conscious and more flexible in their use of language.

1. Present the song after the children have been in school *at least six weeks*. Retain it on a fairly regular basis for the remainder of the term.

2. Allow the children to make up verses. These must usually be rephrased slightly to fit the melody; however, a child should be complimented if he presents a good idea. Sometimes the verse will represent the effort of more than one child. Perhaps one child will have the idea to put the baby on the swing-e-o, but he may not be able to complete the idea. "What should we do with him on the swing-e-o?" Another child may suggest "push him back and forth-e-o."

Eency Weency Spider

Een-cy ween-cy spi-der went up the wa-ter spout [performing finger
D   D   D   E   F#   F#   F#   E   D   E   F#   D
operation].

Down came the rain [down motion] and washed the spi-der out.
F#   F#   G   A   A   G   F#   G   A   F#
Out came the sun [forming circle with hands] and dried up all the rain.
D   D   E   F#   F#   E   D   E   F#   D
Now, een-cy ween-cy spi-der went up the spout a-gain [performing finger
A   D   D   D   E   F#   F#   F#   E   D   F   F#   D
operation].

Children enjoy this song, which is why it is included in the song list. Since it is not so "important" as some of the other songs in the list, however, it should not be introduced early in the year and should be treated as a once-in-a-while treat rather than a regular song.

1. Perform the finger operation of the climbing spider by first placing the thumb on the little finger of the other hand and pivoting until the free thumb and little finger touch, forming a new pivot point.

2. Explain what spiders are and what a water spout is.

What Comes After?

(Tune: *Three Blind Mice*)

First we say a name.
E   E   D   D   C

The name we say is Wednes-day.
E   E   E D D   C   C

Then we ask our-selves
G   G   F   F   E

What comes af-ter Wednes-day?
G   G   F F   E   E

What comes af-ter Wednes-day?
C   C   B-A B   C-G   G

What comes af-ter Wednes-day?
C   C   B-A B   C-G   G

What comes af-ter Wednes-day?
C   C   B-A B   C-G   G

Thurs-day comes af-ter Wednes-day.
E   E   E   D D   C   C

Thurs-day comes af-ter Wednes-day.
D   D   D   D D   D   D

This song gives the children practice in handling a difficult type of statement pattern, in which the statement is completed by changing the beginning. The more familiar statement is completed by changing the ending. "The box is where? . . . The box is *on the floor.*" Questions relating to *before-after,* however, are answered by changing the beginning. "What comes after Wednesday? . . . *Thursday* comes after Wednesday."

1. Introduce the song after the children have been introduced to *before-after* tasks in the language period. Retain it as a regular song for the remainder of the school year.

2. Introduce verses dealing with numbers, days of the week, months of the year, letters in the alphabet: "First we say a name; the name we say is *four*"; "First we say a name; the name we say is *Wednesday*"; "First we say a name; the name we say is *April*"; "First we say a name; the name we say is *j.*"

3. When dealing with a long series of names, such as the names of months in a year or the names of letters in the alphabet, have the children figure out the name before starting to sing. "We're going to sing about March. Ask yourself what comes after March. Figure it out. January, February, *March*—April comes after March. Let's sing."

4. Introduce a series of *before* verses. These should not be presented until the children have become reasonably facile with the *after* verses. Always figure out the name before starting to sing. "What comes before Thursday? . . . Monday, Tuesday, *Wednesday,* Thursday—*Wednesday* comes before Thursday."

Summary

The music program presented in this chapter is designed to be an adjunct to the language program. Culturally deprived children encounter difficulty with certain language tasks. Since some of these tasks are crucial for logical reasoning, the children need a maximum amount of practice in working on them. The music program outlined in this chapter is designed to provide this practice. Specifically, it provides practice in:

1. Translating actions into words, and words into actions
2. Handling class names and subclass names (If it's a car, it's a vehicle)
3. Classifying something according to what it is and is not
4. Handling singular and plural inflections
5. Discriminating between left and right
6. Reversing elements that are "commutative" or reversible (John and Linda)
7. Handling past-tense construction
8. Counting and performing counting operations with fingers
9. Rhyming and blending words from parts of words
10. Reciting difficult series of names—days in a week, months in a year, letters in the alphabet
11. Generalizing word endings (Pappy-o)
12. Processing statements about *before* and *after*

The children also receive practice in creating, in developing lyrics, and in becoming more flexible with language.

The songs presented in this chapter are included primarily because they provide help in specific language problem areas. The list of songs, however, is not exhaustive. Feel free to introduce new songs, but resist the temptation to introduce songs merely because they are supposed to have some musical value. Songs should be selected on the basis of what they do for the language development of the child. Most traditional songs are trivial from this point of view because they present concepts that are not of real significance, and they often present these concepts in stilted language that cannot be readily generalized. The question "Where does the Muffin Man live?" is simply not on the same level of significance as "What kind of Indians are we singing about? . . . Indian *boys*." Before introducing a new song, consider the value of the song and its potential contribution in the race against the clock.

arithmetic 10

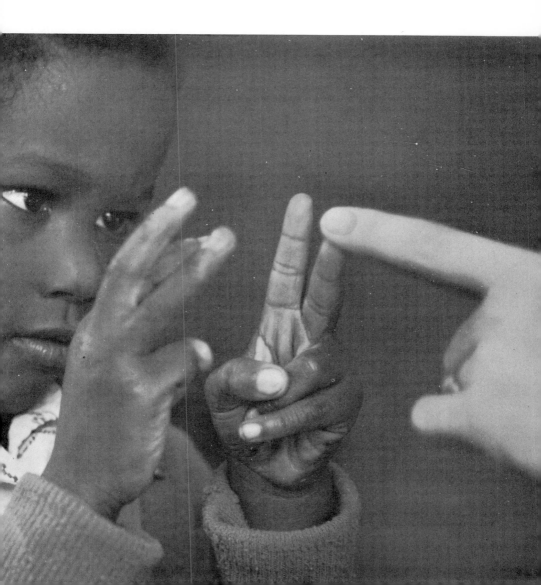

*I*n the present program, arithmetic is taught as a language, as a statement-generating system. Learning the language of arithmetic has two distinct aspects: (1) learning to manipulate and interpret arithmetic statements according to the appropriate internally consistent rules; and (2) learning to use arithmetic statements as models of reality (just as, in the language program, everyday language statements function as models of reality), so as to arrive at true conclusions about reality.

In order to understand the approach taken to arithmetic learning in the present program, it is necessary to recognize that the two aspects of arithmetic language specified above are in many ways quite independent of each other.

1. The logical manipulation and interpretation of arithmetic statements does not require any reference to physical objects or events. It is concerned entirely with numbers and their relationships. The statement $4 + 1 = 5$ specifies a relationship between the numbers 4, 1, and 5, and does not specify an operation with particular objects. Being confined to numbers and their relationships, the language of arithmetic permits much bolder inferences than everyday language does. For instance, if any of the five elements in the above equation were omitted, a person who understands arithmetic will be able to deduce what the missing element is: $4 \_\_ 1 = 5$; $4 + 1 \_\_ 5$; $4 + 1 = \_\_$; etc. This is not usually possible with everyday language statements. The statement "(George) (is) (taller than) (Daniel)" contains four basic elements (indicated by parentheses). If any element were left out, one would not be able to deduce what the missing element should be. There are too many possible reference objects and too many possible ways in which they might be related. Furthermore, it would be necessary, in filling in a missing element, to refer to empirical reality to determine whether or not a particular term was applicable—to determine, for instance, whether it was valid to use the name *Tyrone* for the last element in the statement.

The fundamental knowledge necessary for manipulation and interpretation of arithmetic statements is a knowledge of the counting order of numbers. The truth of the statement $4 + 1 = 5$ depends entirely on the location of the numbers 4, 1, and 5 in the counting order of numbers. Moreover, the several operations of arithmetic all refer to counting operations: the plus sign indicates counting ahead in the number order, the minus sign indicates counting backward, the times sign indicates counting *by* some number (e.g., counting every third number), and the equals sign refers to the end result of the counting operations, the number one ends up with. Thus, the first aspect of learning the language of arithmetic—learning to manipulate and interpret arithmetic statements—must rest solidly on a mastery of the counting order of numbers and various ways of working within that counting order.

2. The second aspect of the language of arithmetic—learning how to use it to make a model of reality—is immensely more complex than the "system" operations noted above. It involves all of the problems in dealing with concepts that were treated in the language program, and, in addition, *it involves learning how to relate real-life concepts to the language of arithmetic.* For instance, the problem "There are five children in one room and four children in another room; how many children are in the building?" involves much more than knowing how to add 5 and 4. It is necessary to realize that one can consider all of the children together even though they are not physically grouped together in one place, and that the operation of going into one room and counting the children and then going into another room and *continuing* to count where one left off is logically the same as counting the same children when they are mixed together in the same room. It is necessary to realize that the two operations must lead to the same result even though the children are not counted in the same order both times. Most important, it requires a knowledge of how the statements that are presented reduce to the operations of arithmetic. Which words—which cues—in the problem tell the child to add? Which cues tell him that the problem calls for the operation of getting more and not of getting less or of counting by a given number? Before the child can translate statements of everyday language into operations of arithmetic, he must understand the basic counting inferences, and he must be equipped with the lexical framework that relates these inferences to conditions expressed in everyday language.

An example of the spectrum of knowledge required to reduce quantity statements phrased in everyday language to arithmetic operations is provided by the following two problems: (1) If a man has three little dogs and two big dogs, how many dogs does he have? and (2) If a man has three white dogs and two big dogs, how many dogs does he have?

The first of these problems is legitimately solved by the arithmetical statement $3 + 2 = 5$, but the second is not. In order to tell whether or not a simple addition operation is appropriate in problems of this kind, it is necessary to grasp whether one is dealing with incompatible (mutually exclusive) concepts or compatible concepts which may be applied to the same objects. A child may understand addition perfectly as it applies to numbers; yet he may lack the concepts necessary to use addition statements in working with real-life concepts.

From an educational point of view, an important difference between the two kinds of arithmetic learning is that the kind which deals only with numbers and their relationships can proceed as rapidly as the child is able to master the limited number of concepts and rules involved; however, the kind that deals with the use of arithmetic in everyday statements of reality cannot proceed any faster than the child's mastery of real-life concepts and everyday language. Because of the culturally deprived child's deficiencies in language skills and concepts, he is greatly handicapped in reality applications of arithmetic learning, but he is relatively less handicapped in the kind of arithmetic learning that involves a special and limited set of concepts and rules.

How rapidly the culturally deprived child progresses in arithmetic learning will depend to a large extent, then, on which kind of learning is emphasized most. The modern trend in mathematics is to regard the kind of learning that involves formal operations with symbols and symbolic statements as the most crucial for an understanding of arithmetic. In an arithmetic program based on this modern point of view, therefore, a culturally deprived child should be able to make satisfactory progress, in spite of his weaknesses in other concept areas.

Unfortunately, the contemporary approaches to beginning arithmetic instruction, including those that are identified with the "new math," are not designed in a way that is consistent with this modern viewpoint. They begin with concrete objects and operations involving these objects, and only after the child has learned (or in some cases "discovered") some general principles of sequencing, combining, and counting are arithmetic symbols, statements, and statement rules introduced. Thus, these approaches begin by emphasizing the arithmetic as it relates to reality, and they use reality relations as a basis for teaching the more fundamental concepts about numbers and number relationships. In this way, all progress for a child becomes dependent on his ability to abstract general principles from concrete examples, to recognize contradictions and correspondences between statements and examples, and to use language precisely and logically. These contemporary approaches to arithmetic, therefore, subject the culturally deprived child to an unnecessary double handicap: they emphasize the kind of learning that he is least equipped to handle, and they make language-concept learning a prerequisite for the kind of learning that is actually more basic and easier for him to learn.

The present program is designed to capitalize on the relative simplicity of number concepts and relationships. The goal is to make it possible for the naïve culturally deprived child to build a solid foundation of concepts and skills for handling arithmetic statements while he is still acquiring the more general language concepts and skills necessary to use arithmetic as a representation of reality. The program starts by teaching the counting operation. It then teaches the various arithmetic statement forms in such a way that their relationship to counting operations is made manifest. The more complex task of producing arithmetic statements in response to real-life situations and using these statements to answer questions about the real world is introduced only gradually as the child's fund of language concepts and skills becomes adequate to the task. This approach is not only more consistent with the abilities of the young culturally deprived child, but also more consistent with the opinions of mathematicians as to what is of primary importance in the conceptual structure of arithmetic.

The Culturally Deprived Child and Arithmetic Skills

The language of arithmetic and everyday language are similar in many respects: both employ statements that are made up of parts, that imply questions, etc. It follows, therefore, that the child who is relatively weak in the ability to handle everyday language statements will also be relatively weak in the ability to handle the language of arithmetic. The culturally deprived child will have trouble repeating the statements (since they are basically unfamiliar); he will have trouble relating the statements to an operation; he will have trouble with the questions that are implied by statements. In other words, he will have trouble with the entire system. It may take him several weeks to *repeat* a seemingly simple statement like "Three plus two equals five," weeks to learn the answer to the question "What's another way of saying 'Three plus two'? . . . Two plus three," and perhaps months to remember a simple addition fact such as $2 + 2 = 4$. He may be apparently unable to hear the parts in a question such as "Three plus zero equals *how many?*" And he may vacillate for months between an accurate information-processing language and wild guesses.

However, the culturally deprived child can be expected, after a slow start, to progress more rapidly in basic arithmetic operations than he does in language or reading. By the end of nine months, the children in the Bereiter-Engelmann preschool experiment had progressed approximately twice as far in arithmetic as they had in reading or language, as indicated by results of achievement and aptitude tests (see Chapter 3). From about the third month onward, the disadvantaged children in this experiment were progressing at a rate that, in the writers' judgment, would compare favorably with the rate expected of average middle-class children under the same circumstances. It was not until the children had entered kindergarten (nearly a year later), however, that many of them had begun to show much facility in relating arithmetic to the physical world. This discrepancy between the children's ability to handle arithmetic at the formal level and their ability to relate it to concrete reality may be distressing to educators who place great emphasis on the latter ability. From a more positive point of view, however, it may be observed that the present program made it possible for the children to progress as far in the mastery of fundamental arithmetic concepts and operations as children usually progress in the first two elementary grades —and to accomplish this in a time during which one would otherwise have had to wait for the children to become "ready" to begin an ordinary arithmetic program.

Basic Operations

Counting out loud.

Some children entering preschool may know how to count; most probably will not. Counting is the first step in arithmetic training because counting is the means by which the various elements in the arithmetic statement are defined. Just as the vocabulary of everyday language consists largely of the names of such things as *stoves* and *balls,* the vocabulary of mathematics consists of the names of such things as 2 and 5. These names have meaning only in terms of the counting series, 1 2 3 4 5 6 7 8 9 10. This series is, then, the foundation.

1. Demonstrate the operation. "Watch. This is counting to five." Clap hands together five times at a moderate pace. Without breaking the cadence, beging counting in a loud voice, "One, two, three, four, five." Clap extra loudly on 5 and emphasize the name. Ask the question "What is this called?" Answer "Counting to five." Repeat the demonstration, placing increasing emphasis on the question about the operation.

2. Invite the children to count with you. They may have trouble pronouncing the numbers 3, 4, and 5. To help them with 3, have them stick their tongues out and then sizzle the "thhh," pull the tongue in, and say "ree." So then the word is produced in two distinct parts. "Thh-ree." Some children may say "pour" and "pibe" for 4 and 5. Show them how to make "buck teeth" and say the *ffff* sound.

3. Remind the children of a rule about counting. *"You always count the same way. You always start with* one. What do you start with when you count? . . . *One."* Use the rule liberally. Use it to correct mistakes in counting. "You always count the same way. One, two, three, four, five. Your turn."

4. Demonstrate that it is possible to count to any number from 1 to 5. Use the clapping and voice to make the children aware of *the last*

number in the counting series. Present the verbal rule for counting to a given number. "To count to *three,* I must say 'three.' One, two, three."

5. Introduce *yes-no* questions to help define the meaning of a statement. "Is this counting to three: one, two? . . . No, I did not say 'three.' Is this called counting to three: one, two, *three?* . . . Yes, this is called counting to *three.* Counting to three. Say it."

Do not count to 3 as a regular exercise, and try to de-emphasize the instruction "Count to three." The reason is that the children may form a spurious rule about counting. They may come to think that the instruction to count to a number should be responded to with a three-word answer. "Count to three." (One, two, three.) "Count to five." (One, two, five.) "Count to seven." (One, two, seven.) These responses can be avoided by avoiding the task of counting to 3 (which is the core of the analogy) as much as possible.

6. Distinguish between *counting to a number* and *saying a number.* Present this task after the children have some grasp of counting to a given number. "Listen big, now. Linda, *count* to three. . . . Yes, one, two, three. John, what is that called? . . . Yes, counting to three. Now, John, say 'Three'." If the child counts, correct him. "No, that's *counting to* three. Here's how to say 'Three': Three." This task is not particularly easy; however, it is very important and should be worked on briefly every day until the children have learned the rule for *count* instructions (Count to five) and *say* instructions (Say "Five").

7. Introduce action tasks after the children have fairly well worked out the *count* and *say* rules.

a. Demonstrate how to clap on signal. "When I say *clap,* you do it. Here we go: *Clap.*"

b. Introduce clapping as the terminal act of counting to a given number. "When I count to five, clap. Here goes. One, two, three, four,
[clap]
five." Repeat the demonstration and encourage the children to clap with you.

c. Play a pausing game. After the children have learned how to "Clap when I count to five," break the cadence of the counting series and try to trick them. The purpose of the game is to demonstrate that the clap is not simply something produced when the teacher stops talking. "Okay, clap when I count to five. Here goes. One, two, three, *four.* Oh, oh, did I count to *five?* . . . Did I say 'Five'? . . . No, so I didn't count to five. I fooled you. Let's try it again. One, two, *three.*"

8. Introduce a discrimination task involving the words *count* and *say.* Tell the children either that they should clap when you count to a given number or that they should clap when you say a given number. "When I count to four, clap. Here goes. *Four.* Did I count to four? . . . No, I did not. I said 'Four.' I fooled you on that one. Let's see if I can get you

again. When I count to four, clap. Here goes. One, two, three, *four*. Good."
When the task involves saying a number on cue, try to "fool" the children by presenting the names of different numbers. "When I say 'Five,' clap. Ready? Six. Three. *Five*. Good."

9. Let the children take turns at giving the action signals. "When John counts to two, clap. Okay, John, you do the counting." After the children have mastered the counting series from 1–5, extend the series to 20. Increase it first to 10, presenting tasks about saying and counting. After the 1–10 series has been mastered, introduce 11–15 and finally 16–20. Counting should be made a brief ritual of no more than three minutes at the beginning of each arithmetic session.

Counting objects.

The counting tasks in the previous section do not specify how the counting numbers are related to the act of counting things. The preceding tasks centered around the mastery of something that is much like a poem. Counting objects is a much more difficult task. In order to count a number of objects the child must learn to:

1. Coordinate the rote counting series with the act of pointing to objects

2. Consider each of the objects to be counted once and only once

3. Use a number in the counting series to describe each object, with the understanding that the order of the objects is irrelevant while the order of numbers in the series must not be violated

4. Stop reciting after the last object has been described with a number

5. Understand that the final number does not refer merely to the last object counted but to *all* of the objects submitted to the counting operation. When the fourth and final block is counted, the child is supposed to understand that he has counted four blocks.

The following exercises help define each of the conventions associated with object counting.

1. Demonstrate object counting by using the children's fingers. This demonstration runs contrary to the old-time arithmetic principle "Don't count on your fingers." However, the conventions about not counting an object twice and counting every object once are more easily learned if the children are provided with a dramatic means of checking their performance. Touching the appropriate finger provides this check. The children can feel whether or not they have touched a given finger before. (The statement of correction "You already counted that one"

therefore has more meaning.) Equally important, fingers are easier to work with and less distracting than other physical objects. Also fingers are available and handy.

a. Demonstrate finger counting. Instruct the children to extend all of the fingers on their *left* hand. *(Show them* which hand they should work with.) Identify the fingers. "This is a finger. This is a finger. This is a finger. These are fingers. Say it."

b. Demonstrate the counting procedure, touching each finger as it is counted. "One, two, three, four, five."

c. Count them again in a different order (perhaps beginning with one of the middle fingers) and again still a different order (perhaps beginning with the thumb).

d. Describe the operation. "I *counted the fingers on this hand.* What did I do? . . . I counted the fingers on this hand."

2. Introduce the question "How many?" and the appropriate answer. The children probably do not know that the answer to "How many?" is the name of *one number,* the last one in the series. To make this point, present the question and its answer as part of the counting operation. Have each child hold up three fingers. "I'm going to count these fingers. One, two, three. *How many* fingers? . . . *Three* fingers. *How many* fingers? . . . *Three* fingers." The child may at first answer the question "How many?" by counting "One, two, three."

3. Show that counting is not limited to fingers. Demonstrate by counting the children in the room, chalk marks on the chalkboard, windows in the room, and so forth. The idea to get across is that *counting works for anything.*

4. Introduce the basic question-answer pattern for counting.

a. Have the children count a finger presentation. "Count these fingers."

b. After the children have counted (One, two, three, four), ask the question "How many?"

c. Introduce *yes-no* questions and the *not* statements. "Did you count six fingers? . . . No, you did not count six fingers. Did you count nine fingers? . . . No, you did not count nine fingers. *How many fingers* did you count? . . . You counted *four* fingers." This is a basic and important pattern. It must be learned thoroughly.

5. Introduce the concept *zero.* The children will probably find this word difficult to pronounce. (The usual mistake is to call it something like "Jeero.")

a. Hold up one finger. "How many fingers are here?"

b. Present a closed fist. "How many fingers are here now? . . . I don't see any. None. And we call that zero."

c. Define the concept further by asking "How many dogs are in this room? . . . Come on, look for them. Count them. There are *no* dogs in this room. *Zero* dogs." Repeat with different entities—old men with beards, airplanes, T.V. sets, Huckleberry Hounds, etc.

d. Inject an occasional nonzero question so that the children do not get in the habit of answering without looking. "How many chalkboards are in this room? . . . One."

The number symbols.

Staring in the first week of the arithmetic program, three to six minutes of each session should be devoted to symbol recognition, continuing until the children have learned the symbols for the numbers 0–20 and the signs +, −, and =.

1. Introduce three symbols at a time, beginning with 1, 2, and 3, and following with 0, +, and =.

a. Introduce distinguishing characteristics for each number:

> 0—Looks like a doughnut
> 1—Looks like an extended, upright index finger
> 2—Has a flat bottom. Hold hand parallel to the bottom of a large chalkboard 2 to demonstrate the flatness.
> 3—Has two humps, one over the other. Place finger on the point at which humps join (·3) and point out "See? A hump up here and a hump down here."
> 4—(To be introduced after +) 4 looks like + with a corner added
> 5—Has a flat *top*. Stress the difference between *bottom* and *top* to avoid confusion with 2.
> 6—Has a big top with a little zero on the bottom
> 7—Is a big corner
> 8—Has a zero on the top and a zero on the bottom
> 9—Has a zero on the top and a big bottom
> 10—A 1 and a zero stuck together (Analogous rules apply for the numbers 11–20)
> 11–19—A 1 stuck together with a familiar number
> 20—A 2 and a zero stuck together
> +—Stands up straight with arms out to the side. Have children make themselves look like plus signs by standing at attention and extending arms to sides.
> =—Lines going together like railroad tracks—always lying down and never standing up.

b. Present each number as a member of a class. Print the numbers 1–10 on a large card or near the top of the chalkboard. Identify each number with the statement "This is number _____." (After all have been identified as numbers, introduce the plural statement. "These are numbers.") Then, identify the numbers by name. "This number is *one.* This number is *two.* This number is *three.*" Work on three numbers at a time. Encourage the children to answer *yes-no* questions about the class of things called numbers. "Are these dogs? . . . No, what are these? . . . These are *numbers.*" Also ask the *what* question. "What are these things called? . . . These are _____."

c. Introduce + and = as *signs.* "These are signs. This sign [+] is *plus.* This sign [=] is *equals.*" Present exercises in which the children must identify the members of a group of symbols (3, 1, +, 2, 1, =, 3, 2, +, 3, 1) as *signs* or *numbers.* Unless the children learn the distinction between signs and numbers, they may have trouble learning that "How many?" demands a *number answer* and not, for instance, the word *equals.*

d. Do not spend a great deal of time on the verbal description of the numbers and do not expect the children to use these descriptions effectively when trying to identify numbers. The verbal rules merely provide a limited amount of extra guidance that may be helpful to some children during the early stages of recognition.

2. Demonstrate that a number symbol is a form (shared by many particular things) and not a particular thing.

a. Write a series of number symbols on the board, large ones and small ones, most of which are 1, and introduce *yes-no* tasks. Refer to a 1. "If it looks like this, it is a one." Point to a 3. "Is this a one? . . . No, this is not a one." Refer again to the original. "If it looks like this, it is a one." Point to another one. "So, is this a one?"

b. After the basic *yes-no* task, have the children find all of the big 1's and all of the little 1's. Repeat with 2 and 3. "See the flat bottom. That's number two. Does this one have a flat bottom? . . . *No, so it is not a two.* Is this a two? . . . Yes, this is a two. It has a flat bottom." [Note: Some children who are very verbal and quick in handling verbal learning tasks may experience great difficulty in learning visual discriminations of the kind required for numeral identification. Children of this type should be taken very carefully and slowly through the identification tasks. They should have extra practice in pointing tasks (finding those symbols that have the characteristics of a 1, 2, or 3).]

c. Present tasks which draw attention to the fact that numbers must be "standing up." Demonstrate the concept with the numeral 1. Draw a 1 on the board. Identify it. "This number is one." Present the idea of standing up. "This one is standing up." Draw a horizontal figure 1. "This one is not standing up. It's going to bed." Present a series of 1's on the board, some of which are standing up, and have the children find those that are standing up. Next, introduce the numeral 2. It is often confused with 5, because the children may think that 5 is merely an inverted 2. Point out that when 2 is standing up, it has a flat bottom.

3. After the children are reasonably proficient at determining whether numerals are the same as or different from model numerals, present the numerals completely out of context.

a. Make a 3 on the board. Before asking the children to identify it, put your finger on the middle member and call their attention to the symbol's distinguishing characteristics. "This number has a hump on the top and a hump on the bottom. What number is this?"

b. If the children give an incorrect response, which is quite possible, show them how to "figure out" the answer. If they indicate that the number is 2, for instance, ask them "Does a two have a hump on the top and a hump on the bottom? . . . No. What does two have? . . . A flat bottom." Draw a 2 and run a finger across the bottom. "This is a two." *Do not insist that the children figure out the name of the number by working from the verbal description. Tell them the name,* but first give them some indication of how the verbal rule can be used to identify numbers. Do not work on out-of-context numbers for more than a minute or two during each session. Even the more visually adept children will quickly saturate and begin to make hideous mistakes. Also, there is a strong tendency for the mistakes of one child to be picked up by the others, especially on visual identification tasks. Incidentally, one of the best ways to reduce the spread of an incorrect response is to call attention to the error tendency. "Oh, oh. John called this three a two. Now, I'll bet I know what will happen. Linda will want to call it a two, and Tyrone will want to call it a two. But is it a two? . . . No, it is not a two. It is a three."

What number comes next.

The number system is not "round" or symmetrical. The counting order 1, 2, 3, etc., does not close upon itself, but instead keeps on going in the same direction. This notion of single direction is extremely important to the logic of arithmetic.

1. Define the operation for determining the number after a given number. "When you count, what comes after four? . . . Let's figure it out. One, two, three, four, *five.*" Repeat the operation several times;

[clap]

then put it into words. "What comes after four? . . . I count to four and then go to the next number." Repeat with other numbers from 1 through 4. The clap helps the child acquire the basic feel of what he is trying to do, *which is to count to the given number in the counting series.* The most common mistake the child makes is to count past the cue number. Clapping to accent the cue number helps to overcome this tendency.

2. Present no more than three or four what-comes-next problems during a session. Encourage the children to answer the basic question, which should be repeated after the counting operation is completed. "What comes after two?" Also require increasing verbalization of the procedure. "What comes after two? . . . How do I figure it out? . . . Do I count to five? . . . Do I count to seven? . . . No, if I want to know what comes
[clap]
after two, I have to count to two. One, two. Now, what do I do? . . . One, two, *three*. Good."

3. Present the series "What comes after _____?" *in the counting order,* beginning with "What comes after one?" "When you count, what comes after one? . . . *Two.* What comes after two? . . . *Three.* What comes after three? . . . *Four.* What comes after four? . . . *Five."* The trick in demonstrating the relationship between identifying the number that comes after a given number and the familiar act of counting is to get the children to hear the counting numbers 1, 2, 3, 4, 5 in the statement series. This can be achieved by asking the questions rather softly and answering them loudly, and by speaking fast, so that the time lapse between statements is as short as possible.

Identity Statements

The preceding exercises teach the skills that are necessary prerequisites to many basic statements of arithmetic. Statements have the same central role in arithmetic that they have in everyday language. In everyday language, the identity statement functions as the bridge between mere object words and subject-predicate reasoning. The parallel to the identity statement in arithmetic is a statement such as $2 + 0 = 2$. It will be recalled that the identity statement "This is a stove" says no more, in one sense, than the simple stipulation "stove." Similarly, the arithmetic identity statement $2 + 0 = 2$ merely says 2 in what might seem to be a roundabout manner, but because of the additional elements in the statement, it can now generate questions that can be answered with information provided by the statement.

1. Write the three identity statements on the board. Always write identity statements with zero as the number following the plus sign:

$$1 + 0 = 1$$
$$2 + 0 = 2$$
$$3 + 0 = 3$$

2. Draw an arrow under each statement.

$$1 + 0 = 1$$
$$\longrightarrow$$

Briefly demonstrate how to "read" an arrow (see page 154). After about the third week of instruction, discontinue the arrow. The children may object. Tell them "You have to pretend that the arrow is there. See if you can remember which way it's pointing."

3. Read the statements very slowly, allowing about a quarter-second lapse between the time a number is pointed to and read. "One   plus   zero   equals   one."

4. After the children have read the statement several times, repeat it at a more conversational speed several times, clapping three times after finishing the statement. "One plus zero equals one. [clap-clap-clap] One plus zero equals one. [clap-clap-clap]

5. Encourage the children to repeat the statement. "Say it with me." They may be unable to say it properly at first. The most common mistake is to eliminate the second number (One plus equals zero). Call attention to mistakes when they are made, but *place the emphasis on listening to the statements, not on saying them.*

6. Introduce the basic *how-many* question. "One plus zero equals
[clap]   [clap]
how many? . . . One plus zero equals *one.*" As pointed out earlier, these questions illustrate the logical basis of arithmetic because, by replacing the words *how many* with the word *one,* the question "One plus zero equals *how many?*" is transformed into the true statement "One plus zero equals *one.*"

7. Introduce *yes-no* questions to demonstrate that $1 + 0$ equals nothing but 1. (This is perhaps one of the most difficult points for a child to learn. At this stage in learning, the child has no basis for recognizing that if $1 + 0 = 1$, it is contradictory to say that $1 + 0$ equals something other than 1.) After presenting the statement $1 + 0 = 1$, ask "Does one plus zero equal three? . . . No, one plus zero does not equal three. One plus zero equals one. Say it. . . . Does one plus zero equal five? . . . No, one
                                                        [clap]
plus zero does not equal five. One plus zero equals *one.*"

8. Introduce a *how-many* question about the *middle term* of the
                                                        [clap]
statement. The accent is quite different. "One plus *how-many* equals
[clap]
one? . . . One plus *zero* equals one." To give this type of question a personality, raise the voice extremely—quizzically—high for the words *how many*. The children find this amusing and, as a result, tend to recognize the verbal pattern of the statement more easily.

9. Include *yes-no* questions about the middle number. "Does two plus three equal two? . . . No, two plus *zero* equals two. Does two plus two equal two? . . . No, two plus *zero* equals two."

Translating Addition Statements Into Counting

Statements of addition can be interpreted either as declarations or as instructions for performing the addition operation. When the statement $3 + 1 = B$ *is interpreted as a declaration,* every element in the statement is assigned its conventional name. The symbol 3 is called "three"; + is called "plus"; and so forth. However, *when the statement is interpreted as a series of instructions,* the entire statement tells one "what to do," and the various elements in the statement take on an *operational interpretation.* The symbol 3 now directs one to "Start out with three," and the + tells him to "Get more." The operational meaning of each element in the statement is very precise.

3	+	1	=	B
Start out with three	Get more	Get one more	End up with	How many?

The precision is important, because the operational interpretation stands as a bridge between the act of counting and the statements of arithmetic on the one hand and the statements of everyday language on the other. The operational interpretation specifies the counting operation needed to answer the question raised by the open statement $3 + 1 = B$. The operational interpretation also functions as a *formula* for reducing word problems to the arithmetic code. For example, a problem about a farmer who has three bull calves and buys one more is reduced to: He starts out with three bulls; he gets more; he gets one more; he ends up with—we don't know. This reduction translates into $3 + 1 = B$.

The tasks in this section are directed at establishing the basic operational meaning of the addition statement.

1. Introduce symbols for unknown numbers. At least two symbols should be introduced, and they should be used in problems more or less randomly.

a. Initially, introduce a △, referred to as "triangle," and a *B,* referred to by name.

b. Demonstrate that different symbols for unknown quantities are interchangeable. Draw an arrow on the board from left to right. Above it, present the problem $2 + 1 = B$. Read it slowly. "Two plus one equals *B.*" Ask the question "What's *B?* . . . We don't know. Whenever you see a *B,* you have to figure it out." Repeat this rule, pointing to the *B.* "The *B* just asks 'How many?' We have to figure out how many." Erase the *B* and introduce the triangle. Read the problem. "Two plus one equals triangle. How many? . . . We don't know. Whenever you see a triangle, you have to figure it out." Repeat the procedure with different examples: $2 + 3 = \triangle$, $2 + 3 = B$.

2. Present the substitution convention as an answer to the question. "If B equals five, what can we do?" . . . Erase the B and put in a five."

3. Teach the translation of a problem a step at a time.

a. Present a simple problem, such as $2 + 1 = \triangle$ (avoid problems such as $2 + 2$, $1 + 1$, etc.), and draw an arrow under it. Read the problem, concluding with the rule about the triangle. "Whenever you see a triangle, you have to figure it out. But how do we figure it out? Does it tell us what to do? . . . *Yes, it tells us what to do.*"

b. "Look over here. It tells us to start out with _____. What's this number? . . . Start out with two."

c. Erase the 2 and replace it with a 3. "What's this number? . . . Yes, *now* it tells us to *start out with three.*" Erase the number and replace it with zero. *"Now* it tells us to *start out* with zero."

d. Eliminate the possibility that one starts out with another element in the problem by using *yes-no* questions. Present the problem $2 + 1 = \triangle$. "Do we start out with the plus sign? . . . *No, we start out with the two.* Do we start out with the triangle? . . . No, we start out with the two."

e. Teach the operational meaning of the plus sign as "Get more." Show that the statement progresses in the direction indicated by the arrow beneath the problem. "See? We start out with two. Then we go with the arrow until we come to the plus sign. The plus sign tells us to do something, too. It says 'Get more! Get more!' What does it tell us to do?" Indicate that only the plus sign tells us to get more. "Does the two tell us to get more? . . . No, the plus sign tells us to get more. Does the one tell us to get more?" And so forth.

f. Pose the question in relation to the plus sign: how many more? "The plus sign tells us 'Get more! Get more!' But does it tell us how many more? . . . *No,* we have to keep going to find out how many more. We go with the arrow until we come to the number one. That's how many more. One more." Ask *yes-no* questions to help limit the concept. "Do we get two more? . . . No, we get one more."

g. Indicate that the equals sign says "End up with." The function of the equals sign is not of primary importance in these tasks. Therefore, it can be skimmed over using the phrase *"End up with."*

h. Indicate the function of the triangle with the question "End up with *how many?*" "Will we end up with seven? . . . with eight? . . . We don't know. So we say 'End up with *how many?*'"

i. Present a summary statement following the arrow from left to right to indicate the source of each verbal element. "Start out with two; get more; get one more; and we'll end up with *how many?* . . . We don't know how many." Do not expect the children to repeat this statement.

4. Present the counting operation that provides the answer to the *how-many* question.

a. Have a child stand in front of the chalkboard on which is printed a very large $2 + 1 = \triangle$. Place his left hand beneath the 2, his right hand beneath the 1. "I want you to make yourself look like this problem." Identify his hands. Refer to his left hand. "This is the hand you *start out with*. See? It's right under the number we start out with. This other hand [squeeze his right hand] is the hand you *get more with*. It's right under the number we get more with."

b. After the children have had a few turns at "making themselves look like this problem," show them how to work from their seats. Present a problem on the board, written very large, with an arrow beneath it.

$$3 + 2 = B$$
$$\longrightarrow$$

Instruct them to hold both hands out in front at arm's length. Stand behind them and ask them to "Show me the hand you *start out* with." If a child has trouble, help him "aim" his hand at the appropriate number and remind him to "Make your hands look just like the problem."

c. After the children have caught on to aiming their hands at the start-out and get-more numbers, introduce exercises in which the children hold up the hand called for. "Hold up the hand you get more with. Hold up the hand you start out with." This task is not easy. Reminders about the arrow beneath the problem will help them keep from mixing their hands up, but a great deal of repetition may be necessary before the children become proficient. This repetition should be distributed over a number of sessions. In demonstrating, hold up the right hand for "Start out with" and the left hand for "Get more" (the reverse of what the children do), since you are facing the class and must demonstrate in a way that is correct from the children's point of view.

d. Demonstrate how to count fingers. Present the problem $2 + 1 = B$. "The problem says to start out with two. So we start out with two." Extend two fingers [on *your right hand*] as you face the children. "Do it." Direct the children to hold up two fingers on the hand they start out with (the left hand). Refer to the problem. "The plus sign tells us to get more. How many more [point to the 1]? . . . *One* more. Do it." Extend one finger on your left hand. "Start out with two and get one more." *Bring both hands together.* "Okay, count them up." Touch each extended finger as it is counted. Do not always count fingers in the same order, or the children may develop a misconception about counting.

5. After all three fingers are counted, ask "How many?" and answer "Three." *This is very important:* summarize the operational meaning of the statement. "If I start out with two and get one more, how many will I end up with? . . . *Three.*"

6. Relate the answer to the unknown in the problem. "So what do I

know? . . . I know that *B equals three.*" Repeat the final questions. "How many? . . . Three. So what do I know? . . . *B* equals three."

7. The final step: "If *B* equals three, what can I do? . . . Erase the *B* and put up a three."

Plan to spend from five to ten minutes during each of the early sessions working on the addition operation. Always try to work toward a fast presentation in which the children are given increasing responsibility for answering the questions. But do not hurry the children when they are trying to carry out the counting operation.

8. Relate the problem to different objects, thereby demonstrating that the operation is universally valid. Touch the appropriate elements in the problem as they are considered. "If you start out with two shoes and you get one more, you're going to end up with three shoes. Three what? . . . Three shoes? . . . If you start out with two books and you get one more, you're going to end up with three books? . . . Will you end up with four books? . . . No, you'll end up with three books." Encourage the children to furnish different examples. Briefly demonstrate that the statements are true, perhaps by starting out with two lines and getting one more.

Identity Statements as Problems

1. Present five identity problems in the counting order, using different symbols for unknowns:

$$1 + 0 = C$$
$$2 + 0 = \triangle$$
$$3 + 0 = C$$
$$4 + 0 = A$$
$$5 + 0 = \triangle$$

The purpose of presenting the statements in the counting order is to help foster the generalization that if a pattern is true for every number in the counting series, it should also be true for any new numbers introduced into the counting series.

2. Solve each problem using the procedure outlined above.

3. After each problem is completed, present questions about the get-more number and the end-up number. "Three plus zero equals [clap] *how many?*" "Three plus *how many* equals three?"

4. After all of the problems have been solved and the unknown symbols replaced by numbers, treat the equations as statements and read them in order. "One plus zero equals one. [clap-clap-clap] Two plus zero equals two." And so on.

+1 Problems

It is possible to figure out what 31 plus 7 equals, if one knows $31 + 2 = 33$, $31 + 8 = 39$, or any addition fact that begins with 31. It is possible to count from the known fact to 31 plus 7. For example, if it is known that $31 + 2 = 33$, then it follows that $31 + 3 = 34$, $31 + 4 = 35$, $31 + 5 = 36$, $31 + 6 = 37$, and $31 + 7 = 38$. In order to perform this fundamental *if-then* operation, one must start with a known fact that is related to the problem that is given. The identity statement $31 + 0 = 31$ provides a starting point in the figuring-out operation, but the fact which enables the children to move on from the identity statement to the solution of any addition problem is the fact represented by the +1 statement—e.g., $31 + 1 = 32$. By starting with the identity statement and successively applying the +1 operation, the children can generate a series that leads to the solution of any addition problem: $31 + 0 = 31$, $31 + 1 = 32$, $31 + 2 = 33$, $32 + 3 = 35$, etc.

The basic rule for the +1 problem is *when you add one more, you go to the next number.*

1. Present the following +1 problems in the counting order:

$$1 + 1 = A$$
$$2 + 1 = \triangle$$
$$3 + 1 = B$$
$$4 + 1 = A$$
$$5 + 1 = \triangle$$

(Do not read these problems too many times—preferably no more than two times—before working them. The child who reads problems with unknowns too many times may come to believe that these statements are the answers, not the questions. When asked "Three plus one equals how many?" this child may say *"A".*) After working each problem, repeat it as a fact. "Four plus one equals five." Ask the appropriate questions. "Four plus one equals how many?" etc. Encourage the children to close their eyes and repeat the statement with you.

2. Select the completed statement $3 + 1 = 4$ and compare it with the identity statement $3 + 0 = 3$.

a. Ask of the identity statement "Does three plus zero equal four? . . . No, three plus zero equals *three.*"

b. Ask a similar question about the second statement. "Does three
[clap]
plus one equal *three?* . . . [point to the problem] No, three plus one
[clap]
equals *four.*" Repeat the question several times.

c. Present comparisons of +0 and +1 problems often. The children may have the idea that the arithmetic statement is much simpler than it actually is. If they are not carefully guided with the proper questions, they may not learn to appreciate that *every part of the statement is important and should be attended to.* Do not expect the children to perform well on comparison questions at first. Lead the children through the questions and let them hear the questions often enough for the questions to acquire some kind of auditory meaningfulness or familiarity.

Continuity Series

These series are designed to help the children hear the differences between the identity and the +1 statements and relate both to the familiar verbal counting series.

1. Recite the continuity series of the identity numbers first. "One plus zero equals one [clap-clap-clap], two plus zero equals two [clap-clap-clap], three plus zero equals three [clap-clap-clap], . . . ten plus zero equals ten." Recite the series several times during each lesson.

2. After the children are able to produce some of the statements in the series, introduce the rule for adding zero. At first, the rule will be only a rote set of words for the children. However, it will acquire meaning as they apply it to an increasing range of statements. *"When you add zero, you always end up with the number you started out with."*

3. Demonstrate the rule on the chalkboard.

a. Write out a familiar identity statement: $3 + 0 = 3$.

b. Ask "Are we adding zero? . . . Are we *adding?* . . . *Can you find a plus sign?* . . . Good. We are adding. Are we adding *zero?* . . . Can you find a zero? . . . Good. We are adding zero." State the rule. "When you add zero, you always end up with the number you start out with. What are we starting out with here? . . . Three. What are we ending up with here? . . . Three."

c. Change the first number in the problem so that the problem now reads $4 + 0 = 3$. "When we add zero [point to the zero], we end up with the number we start out with. What are we starting out with? . . . Yes, four. So what do we have to end up with? . . . Four, *not three."*

d. Repeat the rule. "When we add zero, we end up with the number we start out with. If we start out with four, we end up with four."

e. Repeat the exercise with different identity statements.

4. Apply the rule to statements containing an unknown, such as $3 + 0 = A$. Provide the children with all of the cues necessary to solve the problem. Ask the appropriate questions about (1) whether or not you are adding zero, and (2) what you are starting out with. "If we start out with five and we add zero, we have to end up with _____." Prompt when necessary and acknowledge that the problems are quite difficult.

5. Indicate the appropriate finger operation for the identity series. Perform the operations rapidly.

One ....*plus* ....*zero* ....*equals* ....*one.*			
[Hold up start-out hand with one finger extended.]	[Hold up get-more hand with closed fist.]	[Bring hands together.]	[Wiggle extended finger.]
	[clap—clap—clap]		
Two ....*plus* ....*zero* ....*equals* ....*two.*			
[Hold up start-out hand with two fingers extended.]	[Hold up get-more hand with closed fist.]	[Bring hands together.]	[Wiggle extended fingers.]
	[clap—clap—clap]		

And so forth, through 5 + 0 = 5.

6. Present the +1 continuity series in the same manner as the identity series. Recite the series, in the counting order, separating each statement with three claps. Give strong verbal emphasis to the "plus one" part of the statement. "One plus *one* equals two. [clap-clap-clap] Two plus *one* equals three. [clap-clap-clap] Three plus *one* equals four. [Etc.]" Remind the children that this is not the identity series. "Am I saying 'Two plus zero?' . . . No, I'm saying 'Two plus *one*.' Two plus one doesn't equal two; it equals *three.*" Do not spend time on lengthy explanations. Rather let the rhythm of the pattern make your points for you. Simply point out that "We're adding one, not zero."

To help relate the +1 series to counting, have the children complete each of the statements in order as they are presented *quite quickly.* "One plus one equals _____. [clap-clap-clap] Two plus one equals _____," etc. The children will soon catch on to the fact that if they simply indicate the number that is next in the counting order, they will give the correct answer in each case. They will have learned in a somewhat simplified form the rule for adding one to another number.

7. Present the rule for adding 1 after the children have learned to handle the series of +1 statements. *"When we add one, we go to the next number."* Define the rule further with examples, falling back on the child's knowledge of the number that comes after a given number. "What comes after three? . . . Yes, four. So, three plus one equals *four.*"

8. Apply the verbal rule to chalkboard problems. Present three problems on the board, such as

$$3 + 0 = 3$$
$$4 + 2 = 6$$
$$4 + 1 = 5$$

Remind the children of the rule. "When you add *one,* you always go to the next number." Have the children read the first problem. "Are we adding one in this problem? . . . No one here." The second problem: "Are we adding one here? . . . No, we are not adding one here. So, do we end up with the next number? . . . We do not end up with the next number." And the last problem: "Are we adding one here? . . . Yes, here's a one. Here's a plus sign. So we're adding one. What's the rule about adding one? . . . You always go to the next number." Point to the first number (4) and ask "What comes next—after four? . . . *Five*. So we should end up with five. And we do." The children's major difficulty in using rules is learning when to apply them. The children who have learned the rule for adding zero and the rule for adding 1 will often treat the rules as if they were optional alternatives. They must be constantly impressed with the fact that the choice of rules is not optional. This point needs numerous demonstrations, especially during the initial stages. The children must be shown precisely how one goes about deciding whether or not a rule applies.

9. Make both continuity series (+0 and +1) a part of the daily lesson routine. As the children become more proficient at reciting the series in unison with you, switch the emphasis from repeating to producing the series without help. Follow the identity series with the +1 series. At first, require the children to provide only the last number in each statement (see step 6 above). Later, have them produce the entire series.

If-then Reasoning

The most fundamental *if-then* in arithmetic, simply stated, holds that if $1 + 0 = 1$, $1 + 1$ equals the number after 1, which is 2. This *if-then* is of fundamental importance because it shows how statements are to be linked together.

1. Present the identity statements *out of* the familiar counting order. Preface a question with two quick out-of-context statements. "Three plus zero equals *three*. Nine plus zero equals *nine*. Six plus zero equals _____." From this presentation, the children can hear the pattern.

2. Pose problems involving relatively virgin numbers, such as 20 or 50. Present these only after a quick demonstration of two other identity statements involving virgin numbers. "Thirty plus zero equals thirty. Ninety plus zero equals ninety. Twenty plus zero equals _____." Children do well on these problems because the number in the statement is unfamiliar. The safest answer, therefore, is the number they hear. "Twenty plus zero equals *twenty*."

3. After the children become reasonably familiar with the identity series out of context, present the +1 series out of context.

    a. Pair it with the identity series, "Seven plus zero equals _____. Good."

    b. Ask the question that sets up the +1 fact. "What comes after seven?"

[clap]

c. Draw the conclusion of the (unstated) *if-then*. "Seven plus one equals eight. One more time."

d. After several weeks of presenting four to six pairs of statements during each session, begin to speed up the procedure. "Three plus zero
[clap]
equals _____. Good. So three plus one can't equal three. Three plus one equals _____."

e. From time to time, introduce the +1 statements without reference to the identity statement. "When you count, what comes after five? . . . Sure, six. So, five plus one equals *six*. Say it." As the children become more familiar with this exercise, they will be able to phrase the +1 statement, but this may take some time—perhaps three to four months.

4. Work toward the statement that links the identity statement with the +1 statement. "If three plus zero equals three, three plus one equals _____. What comes after three? . . . Four. Three plus one equals four."

a. Select an identity statement. "Three plus zero equals _____. Yes, three plus zero equals *three*."

b. Clap three times and present the +1 statement that follows. "So, three plus *one* equals four." It helps to hold up your index finger when saying "one," so that the children will have an additional cue for discriminating between this and other statements.

c. Summarize with the *if-then* statement. "If three plus zero equals three, three plus one equals four." Have the children repeat it—at first a small segment at a time and then in larger units until they can produce the entire statement (which again may take weeks).

d. Vary the presentation from time to time, or the children will learn to respond to the order of what is said, not to the content. If the identity fact always precedes the +1 fact, the children may learn, for example, to treat the first statement as if it were an identity statement. Accordingly, when asked "What's three plus seven?" they will answer "Three." To prevent such learning, alter the presentation so that the +1 question sometimes precedes the identity question. "Four plus one equals _____. Do we know what that is?" If the children answer incorrectly, remind them of the identity fact. "Well, four plus zero equals _____. Sure, so four plus *one* can't equal four. Four plus one equals _____. What comes after four?" Expect the children to have trouble with this task for some time. The differences between the identity and +1 statements, and the related contradictions, are often not obvious to the children.

Algebra Problems Involving the Identity Statements

1. Present a question about a familiar identity statement, $5 + A = 5$, and introduce a way of reading the question. We can read the A as "How many?" Substitute different unknown symbols for the A (U, $\triangle$, C), dem-

onstrating that any unknown can be read as "How many." "Five plus
[clap]
how many equals five?"

2. Relate the problem to past tasks. "What are we starting out with?
. . . Five. And what are we ending up with? . . . Five. So, *how many
more* [point to the *A*] did we get? . . . *None at all,* because we're ending
up with just what we started out with. We're getting zero more. This *A*
equals zero."

3. Present a fast method for handling the question. The above analysis
should not be used exclusively. It is helpful, but laborious. The quickest
and perhaps most dramatic way to demonstrate the meaning of the question is to give the children the answer to it. Point to the problem and instruct the children to "Read this as a question. That means read the *A*
[clap]
as *How many*. Five plus *how many* equals five? . . . We know that [clap-
[clap]
clap-clap] five plus *zero* equals five." Repeat the question and answer
three or four times before moving on to the next problem.

Number Pairs

1. Present the number pairs in order on the board:

$$1 + 1 = B$$
$$2 + 2 = U$$
$$3 + 3 = A$$
$$4 + 4 = B$$
$$5 + 5 = U$$

Solve them with fingers in the usual manner.

2. Have the children read the entire series in unison several times.
The children may have trouble stating these number facts, because their
pattern is unfamiliar. Typically, children confuse these statements with
+0 statements (since both kinds have two elements the same), or else
they omit the term after the plus sign (Two plus equals four). To reduce these mistakes, place great initial emphasis on *reading* the problems and less on reciting or answering the questions implied by them.

3. Introduce questions about each fact after the children have gone
through the entire series. Point to the first statement. "One plus *how
many* equals two? . . . One plus *one* equals two." Continue through the
series in this manner.

4. After the children are able to recite the entire number-pair series
with you, have them close their eyes and answer the questions about the
middle term for the entire statement series. "One plus *how many* equals
two? . . . Two plus *how many* equals four? . . . Three plus *how many*

equals six? . . . Four plus *how many* equals eight? . . . Five plus *how many* equals ten?" The children can answer these questions if they listen carefully to the first number in each question. Expect the children to have the most trouble with the number pair $2 + 2 = 4$, because the preceding number pair, $1 + 1 = 2$, is both a number pair and a member of the $+1$ series. The children may get confused about which series they are reciting and say "Two plus two equals three." Forewarn them of the difficulty and make something of a game out of it. "Now think big. Does two plus two equal *three*? . . . No. Two plus two equals *four*." By making the children conscious of the natural mistake, you will be providing them with the means necessary to avoid the mistake.

Algebra Problems Involving $+1$ Facts and Number Pairs

1. Write the following facts on a large chart.

$1 + 0 = 1$	$1 + 1 = 2$	$1 + 1 = 2$
$2 + 0 = 2$	$2 + 1 = 3$	$2 + 2 = 4$
$3 + 0 = 3$	$3 + 1 = 4$	$3 + 3 = 6$
$4 + 0 = 4$	$4 + 1 = 5$	$4 + 4 = 8$
$5 + 0 = 5$	$5 + 1 = 6$	$5 + 5 = 10$

a. Write on the board:

$$2 + A = 2$$
$$2 + B = 3$$
$$2 + U = 4$$

Read each problem as a question; solve it *by referring to the appropriate column of the chart*. Try to work fast.

b. Point out the basis for selecting a particular statement. "Here it is. It starts out with two and ends up with four."

c. Present the question and answer. "Two plus how many equals [clap] four? . . . Two plus two equals four."

d. Repeat the procedure with different triplets:

$3 + A = 3$	$5 + \triangle = 5$	$4 + a = 4$
$3 + A = 4$	$5 + \triangle = 6$	$4 + a = 5$
$3 + A = 6$	$5 + \triangle = 10$	$4 + a = 8$

2. a. Select an identity statement and present it as a question. "Four plus *how many* equals four? . . . Yes, so four plus how many equals five? . . . Yes, and four plus how many equals eight?"

b. Present four or five of these patterns during a lesson, usually proceeding from the identity statement to the $+1$ statement to the number-pair statement. Alter this order from time to time to prevent spurious learning. Expect the children to have initial trouble with the number pairs.

c. Make the children aware of the distinctive nature of the questions that are to be answered with number-pair statements. Accent the final number. "Four plus how many equals *eight?*" Usually, after the pattern has been presented for about a week, the children begin to hear the differences between the questions in the series.

3. After the children are reasonably proficient at handling the exercise outlined in step 2 above, present written algebra problems on the board.

a. At first, present triplets in the regular order—identify statement, +1 statement, and number-pair statement.

b. Next, present an isolated +1 or number-pair statement; $5 + A = 6$. "What are we starting out with [point to 5]? . . . And what are we ending up with [point to 6]? . . . What comes after five? . . . Yes, *so we're ending up with the next number.* That means we're adding one."

c. In analyzing the number-pair problems, point out that they are *not* identity statements and not +1 statements. "Five plus *how many* equals ten? . . . What are we starting out with? . . . What are we ending up with? . . . Is ten the next number after five? . . . No." Demonstrate with the proper finger operation. "Look. Five plus *how many* equals ten? . . . Five plus *five* equals ten."

d. As the child becomes more familiar with the triplets, work toward a verbal handling of the problem. "Read it as a question. That means read the triangle as 'How many?' Four plus *how many* equals five? . . . We know that. Four plus _____." Slap the board over the triangle as the children say *"One."* After the statement has been completed, ask "So, what do we know about the triangle? . . . Yes, the triangle equals one. So, what can I do?"

e. After the child has mastered the number pairs to $5 + 5 = 10$, introduce the following:

$$6 + 6 = 12$$
$$7 + 7 = 14$$
$$8 + 8 = 16$$
$$9 + 9 = 18$$
$$10 + 10 = 20$$

Teach them in the manner outlined above for smaller number pairs. (Exclude all finger operations, however.)

Producing addition statements.

The arithmetic program moves in two directions from such basic statement operations as "Start out with _____; get more; get _____ more; end up with _____." In one direction, it focuses on the relationship between the statement and the *act of counting*. In the other direction, it focuses on the relationship between the statement and more complicated statement presentations—*word problems*. The first step in this latter direction involves learning how to translate words into numerals and signs—to reverse the familiar symbol-to-word direction. This step is a difficult one.

1. Introduce the two-part box—a divided rectangle, which is said to be "a box." "This box has two parts—here and here."

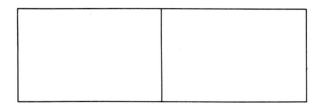

2. Formulate simple addition problems with the box.

a. Draw four or five balls in the box, distributed so that not all are in one compartment.

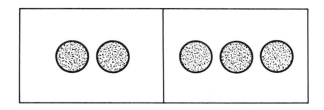

b. Ask "How many balls are in this box? . . . Let's count them and see." Remind the children "We have to count these on this side *and* these on this side."

c. Indicate the total number of balls by writing the number above the box. Then indicate the function of this number in the formulation of equations. "When we count all these balls, we always end up with five. No matter how I move them around, there are five balls in the box."

d. Move a ball at a time from the left side of the box to the other (by erasing and redrawing), calling attention to what is happening. "I'm going to move this ball over to the other side of the box."

e. After each ball has been moved, ask "How many balls are in the box? . . . Yes, there are still five balls in the box. Count them."

f. After many balls have been moved in this manner, demonstrate how it is possible to express the arrangement of balls as an addition statement.

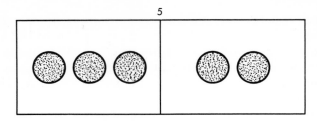

(1) Point to the left compartment and ask "How many balls are in this side of the box? . . . Yes, three." Write "3" below the left compartment.

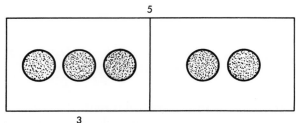

(2) Point to the right compartment and ask "How many balls are in this side of the box? . . . Yes, two." Write "2" below the right compartment.

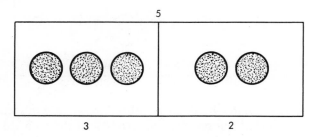

(3) Ask "How many balls are in the box? . . . Yes, five. When we count all of them, we end up with five." Write "= 5" after the 2.

(4) Return to the two compartments. "If we count these *plus* these, we'll end up with *five*. Three *plus* two equals five." Insert "+," completing the statement $3 + 2 = 5$.

3. After the demonstration has been repeated with several other examples, show how to make a systematic series of statements about the balls in the box. Draw three balls in the box, all of them in the left compartment (none in the right), and demonstrate how the statement is made.

a. Remind the children about the number of balls in the box and the function of this number in the statement. "How many balls are in the box? . . . Yes, *three*. We'll always end up with three, no matter how we move them around."

b. Start with the left compartment and ask "How many balls are in this side? . . . Three." Refer to the right side. "How many balls are in this side? . . . Zero. Three plus zero equals _____. How many are in the whole box?"

c. Write the resulting statement below the box: $3 + 0 = 3$.

d. Move the balls, one at a time, to the right compartment of the box, deriving the appropriate statements and writing them beneath the box. After all of the balls have been moved to the right compartment, the statements beneath the box will be:

$$3 + 0 = 3$$
$$2 + 1 = 3$$
$$1 + 2 = 3$$
$$0 + 3 = 3$$

e. Have the children read the statement series. Ask questions about the middle and last terms of each statement.

f. Demonstrate the basic exercise in a way that points out to the children that the number of things in the box can change and that the type of objects used in the box does not affect the basic procedure. Introduce sticks, stick figures, triangles, etc., instead of balls. (In working with the balls, the children sometimes "read" them as zero and thus become confused; sticks are sometimes read as "one." These mistakes can be reduced by filling in the balls with colored chalk and by drawing horizontal sticks.) Introduce no more than four objects in the box until the children become more facile at counting; then increase the total to six.

g. Make the children increasingly responsible for the production of the statements.

4. Introduce the commutative law after the children have become reasonably proficient at producing addition statements.

a. Place three objects in the box; move them one at a time from left to right; and derive the statement series in the usual manner:

$$3 + 0 = 3$$
$$2 + 1 = 3$$
$$1 + 2 = 3$$
$$0 + 3 = 3$$

b. Pair up the reversed elements by connecting them as indicated below:

$$\begin{array}{l} 3 + 0 = 3 \\ 2 + 1 = 3 \\ 1 + 2 = 3 \\ 0 + 3 = 3 \end{array}$$

c. Read the first statement and say "What's another way of saying 'Three plus zero'? [follow the connecting line to the last statement] . . . Zero plus three." As noted in Chapter 2, culturally deprived children typically have trouble in hearing reversed statements. The initial emphasis, therefore, should *not* be on repeating the statements, but on reading them and listening to them. "Listen to the *three*. *Three* plus zero.

[clap]

Turn it around, and it says 'Zero plus *three*.' "

[clap]

d. Present different series. As the children become increasingly aware of what is happening when the statement is reversed, they should be encouraged to repeat statements with the teacher in a rhythmical way. "Two plus one; turn it around; it says 'One plus two.' "

e. During the music period, introduce number exercises such as "Two plus one" in the *Turn It Around* song.

Subtraction

1. Introduce the terminology and the basic finger operation.

a. Present the problem $3 - 1 = A$.

b. Refer to the — as a *minus sign,* pointing out that it looks like part of an equals sign.

c. Work from an operation that is similar to that of the addition problem:

3	—	1	=	A
Start out with three	*Get less*	Get *one less*	End up with	We don't know; we have to figure it out.

d. *Start out* in the usual manner, holding up three fingers on the left hand. *Get less* by "getting rid" of the appropriate number of fingers. "The minus sign tells us to get less. It says to take some away."

e. Help the children with the finger operation. They may try to return their index finger to their fist, which is not easy to do while holding down the little finger.

f. After the children get one less, ask "How many do we end up with? . . . Count them." Be very careful during the initial exercises not to ask "How many are left?" The children may confuse this word with *less* in the instruction "Get less," the result of which is rather thorough confusion. After the operation has been fairly well mastered, the question "How many are left?" can be introduced, prefaced with a warning that the word *left* is not the word *less.* "When you get one *less,* these are *left.*"

2. Introduce the subtraction identity statement.

a. Present the problem $3 - 0 = A$, and work it in the manner described above. Explain the meaning of "Get less; Get zero less" by pointing out "It says to take some away, but when it says 'Take *zero* away,' you take none away. That's a joke, isn't it?"

b. Point out that the subtraction identity series is similar to the addition identity series. Present the subtraction identity statements in the counting order and relate the various statements to familiar addition statements. "Three *plus* zero equals how many? . . . Three *minus* zero equals how many?" The children should have little difficulty with the series.

3. Use the two-part box to demonstrate how to formulate subtraction statements.

a. Introduce a box containing three balls, two in the left compartment and one in the right.

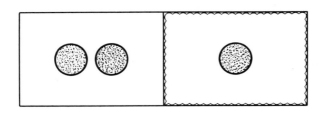

b. Outline the right compartment with a colored chalk line.

c. Count the number of balls in the box and enter the number above the box.

d. Introduce the words *whole* and *part*. Embrace the entire box and say "There are three balls *in the whole box*. There are two *in this part* and one *in this part*."

e. Point to the right compartment and say "I want to *end up with* this part. How many are in this part? . . . Yes, one. I want to end up with one. How can I write that? . . . *Equals one.*" Below the box and to the right, enter

$$= 1$$

f. Pose the problem. "I want to end up with one, but I'm starting out with the whole box. How many am I starting out with? . . . Yes, three. How can I write that: Start out with three? . . . Put a three over here."

$$3 \quad = 1$$

"I'm starting out with three, but I want to end up with one. What can I do?"

g. Point to the left member of the box. "I've got to get rid of the balls in this part. How many are in this part? . . . Two. I've got to get rid of two—like this." Erase the left part of the box. "Now I end up with one." Complete the statement.

$$3 - 2 = 1$$

h. Summarize with the rhythmical statement "If you start out with three and get two less, you're going to end up with one." From time to time, this statement can be expanded. "If you start out with three pigs and you get two less, you're going to end up with one. One what? . . . One pig." Or "If you start out with three boys and you get two less, you're going to end up with one boy."

i. Introduce different problems and work toward an abbreviated presentation. "How many are in the whole box? . . . Yes, four. And how many do I want to end up with? . . . Yes, three. So what do I have to do? . . . Give me the whole statement. . . . Four minus one equals three."

Multiplication

Multiplication is presented here simply as a way of counting. If there are four objects to be counted, they can be counted by ones, in which case the person who is doing the counting would count four times. The objects can be counted by twos, in which case the person would count two times. Or the objects can be counted by fours, in which case the person would count only one time. Accordingly, a multiplication problem such as $4 \times 1 = 4$ is expressed operationally as

$$4 \times \qquad 1 \qquad\qquad = \qquad 4$$
Count by fours   one time;   end up with   four.

This operation expresses the logic of multiplication, and it ties in nicely with various word problems.

1. To introduce multiplication as counting, demonstrate how to count by different numbers. Count from 1 through 10 slowly, clapping once as each number is produced. Next count to 10 by twos, clapping only for every other number. The numbers 1, 3, 5, 7, 9 receive finger snaps, and the numbers 2, 4, 6, 8, 10 receive claps. Explain "Talk big when I clap. Whisper when I snap. Here we go.

[snap]   [clap]   [snap]   [clap]   [snap]   [clap]   [snap]   [clap]   [snap]   [clap]
One,   *two,*   three,   *four,*   five,   *six,*   seven,   *eight,*   nine,   ten.

Repeat the series, making the clap numbers louder and the snap numbers softer, until the children are scarcely saying the snap numbers.

". . . two . . . four . . . six . . . eight . . . ten." Explain that they are counting by *twos*. Demonstrate that it is possible to count by any number simply by controlling the snaps and claps. Counting by fours, for example:

[snap]	[clap]	[snap]	[clap]	[snap]	[clap]	[snap]	[clap]
One,	two,	three,	*four,*	five,	six,	seven,	*eight.*

2. Present two rows of numbers.

1 2 3 4 5 6 7 8 9 10 11 12 13 14 15 16 17 18 19 20
2 4 6 8 10 12 14 16 18 20

Point out that the top row is "counting by ones." Explain "When you count by ones, you count every number. You clap for every number. But you don't have to count by ones. You can count *by any number.* Let's count by twos. Let's clap for every two numbers." Count with the snap-clap pattern and underline every clap number (2, 4, 6, 8, 10, 12, 14, 16, 18, 20) in the top row. Read the underlined numbers and then refer to the bottom row in which they are written out. "Here are the numbers you say." Later, the children can be shown how to count coins, blocks, etc., two at a time. Initially, however, the explanation should be limited to the counting order of numbers.

3. After reading the 2-series several times and asking the appropriate question ("Is this counting by ones? . . . No, this is not counting by ones. This is counting by twos"), introduce a sample multiplication problem, $2 \times 3 = A$.

a. Point out that this is not an addition problem. "Look at this sign. Is this a plus sign? . . . No. This is a *times sign.* Say it."

b. Read the problem. "Two times three equals *A.* Whenever you see an *A,* you have to figure it out. Does it tell you what to do? . . . Yes. But wait a minute. *It doesn't tell you to start out with two.* [Point to the times sign.] The times sign tells you *to count.* Count. [Tap the board rhythmically over the 2.] It says count by twos [slap board hard over the 3] three times. . . . Again. Count by twos three times."

4. Demonstrate the operation by referring to the two rows of numbers on the board. "It says to count by twos. So we find the row that *starts* with two. The top row starts with one. The bottom row starts with two. [Refer to problem.] It says count how many times? . . . Three times. So here we go. One time [slap over 2], two times [slap over 4], three times [slap beneath 6]. Read it. . . . Yes, six. So what do we know about *A?* . . . *A* equals six. So I can erase the *A* and put up a six." When addition was introduced, the children probably worked hard for weeks before mastering the operation. The same children may master the basic multiplication operation in a matter of ten minutes. (This, of course, is not true of the less verbal child.)

5. Give the child a variety of problems to *interpret,* but not work:

$$3 \times 5 = U$$
$$7 \times 0 = U$$
$$2 \times 4 = U$$
$$9 \times 5 = U$$

"What does the first one tell us to do? . . . It says [tap over the 3] count by threes [slap board over 5] five times."

6. Introduce problems involving ones and zero:

$$1 \times 3 = U$$
$$1 \times 0 = U$$

"The first one tells us to count by ones three times." Refer to the "1" row. "Here we go, counting three times. One time, two times, *three times. Read it.* . . . Three. When you count by ones three times, you're going to end up with three. What do we know about U? . . . U equals three."

"The next problem tells us to count by ones zero times. Here we go. There [shrug], read it. Read what? I didn't count at all, did I? . . . But that's what it said to do. It said to count by ones *no times at all.*"

7. Present the multiplication chart and demonstrate how it works.

1	2	3	4	5	6	7	8	9	10
2	4	6	8	10	12	14	16	18	20
3	6	9	12	15	18	21	24	27	30
4	8	12	16	20	24	28	32	36	40
5	10	15	20	25	30	35	40	45	50
6	12	18	24	30	36	42	48	54	60
7	14	21	28	35	42	49	56	63	70
8	16	24	32	40	48	56	64	72	80
9	18	27	36	45	54	63	72	81	90
10	20	30	40	50	60	70	80	90	100

To work a problem such as $4 \times 2 = C$, the children must first translate the problem into an operation. "Count by fours two times." They must then relate this operation to the chart. "Count by fours" tells the child to *find the 4 in the left vertical column of the chart.* This is the starting point for the counting operation. "Two times" tells *how many times* to count. The "= *C*" in the problem indicates that the question to be answered is: How many will you end up with? This question is answered by *reading* the number that is reached by counting two times.

Since there are three questions dealing with *how many* (how many times to count, how many times to count by, how many to end up with), this operation is potentially confusing and must be presented carefully.

a. Introduce a problem that involves counting at least three times, such as $5 \times 4 = N$.

b. Ask what the problem tells us to do. "It says to count by fives four times."

c. Ask questions about the counting operation. These are very important. "What does it say *to count by?* . . . Count by fives. Count *how many times?* . . . Count four times."

d. Show how the chart relates to the operation. "We're going to count by fives. So I've got to find the five over here [run hand up and down the left vertical column]."

e. "We're going to count *four times*. Here we go [proceed from left to right and touch the appropriate squares]. One time, two times, three times, *four times*."

f. As soon as the children have finished counting the appropriate number of times, say *"Read it."* Unless they receive this instruction, they may not know what to do, and until they learn that they are dealing with the numbers on the chart both *as objects* (when they count one time, two times, etc.) and also as *numerical values* (5, 10, 15, etc.), they may understandably become confused.

g. After the children have read the appropriate number on the chart, complete the problem in the same way that addition and subtraction problems are handled. "So what do we know? . . . *N* equals twenty. So what can I do? . . . Erase the *N* and put in a twenty."

h. Summarize the operation and have the children read the problem. "If you count by fives four times, you're going to end up with *how many?* . . . End up with *twenty*. Read it. Five times four equals twenty."

8. Present a variety of problems that involve two-place answers. Concentrate initially on the 20's and then proceed to larger numbers. The children usually learn to read two-place numbers with little training. The teacher should prompt them to attack the number from left to right by pointing first to the left element and then swinging to the right.

2   3

She should expect the children to have some trouble with "reversals," such as reading 21 as "twelve." This kind of error is quite natural.

9. After the children are able to state the multiplication operation verbally and carry it out on the chart (with some prompting), introduce

exercises that sharpen the differences between the *how many* questions posed by the operational statement.

a. Present the problem $4 \times 6 = N$ and have the children state the operation. "Count by fours six times."

b. Ask "Does it tell us what to count by? . . . Yes, it says to count by fours."

c. Ask "Does it tell us *how many times* to count? . . . Yes, it tells us to count six times."

d. Ask "Does it tell us *how many* we will end up with? . . . No, that's what we must find out."

e. Move the unknown to the middle term, so that the problem reads $4 \times N = 24$.

f. Explain "This is a different problem." Point to the N. "Does it tell us *how many times* to count? . . . No, that's what we have to find out."

g. Ask "Does it tell us what to count by? . . . Yes, it tells us to count by four."

h. Point to the 24. "Does it tell us *how many* we end up with? . . . Yes, it says that we'll end up with twenty-four."

i. Present different examples. Do not expect the children to answer the questions properly at first.

10. Teach the children how to count by twos, fives, and tens. Present each series in a rhythmically distinct manner, starting with the 2-series and working on it for perhaps a minute during every period until the children are able to recite the series by rote.

a. Initially, refer to the chart to show the source of the series. "We're going to count by twos, so start over here with two and go across: two, four, six, eight, ten, [etc.].

b. Call attention to the relation between the series and the first number. *"When you count by twos, you start out with two.* When you count by fives, you start out with five. When you count by ones, you start out with _____."

11. Present problems in which the middle term is unknown. These should be introduced only after the children have become fairly proficient at distinguishing between the *how many* questions posed by the multiplication problem (step 9 above).

a. Present the problem $6 \times A = 24$ and ask the *how many* questions. "How many times do we count? . . . We don't know. How many do we end up with? . . . It says that we end up with twenty-four."

b. State the operation for this type of problem: "It says to count by six *how many times* to end up with twenty-four?"

c. Ask "What are we going to count by? . . . Sixes. How many times? . . . We don't know. But we know that we're going to end up with twenty-four.

d. Locate the 6-row on the multiplication chart and indicate "We're going to end up with twenty-four, so I've got to find the twenty-four in this row. Here it is."

e. While touching the 6 with the left hand and the 24 with the right, explain "We've got to count by sixes and find out *how many times.* Here we go. One time, two times, three times, *four times.*"

f. Repeat the question. "How many times? . . . Yes, four times. So what do we know? . . . *A* equals four."

g. Present a variety of problems similar to the one above.

Word Problems

Exercises with the two-part box were designed to function as a transition between working a problem that is presented in the form $3 + 2 = C$ and problems that are posed in "reality statements," such as "A farmer has three chickens; two more are hatched; how many does he now have?" The two-part box problems functioned as a transition because they gave the children practice in formulating the arithmetic statement. The problems demonstrated that a presentation such as that in the diagram

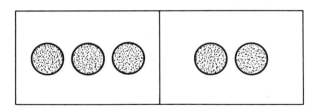

can be expressed not only as $2 + 3 = 5$, but also in terms of the operation "Start out with three; get two more; end up with five." Word problems are similar to the two-part box in the sense that *they are a presentation which can be reduced to a statement of arithmetic.* However, the degree of similarity between word problems and two-part box problems should not be exaggerated. Word problems are more difficult than two-part box problems for two reasons:

1. Word problems are "noisier," since they contain a great deal of extraneous information. Selection of relevant elements requires verbal skill.

2. The solution of a word problem requires that words in the language of arithmetic be substituted for words in the language of everyday statements. The substitution rules are not always simple. For instance, the word *borrow* could imply either addition or

subtraction, depending on whether the person being talked about does the borrowing or whether someone else borrows from him.

These two differences imply differences in the way word problems should be taught. Some of the noise should be removed from these problems at first and the specific links between words and corresponding arithmetic symbols must be clearly defined.

1. Present addition word problems first.

a. Make up problems involving the children in the class. When introducing these problems, phrase them so that they correspond to the familiar operational statement of addition. For example, "Harold starts out with three pennies; then he gets more pennies; he gets two more pennies. How many pennies does he end up with?" The only difference between this statement and the familiar addition operational statement is that the words *Harold* and *pennies* have been introduced.

b. Ask the standard questions about the operation *and new questions about the new words in the statement.* "Who is this story about? . . . Harold. Harold starts out with three whats? . . . Three sheep? . . . No, three pennies. What happens? . . . Does Harold get more pennies or get less pennies? . . . How many more? . . . How many does he end up with? . . . We don't know."

c. Summarize the problem as the familiar operation "Here's what we want to write: Start out with three, get two more."

d. Pose the question "How can I write that?" and answer it, while writing the answer on the board. "How do I write, 'Start out with three?' . . . Make a three."

$$3$$

"How do I write get more? . . . Make a plus sign."

$$3 +$$

"How do I write get two more?"

$$3 + 2$$

"How many do I end up with? . . . I don't know, so I write _____."

$$3 + 2 = B$$

e. After the children have read the problem several times and solved it, remind them of the situation from which the problem derived. "Harold started out with three pennies, and he got two more. How many did he end up with? . . . Yes, five. *Five what?* . . . Five Oldsmobiles? . . . Five Indians? . . . *Five pennies.*"

f. Present a series of operational summary statements which demonstrate that the name of the thing that is added can change without changing the basic statement $3 + 2 = 5$. (The statements in this series should be colorful. The children will probably offer suggestions.) "If you start out with three pennies and you get two more, you're going to end up with five pennies." "If you start out with three Tyrones and you get two more, you're going to end up with five Tyrones." "If you start out with three elephants and you get two more, you're going to end up with five _____." "If you start out with three hamburgers and you get two more, you're going to end up with _____."

2. Introduce problems that involve starting out with more than five or adding more than five. Since these cannot be worked on the finger operation the children customarily use, a new counting procedure should be introduced.

a. Phrase the problem in the usual manner.

$$7 + 3 = B$$

b. Point out the necessity of the new counting convention. "It says to start out with seven. Oh, oh. We can only start out with five fingers. How can we work this problem?"

c. Offer a solution. "Instead of using fingers, I'm going to make lines. It says to start out with seven, so I'm going to start out with seven lines.

IIIIIII

$$7 + 3 = B$$

Then it says to get three more. So I'll get three more lines, like this."

IIIIIII   III

$$7 + 3 = B$$

Draw a circle around all the lines. "We count all of them and that tells us how many we'll end up with." (Note: The relationship between counting with lines in this manner and counting with fingers seems perfectly obvious. To most of the children, however, the connection will be anything but obvious. It will be a great deal like starting over, and every step of the new procedure will have to be taught anew.)

3. After the children have mastered the simplified word problems, introduce different situations that can be interpreted as *getting more*.

a. Demonstrate how the act of buying can be expressed as getting more. "Debby has two dolls. She goes to the store and *buys four more*. How many does she have now?"

(1) Ask "How many does she start out with?" Point out that she started out with two. "Remember, I said that she *has two dolls.*"

(2) Ask the crucial question about the nature of the operation. "And then what happens? . . . Does Debby get more, or does she get

less?" Point out that buying is getting more. "When you buy four dolls, you get more; you get four more."

(3) Work the problem in the manner suggested in step 1 above, asking questions about the dolls.

b. Introduce a variety of problems involving *finding, buying, stealing, and making*. Point out that in each case these words denote *getting more* and therefore can be represented by a plus sign.

4. Introduce subtraction word problems in a manner similar to the presentation for addition problems.

a. Begin with simplified problems that embody the words "Get less." "Harold starts out with four stones, and he gets less; he gets three less. How many does he end up with?"

b. Point out that the problem involves getting *less*, not more. A quick review with the two-part box may be in order.

c. Show in detail how the word problem reduces to the formulation $4 - 3 = A$.

d. Introduce subtraction problems that involve starting out with more than five; also introduce a counting convention for handling such numbers.

(1) Represent the numerical value of the first term by lines, circles, triangles, or letters.

FFFFFFFFF

$$9 \quad - \quad 6 \quad = \quad B$$

(2) To indicate the act of getting less, cross out the specified number. "When I cross it out, we don't have it anymore. The problem says to get six less, so I have to cross out six."

𝕱𝕱𝕱𝕱𝕱𝕱FFF

$$9 \quad - \quad 6 \quad = \quad B$$

(3) Ask "How many are *left?*" and clarify. "These are the ones that are *left*—the ones that are *not* crossed out."

e. Present more complex problems after the children have become familiar with the skeletal problems. Concentrate on problems that involve *losing, throwing away, giving away, selling, and consuming (eating and drinking)*. Point out that each of these actions can be represented with a minus sign, because each is an instance of getting less. "Debby has eight stones and throws five of them away. When she throws stones away, is she getting more or less? . . . She's getting less."

5. Introduce simplified word multiplication problems.

a. Pose the problem "Harold has a lot of pockets. And he has four pennies in each pocket. He wants to know how many pennies he has."

b. Draw a representation of the problem.

c. Make certain that the children understand that each pocket con-

tains the same number of pennies. Point to a big pocket and ask "Does this pocket have more pennies than this little pocket? . . . No, they have the same. They have four pennies." From time to time, make the point that the number of pennies is not related to the size of the pockets.

d. Point out "He can count his pennies by ones, can't he? . . . But there's a faster way." "He can count this four [point to the first pocket], and this four [point to the second pocket], and this four [etc.]. He can count by fours one time, two times, three times, four times, five times. *He can count by fours five times.*"

e. Ask "How can I write that: Count by fours five times?" (4 × 5 = D) At first, the children will probably need a considerable amount of help in phrasing the written statement.

f. Solve the problem in the usual manner, referring to the multiplication chart.

g. Introduce a variation of the problem above. "Tyrone gets two pennies from his mother every time he does a good job in school. I'll mark the days that he gets pennies."

2   X   X   2   X   2   2   2   2   2   2

Explain that the funny marks show the days on which he did not get his pennies. "At first Tyrone had some bad days. But he really got better near the end, didn't he? . . . How can Tyrone count up all his pennies a fast way? . . . He can count by twos one time [point to the 2's], two times, three times, four times, five times, six times, seven times, eight times. He can count by twos eight times." Solve the problem in the usual manner.

6. Introduce area-of-rectangle problems.

a. Draw a grid on the board and identify the parts of the grid as "squares." Explain "We want to count all these squares. First let's count them one at a time."

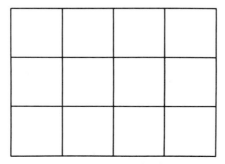

b. After counting the squares and marking the total above the grid, explain "There's a faster way to count. Instead of counting each square, we can count a whole row of squares."

c. Establish the idea that each row contains the same number of squares. Count the squares in the top row, in the middle row, and in the bottom row. Ask "Which one of these rows has more squares? . . . They all have the same. They all have four squares."

d. Conclude "We can count by fours one time [draw a chalk line through the top row], two times [draw a line through the middle row], three times [draw a line through the bottom row]. *We can count by fours three times."*

e. Point out that since lines have been drawn through every square, all the squares have been counted.

f. Have the children solve the problem in the manner described in step 5 above.

g. After the children have begun to master area-of-rectangle problems, show them that the grid can be approached in more than one way. Demonstrate with a sample grid. "If we count by fives three times, we'll

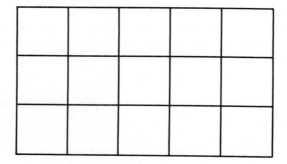

count all of the squares. But there's another way to count." Draw lines through the *vertical columns*. "We can count by threes one time, two times, three times, four times, five times. We can count by threes five

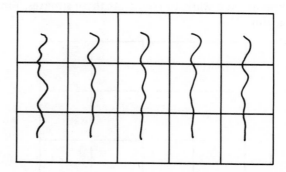

times." Write the two statements on the board, and solve the problem both ways.

$$5 \times 3 = B$$

$$3 \times 5 = B$$

After the solution has been found, ask "What's another way of saying five times three? . . . Three times five."

h. Present a series of grids which must be solved both by counting the rows and counting the columns.

i. After the children have had some practice with grids, present area-of-rectangle problems in which the individual squares are not detailed. Draw a large rectangle on the board and explain that it is a wall or a sheet of paper, asking how many *square* feet or inches it contains. Show the children how large an inch, a foot, and a yard are. Give them practice in indicating with their hands how large these measurements are.

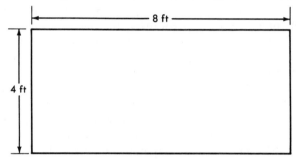

"This wall is eight feet wide and four feet high. The painter wants to know how many square feet are in this wall because he's only got one small can of paint and he wants to know if it will be enough to cover the wall." Work the problem in the usual way, indicating the number of square feet inside the rectangle.

7. Introduce a variation of the problem, in which only the length of the wall is given. "This wall is eight feet across the top. We don't know

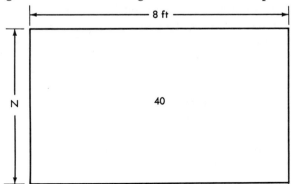

how high it is. This N tells us that we have to figure it out. But we do know that we *end up* with forty square feet after we count all of them. We want to figure out how high this wall is. We can do that if *we count by eights* [point to the 8] how many times [point to the N] to end up with forty [point to the 40]?" Write the problem on the board ($8 \times N = 40$). Solve it by the method outlined on page 262.

Summary

Arithmetic is based on the operation of counting. It is based on the notion that a given number has a successor, that the number's successor in turn has a successor, and so forth. Some operations call for counting by single numbers; others demand jumping in fixed steps, perhaps two numbers at a time, perhaps 20. The understanding of arithmetic must begin with an understanding of counting. Accordingly, the program outlined in this chapter begins with counting by ones—counting as an oral exercise, counting as a way of grouping objects, counting as the operation that answers the question "How many?"

After the counting operations were established, the program introduced the basic statements of arithmetic. These have a dual role, functioning both as declarations of what is true in the world of number and also relating the counting operation that is consistent with the series $1 + 0 = 1, 2 + 0 = 2$, etc. These represent the basic statements for "figuring out" any given addition fact. One may not know what 45 plus 17 equals, but one who is familiar with the rule for identity statements knows that $45 + 0 = 45$. From this point, the question is simply one of counting (according to the conventions of equations) until one has arrived at 45 plus 17.

The $+1$ statement series was introduced after the identity series. The two series helped define the counting conventions of equations. In order to demonstrate the validity of these and other statements, a finger operation was introduced.

Also, a series of "number-pair" addition facts was introduced. Just as statements in everyday language generate questions, statements in arithmetic generate questions. These are the "algebra" questions, which were introduced in connection with the identity series, the $+1$ series, and the number pairs.

The two-part box was introduced to form a bridge between addition and subtraction and also to present the first series of exercises in going from a physical presentation to the appropriate statements of arithmetic. The two-part box, therefore, functioned as the first and most basic kind of reality problem. Instead of translating a statement into an operation, the child was now required to express the physical presentation as a statement. Through the process, he was shown the relationship between the two parts of the box and the "whole" box. The stage was thereby set for subtraction, which was introduced as an operation similar to addition.

Multiplication was presented as counting in fixed steps—counting by twos, by threes, by nines, or by tens. A statement of multiplication such as $3 \times 6 = B$ was translated into the operation "Count by threes six times." The counting operation was carried out on a multiplication chart.

The final series of tasks in the arithmetic program focused on word problems. The primitive type of reality problems had already been introduced in connection with the two-part box. The presentation was expanded so that the presentation from which the child worked was not physical reality but *words*. Statements were carefully programmed, with all but the logical essentials removed. Addition problems were concerned with obvious acts of getting more—stealing, making, buying, etc. Subtraction problems dealt with obvious acts of getting less—losing, selling, etc. Multiplication dealt with counting by fixed jumps—counting by a given number so many times, counting by the number of units of measurement the number of times necessary to count all of the squares in a rectangle.

The arithmetic program outlined in this chapter attempted to provide a basic understanding of arithmetic as it relates to counting. No great emphasis was placed on arithmetic facts, and it would not be unusual for a child to be quite handy at the various tasks presented in the program and yet be unable to specify what 6 plus 5 equals. There are many gaps left by the program; however, the program aimed at what the writers considered to be the areas that must be defined for the child in a way that will be both productive and consistent with future learning.

the reading **11**
program

*I*f a child fails in reading during the primary grades, his chances for success in any other academic area are greatly reduced. It is therefore essential that a preschool program for disadvantaged children do all it can to ensure that the children will succeed in reading when they enter school. Language instruction can go a long way in this direction, but it is not the whole answer. First- and second-grade reading materials, after all, are written in extremely simple English and with very limited vocabularies. A child may be able to understand the materials thoroughly when they are read to him, and yet fail to learn to read. Obviously something more is needed before a child is "ready" to succeed in reading.

The present reading program is based on two principles that have come to be generally accepted by linguistic analysts as fundamental to reading and which have been largely ignored in reading readiness programs. These are: (1) the importance of the word as the basic unit in reading, and (2) the importance of the alphabetic principle in English orthography.[1]

In grammar, the basic unit is the sentence, and discrete words constitute the detail from which the meaning of the sentence is derived. In reading, the basic unit is the word, and the letters constitute the detail. We have noted in Chapter 2 the inability of the disadvantaged child to treat words as discrete units. This handicaps him in grammar by robbing him of the essential details for understanding and constructing statements. In reading, this lack of awareness of words as discrete entities makes him oblivious of the structural wholes which spelling creates.

In the course of his language learning, the culturally privileged child not only masters the syntactical forms of English, but also treats words as entities that can be detached from sentences that contain them. Say to a culturally privileged four-year-old "John did not do a satisfactory job of cleaning up his room," and one will usually not draw a blank stare. The child may ask "What does *satisfactory* mean?" and then, having received a comprehensible explanation, he will put the meaning into the sentence and thus comprehend the sentence as a whole. He may even venture a guess and ask "Does satisfactory mean good?" Hearing "John and Jim went for a swim," he may point out "You made a poem. Jim-swim—they rhyme." Before he goes to sleep at night, he may amuse himself by playing with words that rhyme or alliterate: "Bittle, bottle, beatle, butter, boom." When such a child is told that the set of characters on a sign represents the word *stop,* the statement is likely to mean something to him. For him, words are real things that could conceivably be represented by visual symbols.

Certain traditional reading readiness activities that come under the rubric of "word awareness" seem to point in the direction of getting the child to think of words as independent entities—attaching labels to objects in the classroom and putting the child's name on his chair, his coat hook, and so on. These are worthwhile steps, but they do not go very far. If the culturally deprived child is to come up to the level of the more privileged child in "word awareness," he will need to be put through an intensive course of instruction that will enable him to treat words as things that can be talked about, compared, taken apart and put back together, constructed out of smaller words or word parts, and changed into other words by altering their parts or the order in which the parts are arranged.

Familiarizing the child with the alphabetical principle means, in simple terms, teaching him that words are spelled. It may be some time before the child will grasp that English spelling follows certain rules which make it possible for him to recognize words that he has never encountered in writing before. But if he is to progress in reading at all, he must clearly recognize that it is the spelling and not some superficial characteristic like length or symmetry that determines the identity of a printed word. Again, the culturally privileged child usually manages to pick up during his preschool years at least a vague conception of spelling. The child may learn the letters of the alphabet, may learn to spell his name, and may be informed when he reads off the letters on a cereal box that they spell the name of the cereal. When the culturally privileged child first encounters formal reading instruction, he already has some idea of the nature of the task.

The program outlined here concentrates directly on developing the two kinds of readiness discussed above—awareness of words as distinct entities and awareness of the alphabetical principle. Since awareness of the alphabetical principle requires learning the alphabet and learning to recognize words by their spellings, the program is not a reading readiness program in the usual sense at all, but an actual course in reading. This is a misleading label, however. The program differs from ordinary reading programs in that it devotes the greater part of the time to developing the two kinds of awareness mentioned above, whereas most first-grade reading programs, having been designed for the more privileged child, either assume that the child already has this awareness or that he will pick it up quickly with little help. Perhaps the most accurate way of describing the program is to say that it is a highly intensive nine-month program which covers the amount of material covered in the first half of an ordinary first-grade program, the extra time being devoted to developing the fundamental skills and concepts that the culturally deprived child is believed to require special help in mastering.

Overview of the Reading Program

The approach taken to reading in this program most nearly resembles the linguistic approaches of Bloomfield and Fries.[2] The child is taught to spell out words, words are introduced in clusters that all follow the same spelling pattern (such as *cat, rat, fat, sat*), but there is no effort to teach phonic rules explicitly. That is, the child does not learn to "sound out" words. Only capital letters are used in the first part of the program. This reduces the time required for learning the alphabet, which is a major bottleneck for the child who has not had any previous training with letters. Also, the writers have found that by using only capital letters and using them in systematic exercises where the child always knows what he is looking for, problems of visual discrimination are reduced. Thus, the large amount of work that is usually devoted in reading readiness programs to visual discrimination training can be by-passed.

The program outlined in this chapter makes use of a number of devices for reinforcing the meanings of words and sentences as they are taken up in reading exercises. The teacher should be wary of other techniques which on the surface might seem to add additional meaningfulness to the reading exercises. For instance, it is tempting to bring in pictures or actual objects to serve as referents for words, and when the child has decoded the word CAT, to say "Show me the cat." Such demonstrations can produce grave confusion. When told "Show me the cat," the child does not know whether he should find the word or find the picture. It is not that the child confuses words with their referents (whether he does or not is beside the point here), but simply that he cannot understand what the teacher is trying to get across. In fact, on close analysis, it is not at all clear what is the relevance of sentences like "Show me the cat" to the statement "This word is CAT."

In dealing with individual words, the simplest way to remind the child of their meaning is by asking *yes-no* questions that contrast the given word with related words. "This word is CAT. Is this word DOG? . . . Is this word ELEPHANT? . . . No, this word is CAT." By differentiating the given word (*cat*) from words referring to related classes of objects (dogs, elephants, cows, rats, etc.), the child is reminded of its meaning.

This technique works only for lexical terms (nouns, action verbs, modifiers); but these are the only kinds of words that the child can generally deal with meaningfully in isolation. It is useless to try to establish the meaning of words like *the, is, in, and, not,* and *same* outside of statement contexts, and this should not be done until the child is reading sentences that contain them. The meaningfulness of sentences is best established by treating them with questions as is done in the language program. "MARVIN IS A BIG BOY. Is Marvin a little boy? . . . Is Marvin a big girl? . . . No, Marvin is a big boy. Does it say Marvin is *not* a big boy? . . . No, it says Marvin *is* a big boy."

In the early stages, the reading program contains two separate threads that are followed simultaneously until they eventually join in concerted reading activities. One thread is concerned with developing awareness of words, word recognition, and the eventual reading of sentences. The other thread is concerned with letter discrimination and identification. Once the child has mastered the alphabet to the point where he can spell out words fluently, the two kinds of training merge into reading exercises based on spelling analogies. For clarity of exposition, the sequence of the exercises concerned with words is presented separately from the sequence concerned with letters, but it should be understood that the two are taught simultaneously, a portion of each period being devoted to word exercises and a portion to work with the alphabet.

Besides the usual chalkboard equipment, the materials needed in the early portion of the reading program consist of an alphabet chart and a supply of cards for the presentation of letters and words. The alphabet chart may be printed on a piece of art board approximately two feet square, with the letters arranged according to the phrasing of the alphabet song (see Chapter 9).

```
A  B  C  D  E  F  G
H  I  J  K  L  M  N  O  P
Q  R  S  T  U  V
W  X  Y  Z
```

Ordinary 5″ × 8″ or 4″ × 6″ file cards are suitable for word and letter cards. They deteriorate rapidly and have to be replaced, but this prevents the child from learning to recognize words or letters by telltale irregularities. Characters should be printed on the cards with a marking pen or pencil that does not show through on the opposite side.

Word Awareness and Word Recognition

Production of isolated words.

Even though some of the children may speak mostly in single-word utterances, they are usually not accustomed to treating words as distinct things that can be separated from longer utterances. Printing out words that the children volunteer helps to establish the distinctive identity of words, and it usually arouses the children's interest in words.

1. Print the word HIT on the chalkboard. Teach the rule "This is a word," followed by the statement "This is the word HIT." Insist on the children's producing complete statements and establish the meaning of the statements with questions. "Is this the word PAT? . . . Is this the word TICKLE? [etc., illustrated with gestures]."

2. Invite the children to suggest the next word to write. Be ready with suggestions if the children do not volunteer. "How about BALLOON? Would you like me to write the word BALLOON?" After a few suggestions, the children will usually begin volunteering words. Do only four or five words a day, staving off further requests with a promise to write more words the next day.

3. Print the words in different locations on the chalkboard. As each new word is added, review the identification of the words already printed. "Is this the word HIT? . . . No, this is the word BALLOON. Where is the word HIT? . . . *This* is the word HIT." Do not overdo this exercise, however, by trying to get the children to memorize a whole board full of words. They may be able to do it, but it will encourage them to become too dependent on location cues for word identification.

4. When the children have become facile at producing words to be printed, demonstrate how you construct a word. Set the alphabet board up on the chalk tray. (It is presumed that work with letters will already have begun, as prescribed in the next section.) Explain as you print "I'm going to write the word GUN. I start out with the letter G, here, and make one just like it here." Demonstrate this with each letter in turn, holding your finger by the letter on the chart as you copy it. Then review the identity of the whole word.

5. Have a child help you by keeping his finger on the letter as you copy it.

Spend a few minutes each day on these exercises for a week or two, and then return only occasionally to them to remind the children that any words they think of can be written.

Word-placement exercises.

These exercises are intended to accomplish two things: (1) get across to the children the idea that printed words carry information, that they "tell you something"; and (2) teach the children how to tell whether or not two words are the same. These are important but very limited steps, and the exercises should not be continued after the children have accomplished these steps, for if carried on too long, the activities will generate a narrow conception of words and word meaning.

1. Introduce 5" × 8" cards, each with the name of an object in the room printed on it and each provided with a bit of masking tape for affixing it to the appropriate object. Say, "This card has a word on it. This is the word DOOR." Quickly identify five or more words in this way, setting up each card in the chalk tray.

2. Demonstrate putting a word *where it belongs*. "This is the word DOOR. Let's put it where it belongs. It belongs on the door." Put the card in place on the door and have the children answer the questions "This is the word what?" and "So where does it belong?"

3. Give each child a turn placing a different word, requiring him to answer the above questions.

4. When all the words have been placed, have each child bring back to you a given word, different from the one he placed. Have him identify the word and the location, both before and after he fetches the word card.

5. After the children have mastered this task (usually in one to three days), switch from identifying the words directly to making identification dependent upon matching the word on the card with a word on the chalkboard. Put two word cards up on the chalk tray. Print one of the words on the chalkboard in letters the same size as those on the card. Review the statement "This is a word" for each of the three words. Then present the rule "If all the letters are the same, the words are the same," drilling the children on rhythmic repetition of it and its converse, "If all the letters are not the same, the words are not the same."

6. Demonstrate how to check whether the letters are the same. Place the matching card under the word printed in chalk and, proceeding from left to right, compare the letters one by one. "Are these letters the same? . . . Yes." Conclude "Are *all* the letters the same? . . . Yes, all the letters are the same. What's the rule?" Using the other word card, demonstrate that the words (on the chalkboard and on the card) are not the same.

7. Drill on the concluding statements. "Tell me about these words. These words are [or are not] the same." Then, without explanation, add a second part to each statement. "These words are the same. This is the word TABLE, so this other one is the word TABLE." Also "These words are *not* the same. This is the word TABLE, so this other one is *not* the word TABLE."

8. End the drill with the positive statement "This is the word TABLE, so this is the word TABLE." Pick up the card. "This is the word what? . . . So where does it belong?" Then have a child place the word, as in the preceding exercise.

9. Replace the word with another word and repeat steps 5 through 8. As the task becomes mastered, put up more than two word cards at a

time. Identify the chalkboard word before starting. After one or two words have been checked that are not the same, say "Let's try to find a word that is the same." If a child locates the correct word, check it as before, going through the full series of statements, and then let the child who located the word place it. Soon the children will be able to locate the correct word immediately. When this stage has been reached, the exercise should be discontinued.

10. While the children are working on word matching, change one or two of the words each day so that the children do not merely learn to distinguish among a small set of words.

Word-identity exercises.

These exercises are intended to give the children a small sight vocabulary and lead them as quickly as possible into the reading of simple sentences. As a crutch, during the stage when the children's ability to recognize and remember a number of words is very limited, each of the words used in a given exercise is assigned to a different child so that, cooperatively, the group as a whole can decode a whole series of words or a sentence, even though each individual child can identify only one word in the series.

1. Teach the children to recognize their own names.

a. Have the names printed on cards. Identify a name (James) and have the whole class repeat the statement "This is the word JAMES." Tell James that it is his job to remember that word. Do not make an issue of its being his name. Hold it up for him to look at closely and then place it on the chalkboard in front of him. Have the whole class make the identification statement again. Assign the rest of the words in the same way, one at a time, placing them in a row in the chalk tray *so that they correspond to the seating order of the children.* As each new word is put in place, have the whole class review the identification of all the words from left to right.

b. When all of the words have been put up, have the children identify the words as you point to them in an irregular order. Drill on this until the children can quickly identify every name (allowing time for the children to process what they see).

c. Remove all but two of the words. Review the identification of them. Then print one of these words on the chalkboard and go through the same, not same, and identification procedures outlined in steps 6–8 in the preceding section.

d. Print about five examples of each word, varying the size and scattering them randomly over the whole chalkboard. Identify each one as you print it. Then drill the children on calling out the word as you slap the chalk board beneath it. Work on this until the children are responding very rapidly. Make the slaps very dramatic so that the children are in suspense as to which word you are going to slap.

e. Add a third word and repeat the above steps, then additional words until the whole set of names has been learned. Some groups will be able to handle five or more words almost immediately, but others will need to work up to it gradually. If the children show signs of guessing, retreat to a smaller set of names.

f. Print the whole set of names in a row on the board and draw an arrow under the row that points toward the right. Say "First let's count the words. What way does the arrow tell us to go?" (The children should already be familiar with this procedure from the arithmetic program.) Have them count "One word, two words, three words, [etc.]." Then have the children read the words in the left-to-right sequence until they are able to do so without prompting.

2. Repeat the steps of exercise 1 using a set of body-part words, e.g., NOSE, HAND, LEG, HEAD, FOOT. It will be necessary to emphasize even more strongly to each child as a word is assigned to him the need for him to remember it. Also point out to the rest of the class "When you try to remember this word, just think about Oscar. What's Oscar's word? . . . LEG." Do not comment on the meaning of the words. As you assign each word to a child, simply touch the part of his body to which the word refers. The children may have more difficulty remembering the words when they are all placed on the chalk tray. If they falter, call on the child who was assigned the word. If he does not remember either, say very firmly "You've got to remember your word. Your word is NOSE," pressing the part of the body indicated as you say this. The harder you press, the more likely the child is to remember his word the next time around.

In drilling on step *f*, reading the words in sequence, work toward the gradual elimination of pointing cues. Start out slapping each word in turn, then pointing, then pointing less and less directly as the children are able to move from word to word on their own.

3. Introduce new body-part names and mixed sets of body-part names and children's names until the children have become proficient enough at the exercises to master a set of five words in ten minutes. (Do not expect mastery to carry over to the next day, however.)

4. Assign a new set of words that can be combined to make sentences. A good set to begin with is IS, NOT, BIG, plus the names of a couple of children in the group. Assign the names to the slower of the children. Go through steps *a–f* as before, but in step *f* arrange the words to make a statement, such as "HENRY IS BIG." After the children have read the words in sequence one time, tell them "Listen, this tells you about Henry." Have them read the sequence aloud again and then ask ques-

tions. "Does it say Henry is big?" . . . "Does it say Henry is little?" Recombine the words to make several different statements. "JAMES IS BIG." "JAMES IS NOT BIG." "HENRY IS NOT JAMES."

5. In subsequent lessons, introduce a couple of new words each time to make possible the construction of different sentences. "THE CAT IS FAT; THE CAT IS SKINNY; THE CAT IS NOT FAT." "SUPER-MAN IS FAT; SUPERMAN IS SKINNY." "DIANE SAT ON THE CHAIR; THE CHAIR SAT ON DIANE." "A DOG BIT THE CAT; THE CAT BIT A DOG; TONY HIT THE DOG."

a. When a word has been used often enough that the children remember it from preceding exercises, include it in sentence-reading drills, but do not use it on a word card. Write it at the top of the chalkboard and say "Everybody should remember this word. This is the word _____." The children's own names should be learned as sight words in this way, and eventually the words THE, IS, NOT, A, ON, and IN. Presenting less familiar words on cards and combining them with these sight words can lead the children to read a variety of little stories and sentence sequences.

b. To ensure that the sentences are conveying meaning, have the children close their eyes after they have worked over a sentence and "Get a picture of 'Superman is fat.' " When the children claim that they have a picture, make a sketch on the chalkboard. Ask "In your picture, did Superman look like this? . . . Or was he big and fat—like this?" This "getting a picture" technique is especially important for statements describing action, like "Tony hit the dog."

It is also a good idea, after the possible meaningful arrangements of words have been worked through, to present a nonmeaningful sequence like DIANE CHAIR THE ON. Ask "Does it give you a picture? . . . No. Does it tell you about Diane? . . . No. Does it tell you about the chair? . . . No." The children may not catch on immediately, but with continued examples they will. This exercise is important in establishing the value of word order. After the basic idea has been grasped, show that going through a meaningful sentence backwards does not give a picture (being sure that sentences are chosen which do not make sense backwards). "THE CAT IS FAT; FAT IS CAT THE."

c. When longer sentences or stories are introduced, use the procedure of "counting with the arrow" to establish the correct way of reading words that run on for more than one line. Draw an arrow under each line and show that when you have finished counting the words on one line, you have to go all the way back to the other end to begin counting the words in the second line. Dramatize the operation of going back until the children have become accustomed to it. "One word, two words, three words, four words. Now we go *all the way back* and keep counting. Five words, six words, seven words, eight words."

Alphabet Learning

The above exercises provide training in letter discrimination, and, in addition, they get across the idea that letters are important for identifying words. The major problem in learning the alphabet, however, is learning to connect the letters with their name.

Rote recitation of the alphabet.

The alphabet song (see Chapter 9) should be introduced in the music program as soon as the children have indicated that they can begin to follow the lyrics of a song. Use the alphabet board and point to the letters as they are sung. Brief drill on recitation of the alphabet should be given in each reading class period also, using the same rhythm as the song, but without the tune. In the reading class, individual children should be given a chance to recite. When a child is able to recite the first line (A B C D E F G), have him stand up at the alphabet board and recite it as you move his hand from letter to letter. Then have him try to say it while pointing by himself. Success in this task should be praised highly. In the child's eyes, its only value can be as a difficult feat to perform, and you should treat it as such. Learning to recite the letters does not in itself provide most children with any basis for identifying the letters. What it does is provide a child with the appropriate repertoire of responses which can then be linked up with the visual stimuli that will have become familiar to him through work on the preceding exercises.

Letter-familiarization exercises.

These exercises give the children a great deal of rapid-paced practice in using the names of letters and in locating their distinguishing characteristics, without immediately imposing the burden of memorizing the letter names. They should therefore be used extensively in the early stages of alphabet learning.

1. Identify the letter A on the chart and quickly print a number of A's on the chalkboard—some large, some small, but all capitals. Have the children identify each one by the statement "This letter is A." Ask the children to find a big A, then a little A. Point to the different A's in turn and have the children give the appropriate statement. "This A is big" or "This A is little."

2. Teach the statement "This A is standing up." Point out "See how it has a point at the top." Then print a succession of A's leaning farther and farther to the side until the A is in a horizontal position. Explain that the A is tipping over. Then, indicating the horizontal A, say "This A is not standing up. Is the point up at the top? . . . No, the point is

down here. This A is not standing up. This A is lying down." Print a variety of A's standing up or lying down and have the children make the appropriate statement about each one in rapid succession. "This letter is A. This A is standing up (or lying down)." Keep inserting the question "Is the point at the top?"

3. Repeat the exercises with other letters, supplying a simple clue for telling when each letter is standing up.

B—The bumps come together here (middle of the upright line).
C—It has a piece missing over here.
D—It's flat on this side.
E—Three lines stick out this way.
F—It's flat on top.
G—It has a little place to sit down here.

4. Work with two and then three letters at a time. Do not stress memory for the letter names, however. Identify each letter before asking a question about it. "This letter is C. This letter is what? . . . Is this C standing up?"

5. Introduce the concept *upside-down* in the same way as *standing up* and *lying down,* but use it only for letters that have distinctive tops or bottoms, such as A, F, G, and J.

Letter-identity exercises.

These exercises are structurally identical to the word-identity exercises outlined in the preceding section (page 280) except that letter cards rather than word cards are assigned to the children. Letters are much harder for the children to remember than words, however, and these letter-identity exercises should not be introduced until the children have become quite proficient in the word-identity exercises. Employ the following six steps:

a. Assign a different letter card to each child, arranging the cards on the chalk tray to correspond to the seating order of the children.

b. Drill on identification of the series of cards in the tray.

c. Compare the letters on the cards with a letter on the board to determine whether or not they are the same.

d. Name the letters printed all over the chalkboard.

e. Increase the number of letters worked with at one time.

f. Name the letters in left-to-right sequences.

Work with a given set of letters until some of them are mastered. Each day, as you assign letter cards to the children, check to see how many children can identify the letter on the card before you name it. When the children show that they remember a certain letter from one day to the next, replace it with another letter card, but continue to use the letter in steps *d* and *f*. In this way, a repertoire of memorized letters will gradually be built up.

Rhyming word patterns.

The ability to recognize words that rhyme is the basis for subsequent learning of the relationship between the pronunciation and spelling of words. For the disadvantaged child, who has not had years of exposure to nursery rhymes, the recognition of rhyming sound patterns does not come easily. It is best approached through the use of "overrhyming"; i.e., using words that rhyme in more than one syllable. It is easier to recognize the similarity between BUTTERFLY and SUTTERFLY than between BIG and SIG.

1. *From the first day of class,* devote a minute or two of each period to having the children say words that rhyme. Have the children say a word like SUPERMAN. Then say "Here's a word that rhymes with SUPERMAN: BUPERMAN. What's another word that rhymes with SUPERMAN? FUPERMAN." Have the children repeat each word. Try to make the exercise entertaining and amusing. "Here's a funny one—PUPERMAN." Bombard the children with examples: TUPERMAN, NUPERMAN, ZUPERMAN, RUPERMAN, LUPERMAN, etc.

2. On subsequent days, give a few examples from the day before and then fire the question at individual children. "What's a word that rhymes with SUPERMAN? . . . Good. Harold, what's another word that rhymes with SUPERMAN?"

3. Have the children repeat the words after you. Once they have started responding rapidly, give them the initial sound and see if they can finish it, but do not halt the drill if they cannot provide the word. "MmmmOOPERMAN."

4. After the first couple of days, introduce a different rhyming pattern on each subsequent day, using high interest words of at least two syllables and preferably three, such as BUTTERFLY, ALLIGATOR, DINO-SAUR, HALLOWEEN, UMBRELLA, names of cartoon characters, and names of children. Return from time to time to words that the children especially enjoyed or invite them to choose the word to work with for the day. Quickly drop any word that fails to interest the children.

5. When the children are able to generate some variations of their own on given words, introduce work with initial consonants. SUPER-MAN is a good word to begin with if the children are acquainted with and interested in the character. Draw a large picture of Superman on the chalkboard, including the shield on the chest with a large letter S in it. Have the children identify the character and then point out the letter. "This letter is S. S is in SUPERMAN. Say that." Then erase the S and put in a B. Explain "This isn't Superman anymore. Now it's

Buperman. Here's how you can tell. This letter is B. B is in BUPER-MAN." Go rapidly through about ten variations on the name, changing the consonant each time, identifying it, and having the children say with you "T is in TUPERMAN," etc.

6. Limit the presentation to the consonants B, D, J, K, P, T, V, and Z. These are consonants in which the name of the letter begins with the letter sound (Bee, Dee, etc.). They therefore enable the children to anticipate the word that goes with the consonant. Drill on these variations of SUPERMAN until the children are able to give the appropriate word as soon as the letter has been identified. This drill will also help the children a good deal in learning the names of consonants.

7. Move on to some other high-interest figure that can be drawn recognizably. Names of currently popular television characters are usually the best possibilities, but certain nouns such as DINOSAUR or MOTOR-CYCLE may also be used to advantage. There should always be some way to display the initial consonant somewhere on the figure. Encourage the children to anticipate the word as you introduce variations for the first time. This they should eventually be able to do by generalization from preceding examples.

8. Introduce variations involving the consonants F, L, M, N, R, and S. These consonants are a little harder to use, because the consonant sound comes at the end rather than at the beginning of the letter name (eF, eL). Only after the children have shown definite signs of generalizing the letter-sound relationships for these consonants should the remaining set of consonants—C, G, H, W, and Y—be introduced. These are consonants where the letter names provide no clues to the consonant sounds, and thus they must be learned by rote.

9. Finally, introduce words that permit variations on the long vowel sounds. ICE CREAM, EASTER EGG, and OVERALLS are words of this kind; for example, ACE CREAM, ECE CREAM, ICE CREAM, OCE CREAM, and UCE CREAM. If the name of some person or character can be used for this purpose, so much the better, but it must meet the criteria of having several syllables and starting with a long vowel sound, preferably followed by a gliding consonant sound—F, J, M, N, S, or V.

10. Gradually adopt shorter words until the children are able to perform the exercises with one-syllable words like PIG, DOG, RAT, MOON, SUN, etc.

Spelling Patterns

Until the children have mastered the alphabet, a systematic attack on the basic spelling patterns is not possible. However, certain lower-level tasks should be introduced from time to time that will provide a gradual introduction to spelling.

Counting letters.

In the word-identity exercises, occasionally introduce the task of counting the letters in the words. Print two words on the board. "This word is TABLE. Let's count the letters in the word TABLE. One letter, two letters, three letters, four letters, five letters. There are five letters in the word TABLE. There are how many letters in the word TABLE? . . . This word is DOOR. There are how many letters in the word DOOR? . . . Let's count." Always have the children repeat the statements. "There are five letters in the word TABLE." "There are four letters in the word DOOR." Introduce words that have the same number of letters also, so that the children do not get the idea that different words necessarily have different numbers of letters.

Locating and counting specific letters.

Print several words that the children are able to identify. Then print a single letter above them. "This letter is O. How many O's in the word DOOR? . . . Here's an O and here's an O. Count them. One O, two O's. How many O's in the word DOOR? . . . There are two O's in the word DOOR." Do this for several words, including at least one that has no O's. In this case, the answer to the question "How many O's?" is "Zero O's."

Starting and ending.

1. Print a familiar consonant on the board and beneath it a word beginning with that consonant, drawing a left-to-right arrow under the word. Begin by counting the letters in the word, asking "Which way does the arrow tell us to go?" and "Where do we start out?" After counting the letters, ask "Where did we start out? . . . Here. What letter is this? . . . This letter is T. This word starts with T." Present another word starting with T, but bypass the counting, going directly to "Which way does the arrow tell us to go? . . . So where do we start out? . . . Does this word start with T?" Present negative instances that do not contain the letter T until the children have caught on to the task and can make the appropriate statements. Introduce a word that ends with T. Acknowledge that there is a T in the word, but ask "Where do we start out? . . . Here. Is this letter a T? . . . No, so this word does not start with T." Drill on words containing T in various locations until the children can reliably state whether or not the word starts with T.

2. After reviewing the above exercise, print a word ending in T and have the children count the letters. "Now listen, when we count with the arrow, where do we end up—*end up?* . . . We end up here. What letter is this? . . . This letter is T. This word ends with T. Does this

word start with T [point to the first letter]? . . . No, this word does not start with T. This word ends with T." Drill on words that start with T, end with T, or both, or neither. Have the children make the appropriate statements about each word.

3. Print several words in a row, with a single arrow running under the whole row. For each word in turn, have the children make the statements "This word starts [or does not start] with T. This word ends [or does not end] with T" in response to the command "Tell me about this word."

4. Repeat the exercises, using other letters, and then work with two letters at a time so that instead of using the *not* statement, the children answer either "This word starts with T" or "This word starts with N."

5. When the children have become proficient at making the correct statements, include the identification of the word. "This word is CAT. Tell me about the word CAT. . . . CAT starts with C and ends with T."

Before *and* after.

When the children begin to work on the concepts *before* and *after* in the language program (see Chapter 7), they should receive drill on applying these concepts to pairs of letters. Put two letters on the board with a left-to-right arrow running under them. Put the children through the same exercises that are employed in the language program.

The concept of spelling.

1. Print a familiar word, all the letters of which are known to the children. Draw a left-to-right arrow under it and locate and identify the first letter, as in the starting-and-ending exercise above (see page 287). "Now I'm going to spell the word CAT. Here's the rule. *When you spell a word, you say all the letters.* I'm going to spell the word, so I say all the letters. I start out with C. C–A–T. Say the letters with me. C–A–T. What's the rule? . . . When you spell a word, you say all the letters."

2. Have the children spell several additional easy words. Then drill the children on locating the word you name. "Which word is MAN?" When they are able to locate each word correctly, present the task of spelling the word you name. "Spell the word HIT. First we have to find it." Pretend to be searching for the word HIT. When a child locates it for you, proceed to spell it. Give the children as much help as needed at first to get them to locate the correct word and start spelling in the right place, but later withdraw the assistance until the children are able to quickly locate and spell any of the words on the board that you name.

3. Introduce deliberate errors to clarify the concept. "I'm going to spell the word HIT. H–I. Did I spell the word HIT? . . . No, when you spell a word, you say *all* the letters. Did I say all the letters? . . . I'll try again. H–I–O. Did I spell the word HIT? . . . No, this letter is not an

O." If the children are unable to catch the errors, retreat to straightforward drill on correct spelling until the children have mastered it more thoroughly. A final type of error to introduce after the children have become proficient in spotting the more obvious mistakes is that of spelling the wrong word. After spelling the word HIT several times so that the children have become accustomed to it, say "Now I'm going to spell the word CAT. Listen. H–I–T. Did I spell the word CAT?" This is an important step, for it teaches the children that the correct spelling of one word is not the correct spelling of another.

4. Put a new word on the board without identifying it and have the children spell it. Then say "This is the word BIG. B–I–G spells BIG. What does B–I–G spell?" Then print several familiar words and have the children repeat after you the spelling statements. "C–A–T spells CAT"; "M–A–N spells MAN"; etc.

5. After repeating the spelling statement for each word three or more times, introduce an identification task. "What does C–A–T spell? . . . Let's find C–A–T. Here it is. C–A–T spells CAT." Repeat this drill until the children are able to identify the word from its spelling without your locating the word for them.

6. When the children have worked on a given set of words enough so that they can quickly locate and identify any word from its spelling, have them close their eyes and try to answer questions of the form "What does C–A–T spell?" They may then open their eyes and check their answers with the printed word. Encourage the children to make a picture in their mind of the word as you spell it.

7. Distinguish spelling from reading. In the context of reviewing some of the errors presented in step 3, above, say "I'm going to spell this word. Listen. BIG. Did I spell the word? . . . No, what's the rule? . . . When you spell a word, you say all the letters." Present a number of words, spelling some and reading others, until the children can reliably tell whether or not you have spelled the word. End with a word that you do not spell. "Right, I did not spell the word. This word is MAN. When you read a word, you say what it is. I'm going to read the word. MAN. Read the word with me. MAN. Now spell the word. M–A–N." Go back over each word, having the children alternatively read the word or spell it. Repeat this exercise daily until the children are able to respond correctly to the instructions to read or spell, correcting all errors by referring back to the rules. "When you spell a word, you say all the letters. When you read a word, you say what it is."

Introduce spelling pattern drills.

The spelling pattern drills represent an integration of the preceding exercises on rhyming, word identification, and spelling. The children should have achieved proficiency in all these types of exercises before the integration is attempted. Without such proficiency, the spelling pattern drills can still be performed, but the children will be unlikely to grasp the analogies between spelling and pronunciation that are represented in the spelling patterns.

1. Start with a pattern that has already been worked with in the rhyming exercises; for instance, words that rhyme with CAT. Print the word AT on the chalkboard and identify it. "Now let's make some words that rhyme with AT. AT, RrrRAT. Good. R–A–T spells RAT." Print the word RAT below the word AT and go on to other words that rhyme with them, using any words the children suggest, even if they are non-sensical (like JAT), so long as they rhyme.

2. When four or five rhyming words have been produced, say "Let's spell the words. A–T spells AT, R–A–T spells RAT, [etc.]." Review the subtasks of the preceding exercise. "Spell the word." "Read the word." "Spell the word FAT." "What does S–A–T spell?"

3. Cover up the first letter of one of the words. "Spell this part. A–T. What does A–T spell? [Point at AT at the head of the list.] A–T spells AT." Uncover the first letter. "Spell the whole word. R–A–T. What does R–A–T spell? . . . R–A–T doesn't spell AT; R–A–T spells RAT." Go through the whole list of words in this way.

4. Add an additional rhyming word not in the original list. "Spell this word. . . . Do we know what P–A–T spells? . . . No, not yet. But we do know what this part spells. Spell it. A–T. A–T spells AT. Now listen. If A–T spells AT, then P–A–T spells PAT."

5. On subsequent days, start out with AT again and identify it, but put the next word on without identifying it. "Here's a word that rhymes with AT. Spell it. F–A–T. What does F–A–T spell? . . . Does anyone remember?" If the children do not remember, apply the operation of step 4, above, ending with the rule "If A–T spells AT, then F–A–T spells FAT." Reintroduce each word in this way and then repeat the exercises of step 2, above.

6. End each session of drill on the spelling pattern with the reading of a sentence that incorporates several of the words used in the drill.

Drill on more than one spelling pattern.

1. Introduce a set of words rhyming with UN, following the same sequence of steps as in the exercise on spelling pattern drills (see page 289). Keep reviewing the set of words rhyming with AT so that they are retained while the -UN words are learned, but do not mix the two drills at first.

2. After the -UN words have been learned, start out with UN and reintroduce two rhyming words, as in step 5, above; then shift to AT and

reintroduce two words that rhyme with AT in the same manner, starting one list on one side of the board and one list on the other. Then in the middle of the board print an -UN word that is not one of the two rhyming words already on the list. If the children cannot identify it, cover the first letter and say "Spell this part. . . . U–N. What does U–N spell? . . . U–N spells UN. If U–N spells UN, then R–U–N spells RUN." If they do identify it, say "How do we know? . . . Because this part spells UN. If U–N spells UN, R–U–N spells RUN." In either case, end by asking "Does RUN rhyme with AT? . . . No, RUN rhymes with UN. So RUN belongs over here with UN and GUN and BUN." Erase the word from the middle of the board and print it in its appropriate list, reviewing the identification and spelling of the whole list. Build up both lists in this way, alternating between -UN words and -AT words in an irregular order.

3. Carry out drills using the spelling statement (C–A–T spells CAT), jumping from word to word within each list separately and then crossing from one list to another. Include pairs of words that start with the same letter (FAT and FUN, SAT and SUN). Then shift to having the children read the words without spelling them. If the children become confused or hesitate on a particular word, cover the first letter and apply the *if-then* rule: "Spell this part. . . . U–N. U–N spells what? . . . U–N spells UN. If U–N spells UN, then S–U–N can't spell SAT. If U–N spells UN, then S–U–N spells _____. SUN."

4. Leaving the lists on the board, print several words in a row across the bottom of the board, using words from both lists. Have the children spell each word and try to identify it. If they have difficulty with a word, have them spell and identify the last part of the word as in step 3, above; then point to the corresponding word in the list and help them identify it with the *if-then* rule. End by having them read the whole list in left-to-right order.

5. Do not introduce a third spelling pattern until the children have mastered the first two spelling patterns to the point where they seldom confuse a word from one pattern with a word from another. Teach the new pattern by itself and then present it in comparison with one of the previous spelling patterns, as in steps 2, 3, and 4, above. In subsequent lessons, present it in comparison with the other previously learned spelling pattern. Thus, only two spelling patterns are considered at a time. This should be the rule until at least five spelling patterns have been learned. By working with only two patterns at a time, you can treat the words in a sense as polar sets, permitting a simplified kind of deduction which helps keep the children from becoming confused by too many possibilities. (Within a given exercise, for instance, the child may be able to conclude that if P–I–G does not spell PAT, it must spell PIG.)

6. The choice of spelling patterns to introduce should be guided in part by the spelling patterns used in the reading books that the children

will eventually be working with (see the next section for a discussion of the selection of reading materials). Some of the most useful spelling patterns (in the sense that a number of easy words can be built from them that are useful in sentences and stories) are those employing the endings AD, AN, AG, ET, ED, ID, IG, IT, IP, OT, OP, UT, UG, ENT, ALL, ELL, and ACK. Use only words that are formed by putting a single consonant on the front and that rhyme with the ending; (for example, BUT, NUT, and CUT, but not SHUT or PUT).

7. Even though only two spelling patterns may be worked with on a given day, always review the entire set of endings that have been learned to date each day. Since these endings serve as the reference by which word identifications are recalled (If U–T spells UT, then C–U–T spells CUT), it is important that they be overlearned.

8. After five spelling patterns have been studied, it is no longer practical or profitable to stick to comparisons of two spelling patterns at a time. Devote a portion of each lesson to work on a new spelling pattern and a portion to review of words previously studied. For this review, print the words in a row, with the ending printed above each word:

ID	AN	AT	IN	AN
DID	PAN	FAT	PIN	FAN

First apply the *if-then* rule to each word. If I–D spells ID, D–I–D spells DID," etc. Then erase the upper row and apply the spelling statement. "D–I–D spells DID," etc. Finally drill on reading the words without spelling. End with the reading of a sentence or story employing some of these words. "THE FAT IS IN THE PAN." "THE PIN IS IN THE FAN."

Transition to Books

The primary consideration in determining when children are ready to begin reading from the printed page rather than solely from the chalkboard is what it will do to their over-all rate of progress in reading. It would be *feasible* for the children to begin using individual printed materials very early in the reading program, but the resultant loss of teacher control over attention and pacing, and the added difficulties that reading by oneself presents would inevitably result in retarded progress in the mastery of fundamental skills. On the other hand, after the children have worked on spelling patterns to the point where the exercises have become somewhat tedious, the added motivational boost of spending some time each day working with individual printed materials will often help to speed up progress. This point will usually be reached after the children have worked through five or six spelling patterns, as prescribed in the preceding section. At this time also the children should begin learning the lower-case alphabet, which will be needed when they make the transition to books. The following exercises should be introduced at the same time the children are going on to learn new spelling patterns. Since the children usually look forward to "paper work," it can be used as an incentive to work hard on the spelling drills. "Work hard on this. As soon as you learn it, I'll hand out some papers."

Paper work.

Materials for these exercises may be dittoed. Initially, the letters should be about ¾ inch in height, eventually shrinking to ¼ inch. For paper work, the children should sit at a table facing the chalkboard.

1. On the chalkboard, print two lines of five letters each, with no two letters alike. Draw a left-to-right arrow under each line. Teach the identity statements "This is the top line" and "This is the bottom line." Point to one of the letters. "This letter is E. E is in the top line. Where is E?" Ask the question about different letters, requiring the full statement "G is in the top line" or "G is in the bottom line." At first, point to the letters and then merely name them. Then hand out papers containing a different set of letters in the same format, with an arrow under each line. Have the children point to the top line and the bottom line, checking to make sure that each child can locate them. Print one of the letters on the board, identify it, and have the children locate it on their paper by pointing. Then say "Where is F? . . . Is F in the top line?" Complete the task in the same way as was done with the letters on the chalkboard.

2. Using the same chalkboard presentation as in exercise 1 above, review the "top line, bottom line" task. Then review the older task of reading the letters with the arrow. "Which way does the arrow tell us to go? . . . So where do we start out?" Have the children say the letters in the series with you several times, repeating the questions before every round. Then hand out papers with letters printed in the same format and go through the same exercise. Put special emphasis on finding the top line and locating and identifying the letter you start out with. Be sure each child has located the first letter with his finger before starting to say the whole series of letters. Then go through the recitation of the bottom row of letters in the same way.

3. Repeat exercises 1 and 2 using familiar words instead of letters. A good deal more time may have to be devoted to the step of locating the various words. For exercise 2, have the children count the words before they read them, both in the chalkboard and in the paper task. To make the tasks easier, use the same words in the chalkboard tasks that are used in the paper tasks, but with the order of the words altered.

4. Use the same procedure as in exercise 3 to review spelling patterns.

5. After a story on the chalkboard has been read, as the final phase of a

spelling drill, present the same story on paper. Have the children locate individual words. Then work through each line of the story as in exercise 3 above. Finally, review the whole story on paper, saying "Read the top line. . . . Now read the bottom line."

6. Extend exercises 3, 4, and 5 to include three-line presentations. After reading the top line, say "Now we're going to read the next line. It's not the bottom line; it's the line right under the top line. Where do you start out?" Be sure every child has located the correct starting place before continuing.

7. Present incomplete stories on the chalkboard; for instance:

> THE RAT RAN.
> THE RAT IS IN THE

When the children have read the words, ask "Where is the rat? . . . We don't know. The story isn't finished. Now here's the whole story on your papers. Let's read the story here and find out where that rat is." The story printed on the papers will be exactly like the one on the chalkboard, but will contain the missing word WALL.

Lower-case letters.

If the children have thoroughly mastered the alphabet of capital letters, they should be able to learn the lower-case letters with only a few difficulties.

1. Write the capital letters A, B, and C on the chalkboard with the lower-case letters beneath them. Point out the lower-case letters and say that these letters look different, but they are really the same. Explain that this is the way letters are written in books and that when the children learn to read this kind of letters, they will be able to read books. Say "These are lower-case letters. What kind of letters are these? . . . These are lower-case letters. Are these [capitals] lower-case letters? . . . No, these are not lower-case letters. This is lower-case A. Say it. . . . This is lower-case B. Say it. . . . Now tell me what this is. This is lower-case _____. C. Good." Leaving the list on the board for reference, drill on single lower-case letters until the children are able to identify the letters, *a, b,* and *c.*

2. Present a new (or altered) alphabet board with the lower-case letters under the corresponding capital letters. Have the children say the whole alphabet as you point to the lower-case letters. Then present a simple spelling word like *cat,* written in lower case. As the children identify each letter, write the corresponding capital letter above it. Then have them spell and identify the whole word (*c–a–t* spells *cat*).

3. Use spelling drills to teach the identification of lower-case letters and the reading of words written in them. When a lower-case letter is not

immediately recognized (about half of the letters should be immediately recognizable), consult the alphabet board to find the corresponding capital letter. After a spelling pattern has been worked over a couple of times, stop printing the capital letters above the lower-case letters after they have been identified, having the children spell and identify the words entirely on the basis of lower-case letters. From time to time, introduce a word with an initial capital followed by lower-case letters to familiarize the children with this pattern, which they will encounter in reading.

4. Avoid using the letter *d* for a while until the children have become proficient in identifying the letter *b*. Then point out the difference between them. (Make an *o* with the fingers on one hand and use the other hand to indicate the line, showing that in *d* it goes on one side and in *b* it goes on the other side; have the children gesture with their own hands to indicate which side the line is on as you present *b*'s and *d*'s on the chalkboard.) Introduce special drills on confusable words; for example, *big, dig,* and *pig.*

5. Shift the spelling drills to words printed on paper and start giving the children familiar sentences to read from papers. The words should be printed in the normal way—capital letters at the beginning of sentences and proper names and the rest in lower-case letters.

Introduction of books

The most important requirement for a set of readers to be used in conjunction with the present program is that it use a vocabulary based upon spelling patterns rather than upon word frequency. In other words, it should not be one of the "look-and-say" readers that present a vocabulary consisting of very common but irregularly spelled words. Unfortunately, most of the new reading series designed especially for disadvantaged, urban, or minority-group children are of this kind. At present, the reading series that is most compatible with the approach taken to reading in this program is that of Fries, Fries, Wilson, and Rudolph.[3] However, several other linguistically based reading series are being developed, and may soon be available.

Whatever series is chosen, the spelling drills and accompanying sentence and story exercises should begin to be slanted toward the particular spelling patterns and vocabularies of the early stories in those books. The children will be ready to begin actual work with the books when they have progressed far enough in the paper work and in the mastery of lower-case letters to be able to read dittoed stories that are printed in the conventional book style—lower-case letters except for the beginnings of sentences and proper nouns. Before introducing books, the first two or three stories in the first book should be presented on the chalkboard and then on dittoed sheets. This is important so that the children will encounter quick and easy success when they begin working with the unfamiliar books.

1. Put the first page or two of material on the chalkboard and review the now familiar sentences. Then hand out the books with some fanfare, telling the children that they now know how to read well enough to read from real books. Help each child find the first page. Have him locate the words from the chalkboard one by one in the book, review the reading from the chalkboard, and then have the children read the same thing from their books.

2. From this point on, follow the general procedures recommended by the authors of the chosen reading series, but continue the same types of spelling drills and sentence-reading exercises that the children have been familiar with until the children are thoroughly at home with the books.

The children will sometimes get so enthusiastic about reading from books that they will want to rush ahead without thoroughly learning the material as they go through it. This is best prevented by confining book reading to the last five or ten minutes of each period, continuing to use the chalkboard for drill on new spelling patterns and sight words and for review of previously covered material.

Instruction in Printing

During the reading period itself, no time is allotted for teaching the children to print letters and words. Printing is useful as an aid in letter and word recognition and in the mastery of spelling rules, but it is a very time-consuming activity, especially for younger children, and therefore is omitted from the program in favor of other activities that can generally produce the same effects in less time. However, it is quite profitable to use a portion of one of the periods of less structured activity for auxiliary instruction in printing. Children usually enjoy it, and it provides a relaxing change from the intensive verbal activities carried on in the academic class periods. It is a good activity to place toward the end of the daily session, since the children can handle it well even if they are somewhat fatigued.

Printing activities are best handled by having the children remain with their study group, each group sitting around a different table with a teacher at each table. The range in initial abilities is likely to be large, even within study groups that are relatively homogeneous in academic skills. Thus, instruction will have to be individualized.

Some children will need to be taught how to hold a writing instrument. Rather than doing this as the first step in instruction, it is a good idea to let the children struggle along as best they can for a day or two. Then they will be better able to appreciate the added power that a correct way of holding the instrument gives them. For the child who does not know how to hold a pencil or crayon, shape his fingers for him and place the instrument between his fingers as close to the point as possible. This gives him greatly increased control. He will later naturally begin to hold it farther back for comfort.

Because printing instruction is a minor and brief activity carried out by all the teachers, it is generally not practical to attempt a highly systematic step-by-step program for teaching it. A simple approach which allows children to work fairly independently and to proceed at different rates is one that is based on letter completion. For each letter, sheets similar to the one illustrated in Figure 2 are reproduced. The complete

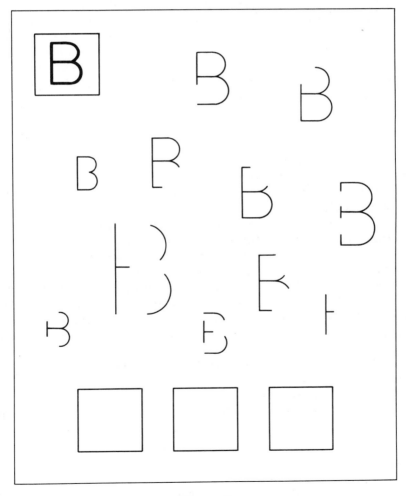

Figure 2

letter is presented in a box at the top of the page. Various incomplete versions of the letter, in different sizes, are scattered about the page, and at the bottom are three empty boxes in which the child may attempt to reproduce the entire letter after he has completed the broken letters. Each child is handed a sheet. If he completes it adequately, he may be given a sheet with a new letter on it. If he completes the sheet, but has not done an adequate job, he is given a fresh sheet with the same letter and is encouraged to make a very nice one to take home.

Each child should be required to make the appropriate identity statement (This letter is _____) when he is handed a work-sheet, when he has completed one, and whenever else the occasion presents itself.

After the children have mastered some letters, they should be given an opportunity from time to time to copy short, familiar words that can be formed from the letters they have mastered. There should be continual review of old letters, *but new letters should be introduced regularly whether or not the children have mastered the preceding ones.* Children who cannot produce letters will gain quite a bit of help in letter recognition from work on completing broken letters.

Summary

The reading program presented in this chapter places special emphasis on developing an awareness of words as distinct entities and on the alphabetical principle: it is the spelling of a word that identifies it and provides a guide to its pronunciation. The early stages of the program are devoted to alphabet drills; to word-identity exercises, in which each child is made responsible for remembering a single word, thus permitting an early introduction to the reading of sentences; and to the teaching of rhyming, which leads eventually to the children's being able to recognize words of a rhyming set by the initial consonants. Once the alphabet has been mastered, the work focuses upon drill with spelling patterns (three-letter rhyming words that are alike in the last two letters) and upon the reading of sentences and stories containing such words.

When this stage is reached, a gradual transition is carried out from reading material presented on the chalkboard to reading from printed sheets and finally to reading from books.

The children's work in the reading class is entirely verbal, but time is allotted in the period of semistructured activity for instruction in printing.

Notes

1. J. B. Carroll, "The Analysis of Reading Instruction: Perspectives from Psychology and Linguistics," in *Theories of Learning and Instruction,* 63rd

Yearbook of the National Society for the Study of Education, Part I (Chicago: University of Chicago Press, 1964).

2. L. Bloomfield and C. Barnhart, *Let's Read, A Linguistic Approach* (Detroit: Wayne State University Press, 1961); C. C. Fries, *Linguistics and Reading* (New York: Holt, Rinehart & Winston, Inc., 1963).

3. C. C. Fries, A. C. Fries, R. G. Wilson, and M. K. Rudolph, *A Basic Reading Series Developed upon Linguistic Principles* (Ann Arbor, Mich.: Author, 1965).

index

A